Praise for *Convinced!*

"To gain assent from others, it's not enough [to be competent] on the topic at hand. It's also necessary to project that competence successfully. With *Convinced!*, at last there's a book that shows us how. We needed this book."
—**Robert Cialdini, author of *Influence* and *Pre-Suasion***

"In an age of information overload and default to algorithms, the ability to assess and convey true expertise is a critical managerial competency. *Convinced!* will help show you the way."
—**Dominic Barton, Global Managing Partner Emeritus,**
McKinsey & Company

"To land a job, enlist investors, close a deal, or lead an initiative, being the best person to play that role isn't enough. What matters most is persuading other people that you're the one they can count on to deliver what they need. Jack Nasher's compelling new book lays out eight practical principles for positively shaping how others judge your competence. I'm convinced of the power of his advice. And you'll be convinced, as well."
—**Michael Wheeler, Harvard Business School professor and author of**
The Art of Negotiation

"Every second of every day, judgements and assessments of compe-tence are being made. Whatever your role or expertise, *Convinced!* provides fascinating and practical insights into steps anyone can take to engender and promote that all-important sense of confidence and trust. Compelling, highly entertaining, and thoroughly convincing!"
—**Matthew Layton, Global Managing Partner, Clifford Chance LLP**

"You may have your foundation degree and experience. You may even have your MBA. But now you need to go to finishing school and read *Convinced!* An excellent insight into the importance of not just being competent but being perceived to be competent. A compelling read."
—**Andy Palmer, President and CEO, Aston Martin Lagonda Ltd.**

"Perceptions matter. *Convinced!* identifies the behaviors, networks, and narrative strategies that you can use to shape perceptions and create a competitive edge."
—**Rupert Younger, Director, Oxford University Centre for**
Corporate Reputation

"We live and work in a world that often works to very fine margins. This book helps us understand how others judge our competence to help us influence and improve that perception while remaining true and authentic to who we are. It offers the opportunity to gain a marginal, but perhaps critical, advantage."
—**Bill Thomas, Global Chairman, KPMG International**

"As a river runs to the sea, power flows to those who can persuade. Jack Nasher gives you the tools you need to win others over and keep them moving in the right direction."
—**G. Richard Shell, Wharton professor and coauthor of *The Art of Woo***

"Be it in business or diplomacy, convincing people of one's expertise is key to successful negotiations. Radiating that competence also helps leaders gain the legitimacy to lead. Dr. Nasher's book offers scientifically grounded, real-life techniques that should be required reading for public and private sector managers alike."
—**Alexander Vinnikov, Head of the NATO Representation to Ukraine**

"At the heart of Professor Nasher's book is a key central thesis: it is no longer enough to be extraordinarily competent. These days, it is necessary for all top managers—and anyone who aspires to be one— to embrace the responsibility for their own personal PR. The author introduces techniques that allow readers to display their expertise in ways that will earn them the recognition they deserve. *Convinced!* is educational (but never pedantic), engaging, and entertaining. Highly recommended!"
—**Georges Kern, CEO, Breitling SA**

Convinced!

Convinced!

How to Prove Your Competence & Win People Over

Jack Nasher

Berrett–Koehler Publishers, Inc.
a BK Business book

Berrett-Koehler Publishers, Inc.
1333 Broadway, Suite 1000
Oakland, CA 94612-1921
Tel: (510) 817-2277
Fax: (510) 817-2278
www.bkconnection.com

ORDERING INFORMATION

Quantity sales. Special discounts are available on quantity purchases by corporations, associations, and others. For details, contact the "Special Sales Department" at the Berrett-Koehler address above.

Individual sales. Berrett-Koehler publications are available through most bookstores. They can also be ordered directly from Berrett-Koehler: Tel: (800) 929-2929; Fax: (802) 864-7626; www.bkconnection.com.

Orders for college textbook / course adoption use. Please contact Berrett-Koehler: Tel: (800) 929-2929; Fax: (802) 864-7626.

Distributed to the U.S. trade and internationally by Penguin Random House Publisher Services.

Berrett-Koehler and the BK logo are registered trademarks of Berrett-Koehler Publishers, Inc.

Printed in Canada.

Berrett-Koehler books are printed on long-lasting acid-free paper. When it is available, we choose paper that has been manufactured by environmentally responsible processes. These may include using trees grown in sustainable forests, incorporating recycled paper, minimizing chlorine in bleaching, or recycling the energy produced at the paper mill.

Library of Congress Cataloging-in-Publication Data

Names: Nasher, Jack, 1979– author.
Title: Convinced : how to prove your competence and win people over / Jack Nasher.
Description: Oakland, CA : Berrett-Koehler Publishers, Inc, [2018] | Includes bibliographical references.
Identifiers: LCCN 2018011565 | ISBN 9781523095599 (pbk.)
Subjects: LCSH: Self-presentation. | Success. | Body language. | Interpersonal relations.
Classification: LCC BF697.5.S44 N47 2018 | DDC 158.2—dc23 LC record available at https://lccn.loc.gov/2018011565

First Edition
25 24 23 22 21 20 19 18   10 9 8 7 6 5 4 3 2 1

Book producer: Westchester Publishing Services
Text designer: Laurel Muller
Cover designer: Adrian Morgan

Dedicated to the dynamic duo I owe so much to:
my mother Diana & my sister Isabel.

And to my beloved American family—
Շնորհակալություն ձեր անսահման սիրո
եւ աջակցության համար։

CONTENTS

CONTENTS

INTRODUCTION

Every day your clients, superiors, and colleagues must decide to whom they will entrust certain tasks. We constantly and mutually judge others' respective capabilities, although we usually have no idea on what to base those judgments. Despite all this, "competence" continues to be regarded as the decisive factor for evaluating performance and making decisions regarding hiring, promotions, the entrusting of tasks, and, of course, compensation.

The good news is that even when the services and products your competitors and you are offering resemble one another, it is still possible to differentiate yourself and convince others of your abilities. That is what this book is all about: explaining how to achieve an inexplicable advantage over others who can deliver a similar quality.

You can control a large part of what others think about you, an opportunity you should seize. The idea is to become your own PR agent, showing your skills by utilizing effective impression management tools. Not only when giving a talk, writing your resume, or interviewing for a job—always! As groups are typically persuaded by the person who appears to be most competent, it is this *perceived competence* that gives you the power to convince, influence, and lead others.

With the advice in this book you will be able to exhibit your abilities in front of customers, colleagues, and superiors. Whether in meetings, presentations, or crucial conversations, you will be able to convince others of your expertise and be appreciated and respected like never before. At the same time, your perception will be trained to accurately assess the competence of others.

When you understand and implement these techniques and tools, your company will profit just as much, whether you are an executive or a sales representative, because customers prefer to buy from people they consider to be competent. And, as real change only comes from within, your attitude will change accordingly and with it your actual ability.

By learning how to use the eight pillars of competence—the perception of brilliance, the anticipation effect, the power of association, the power of framing, verbal communication, nonverbal communication, the power of attractiveness and popularity, and the power of symbols—to your advantage, you will be poised to prove your competence and stand out in any crowd. Throughout the chapters of this book, decades of research on psychological phenomena pertaining to these aspects of communication are explored and exploited to help you showcase your expertise.

Chapter 1 begins with the fundamental observation that brilliance does not speak for itself: you can, in fact, be the best in the world and no one will notice. Some may even think you are a failure. You need to show your skills. But how can you do this? Since the world around you is unable to evaluate your abilities accurately, what counts, above all, is its assessment of your competence—the perceived level of competence. It is this that determines your success—and serves as the subject of this book. In chapter 1, I show you why competence is the most important single factor for your professional success. And as others are unable to evaluate your abilities accurately, what counts, above all, is its assessment of your competence—your perceived competence. Even success and failure have terrifyingly little influence on this perception of competence. Displaying your competence in such a way that the audience will perceive you as highly competent will also increase your actual competence—through a self-fulfilling prophecy.

In order to display your expertise, your demonstrated level of expectation regarding your performance plays a key role. But what kind of outcome should you predict in order to be perceived as competent? This is the question addressed in chapter 2. Should you dampen the level of expectation from the start and show some sort of noble restraint? Modesty certainly is an honorable trait. And isn't it a nice surprise if people end up performing better than expected, along the lines of *underpromise and overdeliver*? Or should you demonstrate extraordinary self-confidence and predict outstanding results? With this strategy, of course, you run the risk of appearing boastful. So how can we achieve effective "expectation management" in terms of competence? Chapter 2 illustrates how you should shape peoples' expectations of your skills: how to demonstrate optimism when faced with new tasks and how to eliminate anything that could potentially bear negative witness against you. As it is you who must, first and foremost, be convinced of your abilities, a technique called priming will be explored to show you how to radiate competence from inside.

Chapter 3 shows you how to present good and bad news in the way that is most beneficial to you. It asks the question, How can you use your success to the utmost advantage in regard to perceived competence while suffering the least damage to your reputation from your failures? With good news, you should maximize your presence and involvement; with bad news, you should stay in the background and communicate neutrally or, if you are a male and of high status, you can show anger. You should describe public mistakes clearly and concisely, and then move on to optimism as quickly as possible. Start with the positive aspect of an event, then mention the negative (primacy effect); the second-strongest positive aspect, however, should be presented at the end (recency effect). By using certain techniques for delivering good and bad news, you will be able to spin even gigantic mistakes so that they have little or no negative effect on your perceived competence.

In chapter 4, I provide techniques for framing your competence by insulating your competence from the confusion of different influences surrounding it. To do that, you must emphasize, as much as possible, the challenges of the job at hand and point out any unfavourable circumstances that will make the job more difficult. You should not, however, awaken the impression that it was necessary for you to work very hard for your earlier successes. They were, of course, easy for you. Since you are a natural talent, you were born for your special field, and your path was, in a way, predestined. That is why you should also resemble, to some extent at least, the stereotype of your profession, and let people know that you live your profession with body and soul. In this chapter, I condense the research on the effects of a phenomenon called the fundamental attribution error—the fact that individuals will be held personally responsible for the results they produce—and identify methods that allow you to use this phenomenon to your advantage.

Chapter 5 synthesizes research on the role of speech in projecting an image of expertise and provides tips for speaking like an expert. There is possibly no other technique that will allow you to effectively raise your perceived level of competence and be more convincing than employing *power talking*. This chapter lists several hands-on tips for using this strong, self-confident language that you can easily employ in your daily interactions. I explain whether and how you should utilize your vocal range, repetitions, and interruptions. You will also learn a technique that I wish would not exist and that has to do with unnecessary complications in your expressions.

In chapter 6, I examine several studies on the importance of body language in attempts to be convincing. We often under-estimate the role of nonverbal communication in terms of our own external impact and, as a rule, focus more on our words. However, if we deliberately use our nonverbal communication skills, we can strongly influence the specific impressions we make on people and present ourselves in a certain light. This chapter provides a guide for doing so, focusing on how to convey competence by fine-tuning your proximity to others, your location while standing, and your posture while sitting, as well as on how to use eye contact, smiling, gestures, and physical contact to increase your perceived competence and win over your audience. And you will learn about a certain Dr. Fox. . . .

Chapter 7 discusses the research regarding the impact of the halo effect, from which the great importance of a positive overall impression derives. Your popularity and attractiveness are crucial for the overall impression you make on others. Some people appear likable—others do not. Some are consid-ered attractive, while others aren't. The main factors that lead to a particular judgment on your likability and attractiveness are not as obvious as they may first seem. However, you should not waste time making changes to your appearance or behav-ior that have little effect or attempting to fix things about them that cannot be changed; instead, this chapter presents findings—hardly known outside academia—that will help you zero in on what is truly important. By learning how to use these techniques, and by gaining a better understanding of what really matters to others, you can immediately increase your likeability and attractiveness and boost your perceived com-petence in the process.

In chapter 8, I examine the extraordinary impact that status has in our lives. The key to perceived status is *habitus*, described by the French sociologist Pierre Bourdieu as a person's behavior and appearance, including his or her clothing, language, and apparent lifestyle. Whether fair or not, by observing a person's habitus, we can assess his or her status within moments. However, your status is also related to the way you interact with the people around you and, as a "peace maker" for instance, and will directly affect your perceived competence. Thus, in this chapter, I show how certain little-known tactics, such as praise, nonconformity, and a technique that social psychologist Robert Cialdini refers to as "BIRGing," profoundly impact your perceived status. Combining all these factors directly leads to a higher perceived status and, thus, a higher perceived level of competence.

In the conclusion and epilogue, I show how the eight pillars of confidence work together to direct almost everyone's attention specifically to your competence, and I provide tips for detecting competence, and especially intelligence—which is closely related to competence—in others.

Most of the methods I describe in this book can be applied immediately, others need some practice, but none of them call for you to change your personality: authenticity is key in order to appear as a luminary. In order to be sustainable, change must come from within. By using the techniques I present, you will be able to display your expertise so that you receive the recognition you deserve.

CHAPTER 1

THE PERCEPTION OF BRILLIANCE

ACTUAL VERSUS PERCEIVED COMPETENCE

If a man today were to take one day away from his current engagement and spend that one day learning the professional approach he would be doing himself and the firm a much greater service than he would be to produce seventy-five, a hundred, or a hundred and fifty dollars a day of income for McKinsey & Company.

—MARVIN BOWER (1965)

The Experiment

What do you think would happen if one of the world's great violin virtuosos performed for over 1,000 people in a metro station, incognito, during rush hour?

This is the exact question *Washington Post* journalist Gene Weingarten posed to Leonard Slatkin, director of the National Symphony Orchestra, in an interview in 2007.[1]

Slatkin replied, "Let's assume that he is not recognized and just taken for granted as a street musician. . . . Still, I don't think that if he's really good, he's going to go unnoticed . . . but, okay, out of 1,000 people, my guess is there might be 35 or 40 who will recognize the quality for what it is. Maybe 75 to 100 will stop and spend some time listening."

"So, a crowd would gather?" Weingarten asked.

"Oh, yes."

"And how much will he make?"

"About $150."

"Thanks, Maestro. As it happens," continued Weingarten, "this is not hypothetical. It really happened."

"How'd I do?" Slatkin asked curiously.

"We'll tell you in a minute," said the journalist.

"Well, who was the musician?"

"Joshua Bell."

"NO!!!"

Yes, the experiment was conducted with none other than American violinist Joshua Bell, who in the course of his fabulous career has been referred to as a "boy wonder," "genius," and even "God"—all by the time he was only in his late 30s. At the age of 4, Bell stretched rubber bands across a drawer to pluck out tunes. At 17, he performed as a soloist at Carnegie Hall and went on to play with the most prestigious orchestras in the world. He has received countless prizes, such as the Mercury, the Gramophone and Echo Klassik, a Grammy, and an Oscar—well, almost: Bell performed the solo part on the soundtrack to the film *The Red Violin*, which won an Academy Award for Best Original Score. Up until that day in January 2007, though, Joshua Bell had never been a busker.

So, early that cold morning, one of the most celebrated violinists of his generation walks down the steps of L'Enfant Plaza Station in Washington, DC. He puts down the violin case and takes out his fiddle, a Stradivarius, to be exact, made by the legendary violin maker in 1713—his "golden era"—and worth about $4 million. Bell lifts the bow, not just any bow, of course, but one from the workshop of bow master François Tourte from the late 18th century. There he stands, this lanky, boyish man, disguised in a baseball cap. Only three days earlier he had filled the Boston Symphony Hall to the last seat with ticket prices starting at $100.

He commences with "Chaconne" from Johann Sebastian Bach's *Partita No. II*, the epitome of violin pieces, about which the composer Johannes Brahms wrote, "If I imagined that I could have created, even conceived the piece, I am quite certain that the excess of excitement and earth-shattering experience would have driven me out of my mind."[2]

So, a world-renowned violinist is now on his Stradivarius playing an epochal piece of music. What happens next?

Ah, one more thing: The publishers of the *Washington Post*—who were staging the event—were very worried about security issues. They feared a tumultuous crowd's reaction and even considered alerting the National Guard so they would be ready to get the situation under control if necessary. They pictured the use of tear gas, rubber bullets, and so on, and yet, the decision was made to go through with this risky experiment.

So Bell begins to play . . . It takes three minutes and 63 passersby before a middle-aged man slows down his walk and seems to notice that someone is making music—but he keeps on walking. Then a woman throws a dollar into the violin case and dashes on. Over the next 43 minutes, 7 people will stand there for a few moments, while 27 others will throw money into the trunk without pausing. No one will applaud.

There is a constant line of people just a few yards away at a lottery stand, but no one even turns in the direction of the music. The lady at the shoe polish stand, an animated Brazilian woman who is also only a few feet away, curses at the noise, but she doesn't call the cops as she usually does on other street performers. Bell finishes playing, packs up, and leaves the station with hardly anyone noticing.

How much did he make? In total, 32 dollars and 17 cents. Not bad for a street musician. However, 20 of those dollars came from the most generous listener: Stacy Furukawa, who recognized Bell and threw the bill in with an utterly perplexed expression.

Bell enjoyed the experience, but there was one moment when he felt particularly embarrassed: the seconds immediately after the conclusion of a set—no applause, nothing. Bell just stood there sheepishly for a while and eventually continued.

"It was a strange feeling," he later recalled, "that people were actually, ah . . . ignoring me. At a music hall, I'll get upset if someone coughs or if someone's cellphone goes off."

So one of the best violinists in the world plays one of the greatest masterpieces of all time on a Stradivarius and almost nothing happens. The organizers had been confident that people would stop and recognize his true greatness because genius speaks for itself.

They were wrong.

Brilliance does not speak for itself: you can, in fact, be the best in the world and no one will notice. Some may even think you are a failure. You need to show your skills.

That's what this book is about.

Research has shown again and again how difficult it is for us to accurately assess others' competence and intelligence in general.[3] Meanwhile, it seems almost impossible to objectively judge, and properly assess, the competence of one's performance, whether a piece of music or a daily task at work.[4]

But don't results speak for themselves? For example, lawyers can win or lose a case. Even in defeat, though, they may still be considered competent at their jobs. The expertise of a lawyer is not really measured by the percentage of cases she's won, just like the competence of a doctor is not measured by the degree of health of his patients. If an ill patient visits a doctor and subsequently gets better, the doctor may have cured her or it may have just been the result of the natural course of the disease. If the doctor's treatment failed, however, it may be that a cure was utterly impossible anyhow. Hence, the doctor could appear incompetent despite her success and competent even though she failed.

The same situation is true with a sales representative: sales may rise, but they could have risen without his effort due to the superior quality of the product or marketing efforts that finally bore fruit. If sales go down, it could have been the result of increasing competition. Just like in politics, where a leader can be perceived as incompetent, despite a strong economy and low unemployment figures, or as competent, even if the economy is on a downswing and unemployment is increasing.

Let me illustrate this phenomenon with an astounding example from the corporate context: In 1983, the then leading communications firm AT&T hired the management consultancy McKinsey & Company to assess the future of the cellular telephone market. As Thomas Sugrue, head of the Wireless Telecommunications Bureau, remembers, "McKinsey & Co. confidently told AT&T that by the year 2000, no more than 1 million Americans would subscribe to cellular services—max."[5] This prediction was not—to put it mildly—accurate.

By the year 2000, over 80 million Americans were using wireless phones, making the prediction off by more than 8,000 percent. This colossal underestimation of the cellular phone market led to a series of ill-advised decisions that cost AT&T billions of dollars, contributing to the former giant's demise.[6] So bad was the company's service that I have heard MCs in Hollywood's Magic Castle nightclub tell their audiences before my show to switch off their cell phones, unless they use AT&T, in which case they need not worry about it since they won't have reception anyway—followed by agreeing chuckles. In 2005, the venerable American Telephone & Telegraph Company, once one of the most admired companies in the world, was acquired by Southwestern Bell—one of its spin-offs.

How did McKinsey & Co. do in the year 2000, when this multi-billion-dollar mistake became obvious? Did they lose most of their clients? Was the company on the verge of bankruptcy, or did they at least take a shameful vow of silence? Not quite. It was a terrific year for the firm, and its reputation did not suffer a bit.

As illustrated, success or failure has surprisingly little influence on the perception of competence. One can appear to be competent despite vast failure and seem incompetent in the midst of immense success.

"Isn't that a little exaggerated?" you may ask. Not at all—it's an understatement! Even in the absence of any actual competence, an impression of competence can remain intact. Until the 20th century, for example, it was usually healthier to *not* go to the doctor at all, as the universal treatment, bloodletting, wasn't only useless but even resulted in infections quite frequently. Yet, at that time, and even in the earliest societies, which had virtually no medical know-how whatsoever, doctors and medicine men were highly respected.

The impression of competence can even last when we should really know better. In 2005, the US psychologist Philip Tetlock asked hundreds of experts from the fields of business, politics, and the military to predict the events of the next five years in their respective disciplines.[7] The disillusioning result: Expertise did not help at all in making valid assumptions. On the contrary, an especially good reputation even had a negative impact on the prediction.

In the midst of the financial crisis, in 2009, just after the collapse of Lehman Brothers, I was living in Manhattan.* When-

---

* I have to admit, it was a great time for a legal trainee. I could afford to live in a doorman building on Park Avenue, and could get a table at every restaurant in town, with heavy discounts: Restaurant Week was extended to last a whole month.

ever you turned on the TV, there was some expert explaining why the crisis was unavoidable: you would see a stern face and hear a precise explanation of why this or that had to happen—alas, only after it happened. A year before, those same experts didn't say a word about these inevitable occurrences.

So common sense is not working here. Poor work does not necessarily lead to a corresponding negative perception. Unfortunately, this idea also applies to good work—it doesn't necessarily lead to a positive perception.

After Joshua Bell's concert in the metro station, some passersby were interviewed. "Yes, I saw the violinist," said a lawyer on her way to work. And her sobering conclusion: "But nothing about him struck me as much of anything."

The Assessment Problem

Is the lawyer who saw Bell playing that morning just ignorant, blind to obvious skill? How about you? Is your assessment of someone's talents or abilities accurate? For example, you may think you have a competent dentist, perhaps one you have even recommended to your friends. But how can you make a judgment if you know nothing about dentistry? Chances are you don't have a clue. Instead, you rely on criteria such as the clinic's cleanliness or the dentist's friendliness, which, as you must admit, have little to do with actual expertise.[8] Even one-on-one conversations do not help us to properly assess others' abilities.[9]

After receiving my law degree, I worked as a legal trainee at the US law firm Skadden. "The Firm," as it is reverently called, specializes in mergers and acquisitions and, according to *Forbes* magazine, is the "most powerful firm on Wall Street." Not feeling much of the firm's might, there I sat 12 hours a day in front of my computer, neatly dressed in a suit and tie—though a tracksuit would have been more adequate, as I never met with

clients; I wrote Share-Purchase Agreements (SPAs), sale contracts for corporate investments. My colleagues in the neigh-
boring offices to my left and right did the same. We all had the
same training and similar grades and in fact looked almost
identical. Yet it would have typically taken me 7 to 10 years to
be made a partner, the highest accolade (and most lucrative*)
in the firm.[10] That's how long the ladies and gentlemen in the
partner offices would have needed to ponder whether I would
be worthy to be considered an equal.

These colleagues—experts in their field—needed almost a
decade to assess their peers' competence. If it takes the best
people at a top firm such an amount of time, then how can a
layman accurately judge the competence of an expert lawyer
quickly and appropriately? And yet, clients set up so-called
beauty contests to assess their prospective legal counsel's expertise after a few meetings—a naive undertaking, but what
choice do they have?

Every day we must decide to whom we will entrust certain
tasks, from our hairdressers to our accountants. We constantly
and mutually judge others' respective capabilities, although
we usually have no idea on what to base those judgments.
Despite all this, "competence" continues to be regarded as the
decisive factor.

In the context of this book, "competence" or "expertise,"
which I use interchangeably, more or less means a combination of knowledge and skills that are needed for the tasks one
faces.[11] A strict demarcation is not very effective because concepts such as "intelligence" and "competence" are so closely
correlated with each other that research habitually combines
them into one single factor.[12] Therefore, a rough idea is suffi-

---

* An annual compensation of $5 million for an equity partner is not unusual, and
this was about nine years ago, which is why I truly hope this book will sell well.
Please recommend it to your friends and do not lend it to them.

cient and gives us time to answer the really important question: Which factors matter in judging others' expertise and which don't?

"Competence" is indeed the most important trait in the professional context, on par with "credibility" and before "likability."[13] Research and common sense agree: competence is the basis for evaluating performance and making decisions regarding hiring, promotions, the entrusting of tasks, and, of course, compensation.[14]

The dilemma: while people regard expertise as the most important quality in any profession, great difficulty lies in properly assessing it. This difficulty is amplified by the exponential growth of knowledge. And as the world's complexity increases, an ever-greater need arises to rely on people who seem to know what they're doing.

What gives us a sense of security in this complex world, however, is not *actual* competence, because it is virtually impossible to rate, but *perceived* competence. If we distinguish between perceived and actual competence, it becomes clear why there are incompetent people who are highly regarded, while some highly competent people are regularly underrated or assumed to be incompetent. Which leads to the key point: it is not so much the actual but the perceived competence that determines an individual's success.

Just World Principle

How do you feel about this idea, that perceived competence is essentially rewarded over actual competence? Chances are, it makes you feel uncomfortable. Deeply rooted in all of us is a faith that has accompanied us since our childhood, a result of the ancient German fairy tales collected by the brothers Grimm, Disney movies, and bedtime stories: Everyone gets what they deserve. The villain gets punished (in German fairy tales, habitually tortured to death) and the heroes get married (to a child, at least, this qualifies as a happy ending).

On that January morning in DC, the one woman who recognized Joshua Bell in the metro station, Stacy Furukawa, just happened to pass by. She stopped in front of Bell and could not believe that she was surrounded by such ignorance: "It was the most astonishing thing I've ever seen in Washington. Joshua Bell was standing there playing at rush hour, and people were not stopping, and not even looking, and some were flipping quarters at him! . . . I was thinking, Omigosh, what kind of a city do I live in that this could happen?"

No wonder Furukawa could identify the virtuoso: She had attended one of his concerts just a few weeks earlier. Yet she clung to the belief that she would have recognized Bell without this favorable circumstance because, she was sure, true greatness speaks for itself—even if only to her out of the over 1,000 people who passed Bell by that day.

Social psychologist Alan Lerner coined this somewhat naive worldview the "Just World Principle."[15] While growing up, it helps us to internalize ethical values, but over time we gradually realize that this charming faith has little to do with reality. Often it is the villain who gets the princess and the good guy who is left empty-handed.

We observe how real life works again and again but still can hardly shake off this childhood ideal. Though this belief was valuable for growing up, it is a hindrance for our later advancement. The just world principle is no more than a delusion that helps us to endure the world's injustice. Some of us who are spiritual or religious may shift our trust to a judgment day, hoping everyone will get what they deserve when the time comes. The rest of us accept the circumstances and make the best of here and now.

Negotiation expert Chester Karass coined a phrase with which I begin my negotiation seminars: "You don't get what you deserve, you get what you negotiate." This statement could also apply to the display of competence—you don't get what you deserve based on your actual competence, but on how you display your competence. Many expect that our bosses or managers at work, who only see us every now and then, instinctively sense how capable we are without us needing to demonstrate our abilities. Nonsense.

Is there something inside you that still rebels against accepting this sheer injustice? Well, you could emblazon slogans on a piece of cardboard and start a demonstration on Main Street, or you could write a postcard to Santa Claus if you are old fashioned—but you won't change the facts. It's better to be prudent and accept the circumstances at hand and even use them to your advantage. As John F. Kennedy supposedly once said, "The world is not fair, but not necessarily to your disadvantage."

True Competence?

This book is not meant to be a manual, as I do not intend to tell you what to do. As is the case with all my books and training courses, it is not my goal to make you do anything. Instead, I want to educate you—it is your choice how you'd like to use this knowledge. In this book, I will show you the most effective techniques to convince others of your worth by demonstrating competence, but it is up to you to decide if and how.

However, I am passionate about you, the individual. I feel sorry for modern men and women living in our corporate world. After having spent half your life trying to acquire the formal qualifications to succeed—high school, college, executive trainings—you should have the necessary skills. But despite these years of hard work, you may have come to realize that, contrary to what was promised, your tediously gained abilities are no guarantee of professional success—hard work just isn't enough. In fact, some twerp outpaces you again and again. No one prepared you to sell your skills!

If you are an executive, you may face a dilemma known as the "Peter Principle." Named after American educator Laurence J. Peter, this principle describes the tendency for people to rise up the career ladder until reaching a position of incompetence—and that's where they stay.[16] Many executives are in a management position not because they are excellent managers but because they were good in their previous jobs as salespeople, engineers, or HR reps. Now, however, these managers are not doing that well, which is why they don't get promoted. So executives tend to spend the most time on the job they are least qualified for. The implications of this system error for the actual leadership abilities of many executives can only be imagined.

Furthermore, you might think that you don't deserve any appreciation anyway. Deep inside, you probably feel that you know nothing, that you really are incompetent. If this is the case, you are in good company: successful people often feel that their success was only achieved illegitimately, that it was only due to a string of fortunate circumstances. This is known as the "Impostor Phenomenon."[17] Nearly 70 percent of successful people describe themselves as con artists. Even the great physicist Albert Einstein considered himself to be an "involuntary swindler" shortly before his death.[18]

This phenomenon increases as we now compare ourselves not only with those around us but with the entire world. As the US researchers Randolph M. Nesse and George C. Williams put it, "In the ancestral environment you would have had a good chance at being the best at something. Even if you were not the best, your group would likely value your skills. Now we all compete with those who are the best in the world. Watching these successful people on television arouses envy. Envy probably was useful to motivate our ancestors to strive for what others could obtain. Now few of us can achieve the goals envy sets for us, and none of us can attain the fantasy lives we see on television."[19] Our feelings of incompetence increases with modern tools of communications, such as social media, and can even lead to clinical depression.

And indeed, only a fool thinks he knows it all. The feeling of inadequacy is in fact a sign of prudence, along the lines of Socrates, who knew that he knew nothing. Indeed, the speed at which knowledge multiplies increases exponentially. The German Max Planck Institute has determined that in 1650 fewer than 1 million people were considered "educated." In 1950 there were 10 million "educated people," meaning humankind needed 300 years to multiply the number of educated people by 10. However, this number increased tenfold in just another 50 years—by the year 2000 there were already 100 million "educated people." All these people think, talk, and write, so the body of knowledge multiplies faster and faster. In fact, there is more technology in a modern smartphone than in a complete 1968 space shuttle.

It is therefore not surprising that never before have breakthrough innovations, or "disruptive changes," a term coined by Harvard professor Clayton M. Christensen, followed each other in such a rapid succession. Entire industries are replaced overnight and new industries are established, making old ones superfluous. Institutions such as the former photography giant Kodak, the once highly profitable Lehman Brothers investment bank, and the mobile phone manufacturer Nokia—once the shining star of the industry—disappeared from the scene. Correspondingly, especially highly qualified individuals, such as bankers, lawyers, and executives, need to be enormously flexible and prepared to change positions, or even industries, faster than ever.

How, then, in light of all this, is it possible to have even the slightest confidence in your own competence? This question had been on my mind since the early 2000s, when I completed my master's thesis on perceived competence at Oxford. Years later, on an evening in New York in 2009, it finally became clear to me.

At that time, as I have already mentioned, I was living in Manhattan and working as a diplomat at the United Nations as part of my legal training. As the world was in the midst of the effects of the financial crisis, and we were right in its epicenter in Manhattan, my boss asked me to write a report on how international institutions could prevent such crises in the future. "Sure," I said keenly, and walked straight into my office to Google, "How to prevent a financial crisis"—one has to start somewhere. One source led to another, and I worked on the topic for about a week and presented it to my boss.

"Abbreviate it," he told me over and over again. And so I learned an important lesson that I preach to all my students: a good paper is not one in which nothing can be added but one in which nothing can be left out. Five pages shrank to a single one—big shots have little time—and my report was accepted at last.

The following day I watched a press conference on TV and saw a very senior member of the German government plead for strengthening the World Bank and the International Monetary Fund to avoid another financial crisis of the same kind in the future. The plan corresponded almost word for word to my short report—with no mention of the author . . .

A week later, on that night in 2009, I was sitting in the Delegates' Lounge at a weekly get-together of UN diplomats with a splendid view of the East River. Next to me sat a senior politician who was there representing his country's stance in some plenary sessions. On day one he talked about the infrastructure of an African nation, on day two about the security situation in the Middle East. But of course he owed his knowledge to a poor fellow just like me who had worked on the topic for days behind closed doors (again, wearing a suit and tie). After two, three, or four drinks I asked, "You didn't know any details on the topics before you came, did you?"

"Nope," he said, smiled, and took another sip.

I couldn't help but blurt out a question that had been on my mind for some time: "Don't you feel like a charlatan?"

He gave me an answer that I recall almost verbatim: "Not at all. Of course I don't know any details. How should I?" His face turned serious. "My job as a leader is to show certainty in an ocean of uncertainty." He then added, "An expert is someone who knows a lot about very little. A leader is someone who knows very little about a lot."

I had an epiphany that evening that has since been illustrated to me again and again, especially when dealing with people at the highest executive levels: successful leaders do not quarrel with their ignorance, they are fully aware of it and accept it.

German sociologist Niklas Luhmann's "System Theory" reinforces this approach, stating that each and every system is isolated from the environment and each system has its own structure.[20] The factory worker acts within his own system, and so does the CEO. Consultants also act within a system and should not feel they have the bird's-eye view simply because there is no all-encompassing knowledge.[21] The world, with its people and organizations, is too complex for anyone to maintain an overview of everything. We can all only act within our own little system.

I am convinced that the awareness that you can only be competent within your own system is one of the keys to long-term success—and to mental health.

A Question of Technique

If you try to display your competence in the midst of all of these adverse circumstances and dilemmas, you will most likely fail. Common sense may help us ingratiate ourselves to others, but it hardly helps in coming up with effective techniques to increase our perceived competence. Though we seem to know how to be friendly or congenial, time and again we exhibit an inability to showcase our expertise in a positive, productive, and effective way.

In an experiment, subjects were told to make their conversation partner like them.[22] Lo and behold, most were successful. Their techniques? They were kind and polite and they smiled a lot. Easy.

Then they were asked to make a competent impression. Now they failed miserably. Their "techniques"? Their body language became stiff and stilted, and they spoke in a pompous manner and tended to disagree more with their conversation partner. Accordingly, they were rated not only as less competent but also as unlikable and cold.

We instinctively know what makes us pleasant, but we have no idea how to show our competence.[23] That's what this book is about: the most effective ways known to radiate competence. These are techniques of *impression management*, the conscious influence of our impression.[24] And there's more good news: these techniques aren't just beneficial for you, the individual, but for everyone you interact with, thanks to a phenomenon known as the "self-fulfilling prophecy." Suppose a fortuneteller predicts that you will gain 20 pounds in the next few months and you believe him. You would then probably give up your current diet because you would consider it pointless anyway. By quitting, you'll end up gaining weight, causing the fortune-teller's prediction to come true. Studies have also shown a similar process at work in the relationship between astrology and personality: people who are aware of the alleged personality characteristics of their zodiac sign actually behave accordingly.[25] So your horoscope becomes reality, but only if you know about it.

When it comes to competence, self-fulfilling prophecies work like a charm. Patients recover better if they consider their doctor to be competent—with the similar treatment.[26] In fact, in some cases patients can fully recover if they only believe in a treatment, despite its ineffectiveness. Who hasn't heard of the *placebo effect*? A patient is given a pill without any actual medicinal substance whatsoever, and yet it works because the patient believes in it, the pill's effectiveness being influenced by absurd factors such as size, color, price, and shape.[27]

Another example of the phenomenon at work: Students learn more from teachers whom they consider competent and as a result perform better themselves. In contrast, the performance of students who consider their teachers to be incompetent significantly decreases.[28]

When it comes to showing competence, this self-fulfilling prophecy works in both directions, as an increase in perceived competence also increases actual competence. If you are perceived as competent, you will be treated accordingly, which in turn affects others' behavior positively.

We have all experienced situations where we have been labeled by others, whether positive or negative. If you're known as a prankster, every comment you make is interpreted as a joke, causing others to laugh about every little thing you say. In turn, you start to believe in your own sense of humor and give it more credence. If you are considered a "weirdo," on the other hand, chances are that sooner or later, after your neutral behavior is misinterpreted again and again, you eventually start acting "weird."

The same idea applies to competence: When regarded as competent, others will grant you more opportunities to display your abilities. The label and actual competence then merge. The same can happen the other way: if you are considered incompetent, you will face a hostile environment where your skills just cannot bloom—and your performance will become worse and worse.

Interestingly, those who use effective techniques to increase their perceived competence are more accurately assessed than those who do not use such techniques. In other words, the correct techniques help you to show your true self.[29]

Conclusion

Do you remember the last time you had to give an important presentation? You most likely did more than just put a lot of thought into what you had to say. You probably also considered how to say it, what to wear, and how to interact with the audience. Such care should be taken with every type of communication we are involved in, because every interaction is a presentation that works for or against you. And make no mistake: just doing a good job isn't enough. If you bury yourself in work, you will only be noticed when something goes wrong.

The good news is that you can control a large part of what others think about you, an opportunity you should seize. The idea is to become your own PR agent, showing your skills by utilizing effective impression management tools; not only when giving a talk, writing your resume, or interviewing for a job—always![30] Perceived competence gives you the power to convince, influence, and lead others, as groups are persuaded by the person who appears to be most competent. When you are perceived to be incompetent, on the other hand, it will be almost impossible to win people over.[31]

By using the techniques described in this book, you will be able to display your expertise so that you receive the recognition you deserve. Throughout the chapters, psychological phenomena from decades of research are explored and exploited to help you showcase your expertise. Actions like controlling expectations, properly delivering good or bad news, using verbal and nonverbal techniques—most of these methods can be applied immediately, others need some practice, but none of them call for you to change your personality: authenticity is key in order to appear as a luminary.

With the advice in this book you will be able to exhibit your abilities in front of customers, colleagues, and superiors. Whether in meetings, presentations, or crucial conversations, you will be able to convince others of your expertise and be appreciated and respected like never before. At the same time, your perception will be trained to accurately assess the competence of others.

When you understand and implement these techniques and tools, your company will profit just as much, whether you are an executive or a sales representative, because customers prefer to buy from people they consider to be competent. The growing field of "corporate reputation" gives a great role to the employee's perceived competence. Oxford researchers David Waller and Rupert Younger found one of the pillars of corporate reputation to be the employee's perceived character ("character reputation"), along with his or her perceived competence ("capability reputation").[32] In fact, a CEO's perceived competence has a direct influence not only on the company's reputation but also on its actual performance.[33] It is therefore prudent for companies to focus on their employees' perceived competence.

Before moving on to the next chapter, let's return to the amazing story of Joshua Bell and the article about his experience that won journalist Gene Weingarten the Pulitzer Prize. One thing I haven't mentioned yet about this experiment at L'Enfant Plaza Station: a single passerby recognized Bell's virtuosity without actually recognizing the performer. John Picarello, who in his teenage years wanted to become a violinist himself, said, "This was a superb violinist. I've never heard anyone of that caliber. . . . It was a treat, just a brilliant, incredible way to start the day." Picarello stands in front of Bell and keeps looking around in despair, as no one else seems to understand what's going on.

Now imagine that not only one man is left standing, but that 1,097 passersby have stopped as well and they are all watching *you* because they know that they are witnessing something amazing, something brilliant in your performance. And you don't even have to be Joshua Bell.

Competence Compendium
The Perception of Brilliance

✧ The three principles:
   1. We cannot accurately assess others' expertise.
   2. We consider expertise to be the most important trait in the professional context.
   3. It is not *actual* competence but *perceived* competence that determines the impression you give.
✧ Success or failure has little effect on the perception of competence.
✧ Be aware of the illusion of the "just world."
✧ Embrace your incompetence.

CHAPTER 2

THE ANTICIPATION EFFECT

MANAGING EXPECTATIONS TO
SHOW YOUR EXPERTISE

Humans will believe anything you say provided you do not exhibit the smallest shadow of diffidence; like animals, they can detect the smallest crack in your confidence before you express it. . . . If you act like a loser they will treat you as a loser—you set the yardstick yourself. There is no absolute measure of good or bad.

—NASSIM NICHOLAS TALEB

The Richest Man in the World

Albuquerque, New Mexico, 1977. It was Miriam Lubow's first day at her new job as an administrative assistant. The young, unconventional company had made a rather chaotic impression on her, and Miriam had not yet met her boss, who was surely away on a business trip. As she sat at her desk, a young guy with disheveled hair, wearing jeans and sneakers, burst in, walked into the boss's office without saying a word to Miriam, and even proceeded into the inner sanctum—the computer room. Anxiously, Miriam ran to another department: What should she do about this guy who was acting like he owned the place? "Well, you know what," a colleague replied, "he does. He's your boss. He is the president."[1]

The name of this young chap? Bill Gates. He ran the company, which at that time was spelled "Micro-Soft," and he did so pretty successfully. After a few years, Microsoft moved to

27

Seattle, where it grew considerably and would soon receive a group of visitors who would change everything.

According to Microsoft manager Steve Ballmer, this group was a most distinguished one, and their visit was "like having the Queen drop by for tea, . . . like having the Pope come by looking for advice, . . . like a visit from God himself."[2]

It was a team of managers from International Business Machines (IBM), the undisputed giant of the computer industry at that time. But the team wasn't made up of elder statesmen; it was a young, ambitious group on a secret mission that would result in a revolution: a computer for individuals: the Personal Computer. "There is no reason for any individual to have a computer in his home," computer pioneer Ken Olson had said a few years earlier, capturing the prevailing opinion of the time. But the wind had changed, and IBM wanted to be at the forefront of this revolution.

IBM needed an operating system that mainstream consumers could use.[3] The market leader was Gary Kildall with his CP/M operating system, having sold almost 600,000 licenses— at the time a staggering amount. Kildall ranked among the most promising pioneers in the industry, despite being a poor and rather nerdy communicator. He had called his company Intergalactic Digital Research and had only dropped the word "Intergalactic" after much pleading from his wife.

Not very impressed with Kildall, the IBM executives approached Bill Gates. But he, too, wasn't much of an inspiration at first: "We got there at roughly two o'clock and we were waiting in the front," IBM manager Jack Sams recalls, "and this young fella came out to take us back to Mr. Gates' office. I thought he was the office boy, and of course it was Bill."

In order not to appear too uptight at the next meeting, the IBM executives dressed down in jeans and T-shirts, but now

Bill Gates greeted them in a three-piece suit and tie—he was evidently making a real effort. Not in vain: he sealed the deal and laid the foundations for the world's largest fortune.

Gates, a 24-year-old college dropout with a tiny company, had defeated Dr. Gary Kildall, an MIT graduate, the market leader, and the shining star of the industry. How could this be? Gates convinced Jack Sams and the IBM executives of his competence. He had dressed smartly at their second meeting, but the decisive factor was something else: he had assured IBM above all of his self-confidence to deliver a first-rate operating system.[4]

There was, however, one tiny problem: Gates had no operating system up his sleeve, and he wasn't even in the process of developing one. He worried little about this, though, until the IBM team had left. He then quickly found himself a programmer to put together such a system in only a few weeks, and for a handful of dollars, based on Kildall's work—a pirated copy under modern-day laws. And, what's more, a lousy one. The programmer was clearly aware of the system's shortcomings; otherwise he wouldn't have called it Quick and Dirty Operating System (QDOS). Gates apparently liked the name but decided to remove the Q: DOS was born, or, more precisely, MS-DOS (Micro-Soft-DOS).

This anecdote illustrates that you don't need grand offices, a pompous appearance, or a thunderous reputation in order to convince decision makers of your competence. Bill Gates did not even have an outstanding product in the bag—he had absolutely nothing, but he promised extraordinary results and then did what anybody else could have done: he found someone else who completed 100 percent of the work. But the decisive factor was that he knew how to arouse the right level of expectations from IBM—great expectations.

From Modesty to Boasting

You are entrusted with tasks every day: as a sales executive, you must ensure dynamic sales; as an attorney, you need to draw up contracts; as a consultant, you are required to develop intelligent strategies. By now, it should be clear that the mere quality of your work is not the only factor in its evaluation. In fact, your demonstrated level of expectation regarding your performance plays a key role. But what kind of outcome should you predict in order to be perceived as competent?

Should you dampen the level of expectation from the start and show some sort of noble restraint? Modesty certainly is an honorable trait.[5] And isn't it a nice surprise if people end up performing better than expected, along the lines of *underpromise and overdeliver*? According to the Gaussian probability distribution, however, average predictions exhibit the highest probability of occurrence, and accuracy is valued greatly in our society.[6] Or should you demonstrate extraordinary self-confidence and predict outstanding results? With this strategy, of course, you run the risk of appearing boastful.

US psychologists Barry Schlenker and Mark Leary scrutinized this issue in a remarkable, yet virtually unknown, study in which they specifically examined the effect of personal forecasts on perceived competence.[7] Subjects were given a randomly allocated task, but before they attempted it, they had to predict their expected level of performance, ranging from "very good" to "very poor." Outside observers noted these predictions. The participants then had to complete their task. Once the results of how well or poorly they performed had been revealed, the observers assessed the subjects' competence. One might think that they would be rated purely depending on their level of success: if they had performed well, they would be seen as having acted competently; if not, then they would be considered to have acted less competently, or even incompetently.

But a different picture emerged: the evaluation of competence was based not only on the results of the tasks but also very strongly on the basis of the participants' initial prediction.

Perceived competence of the subjects from their statement, performance, and timing (Schlenker & Leary)

Prediction	Actual Performance				
	Excellent	Good	Average	Poor	Very Poor
"Very good"	8.1	7.6	5.6	4.3	4.5
"Good"	7.9	7.6	5.9	4.5	4.3
"Average"	7.4	6.9	5.7	4.3	3.9
"Poor"	6.5	6.4	5.0	3.0	2.7
"Very poor"	7.0	6.5	4.8	3.0	2.7

Note: Competence evaluated on a scale from 1 to 10, with 10 being "most competent" and 1 being "least competent."

The crystal-clear trend with minor deviations is that the subjects' competence was evaluated higher if they had previously raised great expectations (see top row). Whoever made optimistic predictions about their performance was distinctly evaluated as being more competent compared to their modest contemporaries—no matter the outcome. This aspect is illustrated most interestingly in the right-hand "Very Poor" column. Here, the performance was always equally dreadful, yet the competence assessed varies—ranging from 2.7 to 4.5—based merely on the participants' predictions. Therefore, with an optimistic forecast and a horrible performance, the subjects are still rated as almost twice as competent as those who accurately forecasted their poor results. In short, the more optimistic the prediction, the higher the perceived competence.

Considering this finding, when confronted with a task, it makes sense to give a positive prognosis of the expected outcome of your performance. If the actual result you deliver matches your prediction, then you are perceived as being competent anyway. But even with an average or even a catastrophic outcome, by showing confidence, you give a considerably more competent impression than in the case of an accurate prediction of a very poor result. Therefore, if someone asks you how you expect to perform, give a positive, confident response (up to a certain extent, as discussed later in the book).

You must not predict a negative result, for no matter how well the task is ultimately performed—whether in a first-class manner or in a lousy one—you will be perceived as distinctly less competent than if you had provided a positive forecast.

Why is this the case? Unfortunately, causal interdependencies are invisible, but a certain combination of phenomena provides a plausible explanation.

Just Don't Worry!

One of these phenomena is all too human: fear. As a fundamental human mechanism, we do not look for what we like best but for what we fear the least. We have a veritable "loss aversion," which is why we have a greater motivation for avoiding pain than for increasing joy.[8] As a consequence, reducing uncertainty becomes a fundamental driving force of human behavior: when making a decision, we are—above all—trying to avoid making a mistake. And not without reason.

For our ancestors, almost every misfortune was a potential direct path to the afterlife. A simple cold and fever could mean death was imminent. They had to be on guard at all times simply to avoid making a life-threatening mistake. The cowards, our forefathers, survived. This legacy is revealed to us every day in the most trivial situations.

Some years ago, I went to Brussels to visit Sasha, my friend from Oxford, who had just started working for NATO. Sasha was delayed by about an hour—presumably the Third World

War had to be avoided (a five-star excuse Sasha would regularly use)—so I decided to find a café and do some reading. Nearby I had the choice between a small Italian café and, right next door, a Starbucks, which I am not a big fan of. So I asked myself, "Where should I go?"

Unconsciously, my legs led me straight into the Starbucks. When Sasha showed up, he was amazed that instead of choosing Luigi's—which apparently served the best espresso outside Italy—I was sitting in this place that was a spitting image of the Starbucks I could have found back home, right outside my front door. He was right, of course. But it was that fear, passed down by my forefathers, that had driven me toward the Starbucks. Here I at least knew what to expect: a decent cup of coffee. And so I had chosen not what I would have probably liked more but that which I had feared least.

"I'm lovin' it!" Really? Is there any person who truly *loves* the food at McDonald's? OK, there may be some, but they are few and far between. So how does McDonald's keep serving billions? Above everything else, customers want to avoid making a *bad* choice. And they know exactly what a McDonald's burger tastes like. It is this necessity of minimizing the risk for customers that Ray Kroc, the founding father of McDonald's, recognized early on as the key to success. His aim was to offer the "same" burger from Atlantic City to Zaragoza. As he put it, "There is a science to manufacturing and serving hamburgers."[9] This idea—simple but accommodating to our deepest fears—catapulted McDonald's, and the entire franchising industry, into new stratospheres.

The same fundamental principle applies for selling more-complex products. "Nobody gets fired for buying IBM" was a familiar dictum as early as the 1970s. IBM used the fear of uncertainty as the main argument against their small, emerging competitors. This notorious sales tactic, called "Fear, Uncertainty, and Doubt"[10] (FUD), was later adopted by none other than Microsoft and taken to a whole new level: the company deliberately built nonsensical error messages into its operating system that only popped up when using third-party, non-Microsoft software. The company preyed on the fears of its customers to steer them away from competitors' products.

Though it may be possible to offer almost the same burger, cappuccino, or computer anywhere in the world, it becomes so much more complex with services. How can you trust an attorney you have never met before? This is precisely why reducing the level of client or customer anxiety in service-sector industries plays such a significant role. It's no wonder that the worlds of attorneys, auditors, accountants, and consultants are dominated by a handful of big players that consumers trust.

And yet, an attorney from the Clifford Chance law firm in London is unlikely to draft a sales and purchase agreement that conforms 100 percent with the work of his colleague in Shanghai, nor even with the work of his peer next door, because there is no completely standardized procedure for such complex services.[11] The role of individual team members is hence still fundamental. The "rainmakers" and stars at those firms are those who manage to eliminate their clients' anxieties during personal interactions.

The most influential "service providers" are arguably politicians, and reducing anxiety levels is one of their central driving goals. With voters, many times we see a willingness to stick with politicians they know, as compared to electing ones they are unfamiliar with. Current officeholders frequently win in subsequent elections for precisely this reason, known as an *incumbency advantage*.[12] In the US House of Representatives, for instance, between 1964 and 2014, the reelection rate ranged between 85 percent and 98 percent.[13] Every officeholder who put himself or herself up for reelection in these 50 years could be almost virtually certain of victory—it is hard to imagine that the voters dearly loved them, but it is likely that they feared the unknown.

This fear of imminent deterioration plays a decisive factor when any kind of role must be assigned within an organization. Who are the least competent people who work at your company? It may be hard to imagine, but there must have been a moment when the decision makers—possibly even after lengthy consultation—told them, "Yes, you are the right one for the job!" But why? Perhaps their main driver was a desire to avoid an even bigger disaster. It isn't unusual that interns who never stood out positively, but also never left a negative impression, are hired by the company they interned for—at least they didn't burn down the building.

It is important to recognize that, time and again, fear is the key factor in decision making, no matter if we are choosing a hamburger, electing a head of state, or deciding between job candidates.[14] If you want to convince people of your value, you should follow the words of the US marketing strategist Harry Beckwith: "Do not try to be a good choice. Eliminate everything that could make you a bad choice." This statement may sound banal, but it represents a true paradigm shift: no matter whom you want to convince, and no matter of what, if your primary concern is helping them overcome their fear, then you automatically become a more effective salesperson of your own competence. This is especially true if a client or consumer must make a difficult decision in a complicated context, as is the case when a layperson puts his fate in the hands of an expert, such as a family hiring an architect to plan their dream house or a young start-up entrepreneur engaging a tax adviser.[15] So always ask yourself what your clients', your colleagues', or your supervisors' specific anxieties look like and focus your persuasion strategy on eliminating these fears.

In considering this approach, I am reminded of the time I interviewed for grad school at the then newly founded Said Business School at Oxford University. Before the interview I pondered what I was up against: I had studied at Oxford, but in the Philosophy Department, before which I had studied law and psychology. Consequently, there was nothing on my resume that indicated I had ever dealt with business. I assumed that the greatest fear I could arouse in my interviewer was that of accepting a philosopher not concerned with the worldly matters of a business school.

I decided to at least dress "businesslike," so I bought myself a blue shirt and pinstripe pants (I didn't have enough money for the jacket). I will never forget how my future professor greeted me: "Oh, I expected a philosopher. But I see you would fit right in." It worked—even with an Oxford professor.

Transferring this concept to an everyday situation, imagine you are out of town and you need a haircut. You find yourself standing in front of a hairdresser, uncertain whether you should enter, worrying that you could ruin your appearance for weeks to come. As I frequently travel for my advisory work, I end up in this situation all the time. I remember one particular incident: I was in New York City for a few weeks and found a small barbershop that seemed fine, but standing there, pondering, I was still undecided. The barber approached me and told me that I would be in the best of hands. Then, I spotted a few certificates and trophies inside—I was very pleased with this evidence of competence and my fears subsided. As I sat in the barber's chair and he finished washing my hair, he proudly told me about his last soccer tournament and showed me the trophy he had won. Only then did I notice—a soccer ball was displayed on all the awards. It was too late (but turned out ok)!

The first step in displaying your competence is therefore to consider what could potentially speak or work against you, and then to address this fear; reducing uncertainty plays a key role when you are trying to display competence and convince other people of just about anything.[16]

If you are invited for a job interview or you are meeting with a prospective client, then it is obvious your formal qualifications certainly fulfill all the necessary requirements for the position or the work. For them, it's now just a matter of ensuring that they're not making a mistake by choosing you. Such mistakes are costly; it is much more cost effective for a company to overlook an able candidate or service provider from time to time than to pick an incompetent one. US authorities regularly fall back on lie-detector tests when interviewing for government positions, even though they only attribute an accuracy of 80 percent to these tests. The reasoning is that it makes more sense to not recruit a number of highly qualified candidates than to recruit just a few who could pose a potential risk to national security.[17] Accordingly, applications and interviews are, first and foremost, searches for negative information.[18]

"It's good that you are here. I can imagine you must be a bit nervous. But don't worry. I'm very good at what I do." We do not interpret words like these from those whose help we seek as arrogance in critical decisive moments. Rather, they are music to our ears when we are full of anxiety about making a major mistake: choosing the wrong hairdresser, the wrong tax consultant, the wrong construction company, the wrong employee. In those vulnerable moments, there is hardly anything better than hearing someone say, "Don't worry. I'll take care of it." Projecting this type of confidence instills trust and places you at a distinct advantage. Maintaining that confidence is the next crucial step in signaling your competence.

Always Remain Confident

In a fascinating experiment, subjects were given a glass of wine and told that it cost either $10 or $90 a bottle.[19] The ones who were told that they were drinking the expensive wine rated it as significantly higher. The scientists were not satisfied by solely taking the subjects' word and wondered if they really perceived the wine differently. So, when drinking the wine, they measured the subjects' brain function with an fMRI scanner. Lo and behold, their oxygen and blood flow differed even though it was the exact same wine. Thus not only did they say it tasted different but it actually did—solely based on their expectation. The different reactions originated from what is called *confirmation bias*: individuals select information that fits their hypothesis and confirms what they believed from the very beginning.[20] And people usually believe what they are told.[21]

The confirmation bias phenomenon is reflected in our assessment of other people. In one experiment, test subjects were presented with the biographical data of a nonexistent "Jane."[22] One group of subjects was told ahead of time that Jane was shy and introverted, while a second group was informed that she was loud and extroverted. Both groups were then presented with further, identical information about Jane's life and were asked if it matched what they had previously thought about Jane. And indeed, both groups confirmed their diametrically opposed hypotheses: Jane's introverted nature was confirmed by group one, and her extroverted nature was confirmed by group two.

Some time ago, I strolled through picturesque Turl Street in Oxford and discovered a wonderful pair of shoes in the window of a traditional store, made by hand. I went inside and asked the shoemaker just why I should buy this very expensive footwear. Granted, a foolish question, but don't customers constantly ask questions they could answer themselves by reading the company's website or sales brochure? We have an un-conscious need to have someone take away our fear. Good salespeople are aware of this fact—and the shoemaker was cer-tainly one of them. He looked me directly in the eye and re-plied with a straight face, "Because they are the best shoes in the world." Funny, I thought. But naturally, I had to buy them.

Three months later, I was back in the store for the third time: the heel had fallen off one of them . . . again. I wasn't angry but instead felt bad for ruining such a masterpiece.

Had I discovered a twisted seam while examining these "best shoes in the world," I wouldn't have regarded it as evidence of sloppiness but as that of traditional craftsmanship. Had I been told that this was a cheap pair of shoes from some factory, I would have considered the same seam a sign of inferior qual-ity. Again, we subconsciously try to confirm our expectations and interpret ambiguous information to be in line with our assumptions. And even though I began gradually to have doubts, to this day I cannot find it in my heart to throw this pair of shoes away. I somehow still believe that they are the work of a truly masterful craftsman—even though I (should) know better.

As in Schlenker and Leary's study, even the one predicting a "very good" result who then fails is still judged as more com-petent than a person accurately predicting his own failure. In this way, confidence is more important than success. We for-give optimists for their failures and we continue to regard them as part of the solution, rather than as a part of the problem.

In other words, people believe what they are told and are willing to overlook quite a lot to the contrary in an effort to maintain their beliefs. Therefore, signaling your capabilities is actually rather simple: communicate in very clear words that you have outstanding skills in your field and show confidence regarding the task entrusted to you. "Praise yourself daringly," the philosopher Francis Bacon once said, because, as he continued "something always sticks."

If you communicate your expertise and display confidence, others will believe you and will tend to confirm this impression. That being said, note that there are certain cultural differences for which this approach may need to be somewhat tailored. In China, for example, forcefully praising oneself is not recommended, while in Japan, such behavior is even more reserved.[23] This does not mean that these techniques could not be applied in these countries, but only that they must be adapted to the environment in their nature and intensity.

Demonstrable confidence in one's own ability can go quite far. In one experiment, groups of four had to discuss a strategy for how to perform a certain task. The researchers sneaked an actor into the discussion group and told him to be impolite and somewhat bossy.[24] At the end of the debate, when discussing how to divide the joint gains, he boldly claimed the largest share, as he considered his contributions to be the best and the most important. Contrary to researchers' expectations, his competence was rated higher despite, or actually *because* of, this boldness. In fact, the sooner he started behaving arrogantly, the higher his competence was rated, even when he was obviously wrong.

This experiment showed that people are convinced not by who has the best arguments but rather by whoever shows the greatest confidence.[25] Think of it this way: If two of your friends are discussing who won the yo-yo world championship in 1955, and one of them suddenly pulls out a $100 bill and bets on her candidate, who are you more likely to believe? Exactly.

You can also refer to your past successes to substantiate your competence and ensure confidence in your performance. A *Forbes* study of the top 100 high-tech companies unsurprisingly found that earlier successes by individuals are a very significant part of giving the impression of competence later on.[26] We expect people to deal with future tasks the same way they dealt with ones in the past. Some extremely successful managers even send out a slideshow every year, showing their greatest accomplishments and reminding superiors and clients of their capabilities. You do not need to go this far, but it doesn't hurt to inform your boss or manager whenever you have exceeded expectations in terms of speed or quality or if you just received a thank-you email from a client. By doing so, you manifest the impression of high performance, even if they don't recall the particulars. If you think that you should focus on delivering good work instead of selling your work, think again. You will then only hear from your boss or your client if something went wrong.

People are not hired or promoted because of their actual outstanding performance but because of their presumed potential. Others will quickly forget specifically what you have said or done, but they will never forget how you made them feel.[27] A key objective of executive leadership is therefore absorbing the uncertainty and insecurity of the people around you.[28]

Another argument speaks in favor of displaying confidence. Two Canadian psychologists, Donald Dutton and Art Aron, carried out a fascinating study in the 1970s that is now known as the "bridge experiment."[29] Male test subjects were asked to walk across a bridge to the other side, where an attractive female researcher was awaiting them. For one set of subjects, the bridge was a sturdy bridge of average height and width, whereas the other group had to cross a narrow, swaying suspension bridge nearly 300 feet above a terrifying ravine. The female researcher then asked the men to take a test and gave them her phone number in case they had questions. Unknown to the subjects, the main point of the experiment was about the phone number: The men who were thrown about on the swaying bridge tended to call significantly more often than those who weren't. They did not ask her any particular questions but appeared to have developed a crush on her.

The experiment illustrated how context influences our feelings considerably. If we fall in love, for example, a series of physical symptoms takes place: our hearts beat faster and our hands become moist and sweaty. But this idea also works in reverse: if our heart beats faster for other reasons, say, out of fear, then our feelings of love may also increase. You should hence avoid peaceful walks on a date with your prospective sweetheart and should rather pursue activities that result in the symptoms of falling in love—skydiving, bungee jumping, or watching horror movies.

Applying this experiment to demonstrating competence, you should attempt to put the person you're trying to influence at ease. Think about what symptoms people display when they find themselves in the hands of an expert in whose skills they wholeheartedly trust. They should feel relaxed, calm, and confident in the expert's capabilities. You should therefore put your customers, colleagues, or superiors into exactly this state as best you can, both mentally and physically. Create a calm environment with comfortable chairs and without interruptions; above all, radiate confidence. In this way, others will believe in your competence and trust your expertise. The more people are convinced by your confident approach and your ability to dispel their fears, the more your confidence and true competence will grow from within. To get to that point, however, you need to remember that the first person you need to convince of your competence is *you*—if you don't believe in it, no one else will.

Confidence Comes from Within

The bridge experiment showed how context influences our feelings. You can use this phenomenon directly on yourself. Our bodily communication can directly influence our state of mind.

We need to obtain information about our emotions through certain clues—and when we smile, for example, we assume that we are in good spirits. This idea was illustrated by the German psychologist Fritz Strack, who conducted an experiment in which he showed test subjects a cartoon film.[30] There were two test groups: the members of one were supposed to put a pen in their mouths like a straw, under the pretext of investigating "psychomotor coordination." The other group was supposed to fix the pen across their mouths with their teeth—like a dog biting a bone. Afterward, everyone assessed how funny they thought the film was. Behold, those who held the pen in their mouths lengthwise—and thus were forced to "smile"—thought the film was funnier.

Strack showed that people can change their moods from the outside to the inside, not just vice versa. Similar to the bridge experiment, in which the symptoms of being in love led to actual infatuation, we don't only have to be in a good mood to conjure up a smile—smiling gets us in a good mood.[31] We can use this insight to convince ourselves of your confidence. A much discussed study on the effect of the "superhero stance" found that a self-confident body stance has a tremendous effect on your actual feeling of confidence.[32] The researchers tested the saliva of subjects who were holding their body in a "high-power" position briefly and found that it led to lower levels of cortisol (stress hormone) and higher levels of testosterone (the hormone leading to dominance). High-power poses were either sitting or standing. The sitting position was feet on the desk and hands behind head, with the elbows out. The standing pose had the subjects standing with their legs about a foot apart, and the hands leaning over a table. Both positions took up a lot of room. The low-power poses, on the other hand, took up much less space: Now they were sitting straight up, legs at a 90 degree angle, feet on the floor, hands on the lap, with the arms tucked in. Low power standing subjects had their legs crossed tightly, and the arms hugging themselves. So, standing or sitting in a high-power pose, will help you project the necessary confidence. Canadian psychologist Jordan Peterson regards the right stance as the first out of 12 rules for life.[33] He writes: "Maybe you are a loser. And maybe you're not—but if you are, you don't have to continue in that mode." Right and wrong posture have consequences, and you can create a 'positive feedback loop': "If your posture is poor, for example—if you slump, shoulders forward and rounded, chest tucked in, head down, looking small, defeated and ineffectual (protected, in theory, against attack from behind)—then you will feel small, defeated and ineffectual. The reactions of others will amplify that." If you stand up straight with your shoulders back, on the other hand, you will not only be treated differently, but you will feel differently: "You step forward to take your place in the dominance hierarchy," writes Peterson, "and occupy your territory, manifesting your willingness to defend, expand and transform it."

And there is an even more subtle way to alter your own behavior: *priming*. Imagine you are taking part in one of my seminars and are asked to come up to the front of the room and pull a piece of paper out of a box. On the paper is one of the following questions, which you must answer immediately:

• What are you actually good at?
• Why are you suitable for your job?
• What was your greatest professional success?
• What have you ever achieved for your company?
• Why should you, of all people, take on the responsibility for an upcoming project?
• Why should anyone be led by you?

Not easy to answer, are they? But they should be! And yet, you have probably never thought about these questions, even though you won't get a second chance to reply. If you cannot immediately give a good answer to such questions, then it is highly unlikely that you'll be seen as confident—and eventually be competent. If all eyes are on you, you cannot afford to stutter and stammer. No one will blame you if you don't know every detail, but you must know the obvious! Such are the moments that can make or break your career.

When Ted Kennedy ran for president in 1980, the TV journalist Roger Mudd asked him a seemingly innocuous question: "Why are you running for president?"[34] Almost 10 agonizing seconds passed before Kennedy replied, seconds that seemed like an eternity and were considered the beginning of the end of his campaign.

Similarly, when I was conducting interviews of bachelor candidates at Oxford University, I asked each one why he or she should be considered to study economics and management at the school. It was strange how few were able to answer this simple question and how this failure fundamentally shattered the impression they were trying to make.

Even if you rarely encounter such blunt questions, the mere awareness of the answers, the mental preparation technique known as priming, has an effect on your subconscious:[35] the exposure to one stimulus can influence the response to another stimulus. To be more specific, a very brief occupation with an abstract idea can lead to differences in levels of performance. Let me illustrate it with a perplexing study: Test subjects were asked to answer 42 relatively difficult Trivial Pursuit questions. One group had been asked beforehand to briefly consider what it means to be a professor, while the other group concentrated their thoughts on football hooligans. The "professor group" correctly answered significantly more questions (55.6 percent) than the "hooligan group" (42.6 percent).

In another experiment, test subjects were asked to complete a scrambled-sentence task as part of a "language proficiency experiment."[36] The test contained either neutral words or those related to "old age," such as *wise, wrinkle, bingo,* and *Florida.* Unknown to the subjects, their answers to the questions were irrelevant. Once they left the room, another experimenter secretly recorded the time they took to walk down the corridor. And, in fact, the time varied considerably. The subconscious occupation with the idea of age led to an almost 20 percent slower pace. Our thoughts—conscious or not—influence our behavior.

You can use priming to your advantage. Superstar athletes use it regularly to boost their performance. David Platt, the former captain of the England national soccer team, routinely watched video recordings of his greatest goals to prime himself for the upcoming match. Competitive athletes must regularly overcome enormous pressure while being observed by millions—for example, as Serena Williams must do when setting up for a decisive serve at Wimbledon. They learn to deliberately suppress doubts in order to achieve peak performance even in high-pressure situations and instead focus on their strengths and previous accomplishments.

This doesn't mean that you should ignore your weaknesses or stop self-reflection. But this targeted suppression of negativity should be used before key moments, such as a penalty shootout or, when transferred to the corporate context, just before the final presentation in a sales meeting or an interview for your dream job. Before beginning the important high-stress task, and after having thought about how to eliminate any arguments that speak against you, you should visualize your achievements and abilities, suppressing any doubts about your competence whatsoever. Will this priming technique immediately turn you into an Olympic champion? Not likely, but as the British athlete Sally Gunnell, world champion and Olympic gold medalist in women's hurdles, aptly says, "It's the difference between gold and silver."[37]

Inner confidence is more than mere luxury, especially in the workplace. Those who lack confidence develop feelings of inferiority that typically lead to aggression.[38] Managers, for example, become hostile as soon as they doubt their own competence, causing them to speak in an agitated tone and intentionally hurt their subordinates.[39] Priming therefore helps not just the managers to mentally prepare themselves—resulting in increased confidence—but also all other parties involved.

Once you have consciously made yourself aware of your abilities and noted down your answers to the foregoing questions—on your phone or on a piece of paper you keep in your wallet—try giving them a quick look before any crucial meetings. By internalizing your responses, your behavior will change, you will exude more confidence, and, on top of that, your actual performance will improve. And if you are ever asked these questions, you will be prepared to reply immediately with confidence, once again signaling your competence.

Modesty Is . . . ?

As I have expounded on the importance of displaying confidence throughout this chapter, you may have at one time or another wondered to yourself whether overconfidence isn't too much of a good thing. You may be concerned that you'll be viewed as a showoff without any critical self-awareness whatsoever. Maybe you've asked, "What about the virtue of modesty? Is this no longer an honorable and commendable characteristic? Is it not humble people who, after all, enjoy the greatest respect?" These are all good questions, to which I'd like to respond by presenting the following scenario.

Imagine that, following a skiing accident, you are lying with a broken leg in a small-town hospital. The surgeon on duty, a nice guy, tells you that you have had two lots of bad luck: not only is your leg broken but you also ended up with *him* as your doctor. He then lets you know that he isn't "the greatest physician in the world," had enjoyed student life rather too much to give enough attention to his studies, and "actually always wanted to be a musician: jazz!" But he will do his honest best. Would you be pleased with so much modesty? Unlikely. Instead, you would probably try to grab the closest wheelchair and make a quick getaway.

It is very possible that the man is an excellent surgeon and is merely being modest, living according to the maxim "under-promise and overdeliver," discussed earlier. But would you consider him competent? And would you personally like him more for being so modest? Even if the surgery turns out successful, wouldn't you still think it could have been even more successful with a different physician? When you are lying in a hospital, weak and in the hands of fate, the last thing you want to hear from your potential savior is self-doubt. Instead, you would like to meet a confident professional who assures you that you are in the best of hands and will receive the greatest treatment the world has to offer.

Your clients, colleagues, and superiors want to hear the same thing from you as soon as they entrust you with a task. They want to work with someone who is confident enough to face any challenge, not someone who breeds fear and worry with false, or sincere, modesty.

As mentioned earlier in the chapter, people believe what they are told and tend to unconsciously confirm those expectations—positively and negatively. If you behave modestly, people will take your self-doubt at face value and will hardly be stirred from their initial expectation, no matter your performance. You will be perceived as incompetent from the start, and whatever you do will be seen as proof of your inability.

In fact, modesty may be the most commonly observed form of self-destruction in offices and boardrooms. When highly paid managers or experts joke about their supposed incompetence, they immediately ruin their appearance and degrade their skills. Most of us have experienced someone making a self-deprecating comment in jest, such as an accountant saying he never was all that great with numbers. We laugh along with them, but at the same time we likely make a note to never work with this person when something really important is at stake—the joker has irreparably damaged his or her perceived competence. To laxly paraphrase the British thinker Thomas Fuller, "Better to lose a jest than a customer."

Incidentally, modesty is by no means as popular everywhere as it is in Western societies, where it is welcome at least in private settings. For example, in India, it is much more common to praise oneself.[40] The universal fact, no matter the country or culture, is that modesty must be avoided as far as possible in a professional context.[41] In my seminars, I have observed that North Americans and Asians follow this advice more readily; Europeans, however, especially British and German managers, only reluctantly accept that modesty has no place in a professional setting. Many assume that demonstrating too much confidence could have adverse effects on their likability and would therefore somehow reduce their perceived competence. This assumption is flat-out wrong: modesty is associated with uncertainty and cowardice and is seen as being a shield against possible failure.[42]

Indeed, humility often originates from the calculation that in the event of failure, it takes the wind out of any critics' sails—a motivation that is not respectable whatsoever. Why accept the task at all if you believe you cannot perform it? I often hear speakers starting their presentations with some excuse about what's to come: that they are not well prepared or that they did not sleep well. Does the audience immediately like these people? Not at all. Instead, we wonder why they did not prepare better or get more sleep—it's not as if they just found out yesterday that they would have to appear here today. It is hence not surprising that modesty can actually lead to aversion.[43]

Do we have to denounce modesty in all cases as a downright reprehensible characteristic? As always, there is an exception to the rule. If you know ahead of time that you cannot perform an action or task to the required degree, then by all means, be modest. Besides ethical considerations, your credibility will be shattered after a series of failures. However, this should be the only exception. Otherwise, if you feel that you cannot perform successfully on a consistent basis, you may want to reconsider your choice of career.

If you refuse to let go of modesty, even when you know you are up for the task, there is one way to use it to your advantage. The marketing strategist Harry Beckwith describes an experiment in which two similar applications for the same position were sent to different companies.[44]

The virtual applicants were called Dave and John. Their applications only differed by one sentence in the letters of recommendation they had to include: "Sometimes, John can be difficult to get along with." This sentence was not written anywhere in Dave's documents. In the end, John was invited to more interviews than Dave. The tiny negative remark made the whole application appear more credible and John more competent.

A single, slightly negative, or—when describing yourself—modest, statement can therefore be perceived as believable, and in this way, it can increase a person's perceived competence. However, the greatest caution is advised here: humble statements must appear insignificant compared to your strengths and must not interfere with your core competencies. Good examples of modest statements that might work include those that are somewhat superfluous, such as "I am horrible at ping-pong"—unless of course you're trying out for a national table tennis team—or those that take a negative and make it a positive, like "I'm a lousy liar," which also contributes to perceived credibility. A sentence like "I was always bad at math," however, can already be harmful, irrespective of the field or activity, since math is regularly associated with intelligence and in turn serves as an indication of competence. The Princeton psychologist Edward E. Jones gets to the point, saying, "Whenever modesty is used, it must reflect the self-assured acceptance of some weaknesses that are obviously trivial in the context of the strengths."[45]

To summarize, modest predictions of your performance and good-hearted self-deprecating anecdotes that cast doubt on your skills do not help portray competence. Not only will you appear less competent, but you could also make yourself unpopular at the office. People do not appreciate modesty in the professional context, but they are grateful for every sign of confidence. If you feel that you absolutely must inject a little humility into your personality, correspondence, or tasks, then make sure you do so without jeopardizing your core competencies. Remember, some may consider modesty a virtue, but you will get further without it, which leads to the question of whether modesty is a virtue at all.

Conclusion

There is a phrase by management thinker Jim Collins: "Quiet, hard-working, stoic leaders are responsible for really big changes."[46] It is a rather symptomatic view I often encounter—and one that is, of course, opposed to everything you have just read. So who is right? Well, business guru Tom Peters countered Collins's statement with a list of protagonists from world history, such as Pablo Picasso, Wolfgang Amadeus Mozart, Abraham Lincoln, Winston Churchill, Margaret Thatcher, Andrew Carnegie, John Rockefeller, Henry Ford, Jack Welch, Steve Jobs, and more.

Could we draw up an equally impressive list of modest, stoic people? I tried, but I did not succeed, especially when I considered that the people named by Peters are *the* icons, *the* top names in their fields. I couldn't get any further than Mahatma Gandhi and Mother Teresa—and there are anecdotes from their closest confrères that indicate they weren't so stoic after all. Furthermore, Peters's list can grow and grow without end, from Napoleon Bonaparte to Ludwig van Beethoven to the German philosopher Friedrich Nietzsche, who used the following chapter titles in his last work, *Ecce Homo*: "Why I Am So Smart" and "Why I Write Such Good Books." In extreme cases, these people have an almost narcissistic personality disorder, convinced of their own grandeur—and they are extremely successful.[47] A modern example is Donald Trump, who won the US presidential election without any political track record but by displaying an exuberant confidence in his skills.

Political affiliations or industries make no difference: Hollywood actor George Clooney is certain that it was his demonstrated confidence that led to his success:[48] "The best actor never gets the job when they audition. Never." Why? Because of their lack of confidence: "Actors go into auditions thinking, Oh God, they're going to hate me, they're going to hate me."

This insight marked a turning point for Clooney: "I started to come in selling confidence, not even my acting skills." He uses baseball as a metaphor for his transformation: "I realized that I needed to treat acting like I treated baseball. I said, 'From now on, I'm not going to wonder if I'm going to hit the ball. I'm going to knock the hell out of it.'"

So how can we achieve effective "expectation management" in terms of competence?

Eliminate others' anxieties and you will be handsomely rewarded. Demonstrate confidence regarding your skills and underpin this with your successes, whether from past achievements or from experiences related to the current project. Others will believe in you and will unconsciously confirm their assumptions. Prime yourself by focusing on your strengths just before critical moments. Avoid modesty regarding your core competencies. If you follow these steps, even when failing, you will still be rated as competent and likable.

Remember that Bill Gates had no operating system, but he still managed to convince IBM to rely on his competence. Though he used someone else's work, he nonetheless rose to become the market leader, despite the fact that releasing his (Q) DOS led to decades of computer crashes. And what about the software pioneer Gary Kildall? As *Bloomberg News* once put it, he became the man who "could have been Bill Gates."[49] He died an embittered alcoholic at the age of 52 after suffering a head injury in unexplained circumstances at a bar. Bill Gates, however, influenced the thinking and actions of humankind for decades, amassed the largest fortune in the world, and eventually became its most generous benefactor.

Learn from Bill Gates—and at the same time do a good job. You will probably not become the richest person in the world overnight, but then again, the longest journey starts with a single step.

Competence Compendium
Great Expectations

✧ **Reduce anxiety**: eliminate anything that speaks against you.

✧ Demonstrate **confidence** regarding your abilities and the task—**prime** yourself by using high-power poses and being aware of your strengths.

✧ **Avoid modesty** regarding your core competencies.

CHAPTER 3

GOOD NEWS, BAD NEWS

USING THE POWER OF ASSOCIATION

In life, 10 percent is about what happens, and 90 percent is about how we react to it.

—UNKNOWN

The Power of Association

Yes, yes, no, no, yes, no, yes, yes, no, no.

Without counting the number of words on the previous line, take a guess of whether "yes" or "no" appears more times. Keep your answer in mind, as I'll return to this question later (and don't cheat by counting them!).

Do you remember the McKinsey and AT&T story from chapter 1? Though the consulting firm made a gigantic mistake, their reputation was hardly damaged. They were still able to radiate competence despite such a gigantic public failure. It's important to ask, How can any company or individual appear competent in spite of such an obvious bomb? This ability is even more surprising when considering the asymmetry that exists between the effects of good and bad impressions: negative events will normally make a deeper impression than positive ones because they run counter to social expectations.[1] That is why it is particularly important to properly manage bad impressions. However, we should also look at how to convert a success story into the best possible impression of perceived expertise.

When you check out the newest cars at the Detroit Motor Show, you will see plenty of pretty hostesses either stand around the cars or sit right on top of them. It is almost a cliché, but there are still advertisements where a model poses on the hood of a vehicle. Are these 18-year-old models automobile experts whose endorsements should be taken seriously? Probably not. Then why has car advertising been done this way for so many decades?

The answer is, of course, that the attractiveness of the models influences the perception of the cars. With a beautiful girl, the car seems more attractive, faster, and better in every way—that is the power of association. In psychology, this idea is known as the "halo effect,"[2] because like a halo that shines on the saint, one characteristic of an object rubs off on another object— positive as well as negative.

It is also the halo effect that makes celebrity endorsements so powerful: actors wearing watches, singers being the face of a makeup brand. But when the star power of that celebrity begins to fade and is shattered by a scandal, the positive association will disappear, because the golden halo fades or even turns pale. It may therefore be cruel, but it is hardly surprising that companies are so quick to end their sponsorship agreements with dwindling stars.

Another example from the automobile industry is found in car manufacturers that are fond of producing so-called halo cars, spectacular studies in design.[3] They create these works of art in the hope that the attention-grabbing design and the outrageous performance stats of the futuristic prototype will influence the entire brand, even though not a single one will ever be made available for purchase.

Why do major fashion labels like Ralph Lauren or Giorgio Armani sink millions in magnificent and oversize flagship stores on the most expensive shopping streets in the world, such as

Rodeo Drive in Beverly Hills or Via Condotti in Rome? For the same reason that they put on shows presenting their haute couture at the New York Fashion Week, where hardly anything is sold. These efforts are made to connect their brands with the glamour of the Magnificent Mile and the dazzling fashion shows so that hordes of customers will make daily purchases of their trademark perfumes or comparably inexpensive T-shirts with the company's logo, partaking in the glamour of the brand for only a few dollars.

The power of association is enormous—whole bookshelves could be filled with tomes listing examples of its applications.[4] However, for the purposes of this book, I am only interested in how the power of association will help you improve the perception of your competence. More specifically: How can you use your success to the utmost advantage in regard to perceived competence while suffering the least damage to your reputation from your failures?

Delivering Good News

Messengers will always be associated with the message, regardless of whether they contributed to its content or had nothing to do with it at all. In the case of good news, you should make your personal connection to that message as clear as possible. To continue with the car theme, think of yourself as the automobile and the good news as the pretty model. The closer you are to the model, the stronger the positive association. You should strongly align yourself with good news so that the positive information you're relaying reflects on you as much as possible. The key is to demonstrate presence: Deliver good news in person, not by telephone, and certainly not by email. When you are presenting good news in a meeting, stand up, position yourself in the center of the room, and make a short speech. Try to stay visible in that position for as long as possible—every single moment strengthens your ties to the positive information you're providing. Devote as much time as you can to your message by stretching it out, dividing it up into as many parts as possible, and spreading those parts out over your entire presentation.[5] You want the message to come across loud and clear, and you also want people to associate you as much as possible with such excellent news.

If your team is going to highlight its accomplishments and successful work in the next department meeting, volunteer to present the report yourself—you want to make sure that you're the one up front and center. Even though you are praising your team in the highest possible terms, above all, you and your expertise will appear in the strongest light and will be remembered by all those in attendance.

Say your friends and you have saved up for a gift that you're giving to another friend for her birthday. Whichever one of you physically hands her the gift will always be most strongly associated with it. Someone who shows up after the formal presentation of the gift will hardly be connected with it at all; perhaps even less than someone who was not part of the group whatsoever but who was just a lucky onlooker.

It is therefore crucial to put yourself in the best light—literally. If you stand in a bright light that causes you to be the shining center of the room, the audience will be more likely to associate the outcome you're describing with your personal competence than with anything external. Your competence becomes the focal point.

Compare it to a spotlight in the theater: If an artist stands alone in the spotlight, he will be the focus of attention. There is no set design to distract from his presence, no other actors, nothing—in this moment, there is only this one person, and everyone is watching him. Similarly, actors or other performers always want to take their curtain calls in the spotlight after a very successful production. If the performance was less successful, the audience area will often be brightly lit at the end of the show so that the set, all the actors, and even the audience can be seen.

In regard to displaying competence, the following conclusions can be drawn: If you are presenting news about a success, you should always stand in a strong light. Under no circumstances do you want to humbly pull back into some dark corner. When giving a presentation, make sure that you are brightly lit—the presentation will, perhaps, not be as easy to see, but it will be easier to see you. Good lighting also has two more benefits:[6] First, it serves as a memory aid. Audiences tend to remember a well-lit performer better, which is, naturally, what we want for a success story. Second, an individual standing in a strong light is more likely to be perceived as a leader, and perceived authority is very helpful when conveying competence.

Physical movement will also direct attention away from the surroundings and toward your abilities.[7] If you are the bearer of good news, you should not, under any circumstances, stand stiffly in front of the audience; rather, move around and gesticulate in a lively manner, directing the audience's focus toward you and your expertise.

Possibly the most outstanding communicator of modern times, former Apple CEO Steve Jobs masterfully utilized these techniques: In his legendary presentations, Jobs was the sole focus of attention, striding around the stage, constantly gesticulating, speaking at great length about the advantages of a new product, and always bathed in a dazzling light—very much like the image of a holy man. But he also knew how to present bad news. Unfortunately, sometimes you, too, will have to be the bearer of information that others aren't happy to hear.

Bearing Bad News

In ancient Persia, a messenger who reported a victory in battle was celebrated like a hero. If his army lost, he could expect to be executed immediately, even though he had nothing to do with the outcome, of course. (Oddly, there are no reports of messengers lying about a victory and sneaking out after the party.)

Today, meteorologists on TV are regularly subjected to abuse from viewers because of bad weather, as if they had something to do with the forecast aside from reporting it. US psychologist Robert Cialdini mentions an incident in which a weather forecaster entered a bar and was approached by an angry farmer:[8] "You're the one that sent that tornado and tore my house up. . . . I'm going to take your head off." Fortunately, this was a smart weather man, and he replied, "That's right about the tornado, and I'll tell you something else, I'll send another one if you don't back off."

In this case, the halo effect is at work, as something positive or negative directly rubs off on the messenger.

Bad News Can Be Good News

No matter what business you are in or your position in an organization, it is often necessary to deliver bad news. But be careful: people are often far too quick to think that a seemingly negative situation is unfavorable toward them. For instance, if I order a turkey breast salad and the waitress admits to me, with sad eyes, that she is "very, very sorry," but the only salad available is with chicken breast, then she puts herself and the restaurant in a bad light. I will probably reflexively stand up and head to another restaurant. Instead, if she tells me with shining eyes about their chef's extraordinary salad, made with the most tender chicken breast on the planet, I will certainly be intrigued and will likely order it. So even though it's the same problem—chicken instead of turkey—the outcome is completely different depending on how it is presented. It's possible to take a potentially negative situation and turn it into an advantage.

The "framing" of a situation—putting the situation, figuratively speaking, into the proper framework—is crucial. By framing, it is possible to define the perception of a situation.[9] For example, instead of saying, "Unfortunately, we only have fresh rolls for breakfast," you could state, "We have rolls for breakfast." And instead of, "Unfortunately, we cannot show you our new model before November," say, "We can show you our new model in November." The wording makes the frame—and the crucial difference.

An adventurous salesman from the Czech American Bata Shoe Company was supposed to investigate the possibilities for growth in the African market at the end of the 19th century.[10] As the story goes, his colleague had been very upset by the fact that most people went barefoot in Africa, and concluded, "There's no business for Bata here." However, the audacious salesman reframed the situation and cabled the following back to the home office: "Great business for Bata, everyone is barefoot!"

Apply this concept to everyday obstacles: You have delivery problems? Demand is exploding! There is resistance to your decisions? Effective changes are always hard to implement! You lost a customer? A new generation of influential customers is replacing the old one! Even a mistake that hardly can be counted as a success can still be framed so that something positive comes out of it. Did you send out an invitation by email with an incorrect date on it? An excellent reason for a follow-up, which now, with a subject line like "Correction of previous email!" or—even better: "Calling back first email" nearly guarantees that both the original and the follow-up will be read.

Your own perception of success or failure plays a crucial role in how you frame a situation and how you respond to others. Have you ever caught yourself gratefully thanking someone for his work even though the outcome he delivered was far below your expectations? If someone beams at us with pride over a job well done and is apparently convinced that she has been successful, it creates a certain expectation and pressure for us to respond positively.[11] Especially if we like the individual, if she smiles and believes in herself, we will tend to give her performance a better review. In both circumstances, those who did the work are framing the situation in their favor, even if it didn't meet our expectations. The lesson here is that you, too, should be framing your response to a situation in a way that causes the other party involved to see the upsides, or at least still see the positive effort on your part. Therefore, always consider carefully whether the news you are going to deliver really is as bad as you first thought, and then try to frame the news in a way that is as positive as possible.

Bad News Can Also Simply Be Bad News

There are, however, truly bad pieces of news that you cannot turn into anything positive, and do not wish to. For example, maybe you need to get your customers to accept a hefty price increase even though there is no improvement in your product. Or say you lost a contract in a bid that was really important to your company, or you left a folder at a café that contained absolutely confidential information about a factory closing.

What do you do with such bad news? Avoid being associated with it. To put it bluntly: don't show up. Do not be physically present when the bad news is reported. Instead, let someone else do it—an assistant or a team member—or deliver it yourself by telephone or email. By not being there, you will be less strongly associated with the evil tidings. Of course, much tact and finesse must be used in these situations.

When it became known, in 2004, that Shell had nearly four billion fewer barrels of oil reserves than forecasted, CEO Sir Phil Watts practically went into hiding—he stopped nearly all public appearances and made no statements. When I asked him about his approach at a function in Oxford, he told me that he, as CEO, had known nothing of the mistake and that he could not be held responsible for miscalculations made before his accession to the CEO position.[12] He was forced to resign only a few weeks later.

What are the implications of this? When there are truly serious problems, the presence of the leader is absolutely necessary, no matter whose fault they were. People who apologize for an obvious mistake will more likely be thought of as likable, independent of whose failure it was.[13]

However, you must act astutely in such a case, because the halo effect is merciless—anything negative on such a major, public level will always rub off on the most visible person, such as the CEO or president. To minimize the negative effect when having to present bad news, you must, in contrast to the way you present good news, behave as inconspicuously as possible—be present but be invisible at the same time. Lively gestures and any other movements or actions that direct attention to you must be avoided.[14] For example, in a meeting where you're relaying bad news, if possible, remain seated and do *not* place yourself in the middle of the room. Avoid direct lighting and be sure the entire room around you is well lit, so you're not in the spotlight. Darkening the room can also have the same effect, especially if you provide a focal point such as a Power-

Point presentation, video, or other bright visual aid. The main point: direct the attention away from you!

How, you may ask, could these tiny differences have helped Sir Phil justifying the lack of four billion barrels of oil? To answer this question, let's take a look at an even more serious case. On June 1, 2009, the CEO of Air France, Pierre-Henri Gourgeon, held a press conference about Air France flight 447: on the way from Rio de Janeiro to Paris, the plane had crashed and all 228 passengers had lost their lives. No, there was no way to gloss over the event or spin it as a positive. So how was the podium set up at the press conference? Unlike the setup at Gourgeon's excellent presentation of the annual report, he was not in a spotlight this time. Instead, the entire room was brightly lit. There was no Air France logo anywhere to be seen. Gourgeon was not exposed on a stage; instead, the press surrounded him at eye level.

To sum it up, with a success, remain in the center. With a failure that cannot be framed otherwise, be as inconspicuous as possible—depending on the situation, either don't be there at all or position yourself on the edge, almost in the shadows, or disappear in the crowd. In this way, the outcome will more likely be attributed to external circumstances than to your incompetence.

Anger and Neutrality

When presenting truly bad news, there are some other factors that will improve your standing. What feelings should be on display when giving an apology? Or is it best not to show any feelings at all?

The tone of voice plays a decisive role. Sadness, for example, creates the impression that neither you nor anyone else is directly responsible for the outcome. The result is that you come across as weak, a victim of circumstances.[15] And someone who apparently has no control of the situation cannot be very competent.

Showing guilt or shame is even worse than projecting sadness. In an experiment, a doctor presented bad news to a patient while looking ashamed about the circumstances.[16] Shame, however, has a negative effect on the perception of competence, because it does not indicate decisiveness and initiative, but rather self-doubt.[17] Above all, shame signals that the individual feels responsibility and guilt for the negative outcome. Not having control over the situation is obviously bad, but being fully responsible for failure is even worse. There is also, however, an emotion that can have a positive effect when presenting bad news: anger.

One study showed that politicians and CEOs who reacted to their failure with anger were judged to be more competent than ones who remained neutral.[18] Angry behavior creates the impression that you were not responsible for the outcome yourself; rather, the responsibility lies with circumstances that were unusual and outside anyone's area of control. And yet, you are not weak, as anger gives the impression of assertiveness, decisiveness, and tenacity, and it has a correspondingly positive impact on perceived competence.[19]

This "anger rule," however, is not universally valid. In the case of a trainee—a person of rather low status—it did not make any difference whether he showed anger or acted neutral. For women, anger even seems to have a universally negative effect on their perceived competence. The reasons for these reactions can only be guessed. For example, anger in a man with lower status may seem inappropriate and, in a woman, not "ladylike."

To sum up, grief, shame, and guilt should be avoided in all situations, even if your performance was absolutely terrible. Presenting a bad result with an angry attitude is the most advantageous way to do so for men with high status—for everyone else, it is best not to show any emotion. Of course, keeping your emotions in check isn't always easy, especially depending on the content that you are communicating. It is therefore best to follow some simple rules when you know you can't reframe the situation and you have to fess up to a personal or company-wide failure.

The Shift to Optimism

In order to optimally manage particularly bad news, we can gain some insight from how public relations agencies conduct their crisis communications: You should communicate your failure immediately and completely—any hesitation and procrastination will shed an even worse light on you.[20] Mention every point of conceivable criticism as early as possible and express yourself clearly. Calling a mistake by its correct name increases your impression of competence.[21] Playing down the significance of an obviously miserable situation will have a negative impact on perceived competence.

That all being said, there is a way to manage potential fallout from your admittance of failure. You should play down, as much as possible, the importance of the skills that were lacking in this particular case, and you should make it clear that these skills were so special that they are irrelevant apart from their application to this failed task. By presenting the problem this way, you're showing that this event is so specific that it is unlikely to occur again—then there won't be much left for your opponents to say. This response also displays your trustworthiness. In this way, you can move on from this confession as quickly as possible, as every single second it takes will lengthen the time this bad news reflects negatively on you.

You should then immediately turn to optimism—or as the subtitle of a recent book on crisis communication suggests, you should be "Moving From Crisis to Opportunity."[22] As soon as you have dealt with the negative points as quickly as possible, focus on your skills in other areas, which are—of course—much more significant.[23] You must also emphasize what you have learned from the past and what will, as a result, be changed for the better moving forward. Use as much time as you can to explain these positive points. Again, the halo effect will do its work: You will be associated with the positive elements of your presentation, not the negative ones.

Let me illustrate it with a first class fiasco, General Motors (GM) was faced with a few years ago. The instrument panels in Cadillacs went up in flames because the lids of the ashtrays in the cars had not been properly installed.[24] A spokesperson for GM was subsequently a guest on *Good Morning America*, one of the nation's most popular TV programs. He immediately accepted all responsibility in the name of GM and denied nothing—this only took a few seconds. He then used the remaining time to explain what GM had learned from the incident and what new products were being developed. At the end of his appearance, despite the recent disaster, the audience had received a very favorable impression of him as an individual, and of GM as a company.

Another example can be seen in an event that occurred in New York City on Valentine's Day in 2007. It was bitterly cold, and the airport was, for the most part, covered by snow and ice. Quite a few flights were canceled. The airline JetBlue was affected the most: over 1,000 of its connections were canceled and some passengers had to endure up to nine-hour delays, sitting in airplanes on the runway. The airline could not get back on schedule for nearly a week, and the result was a storm of criticism. JetBlue's CEO David Neeleman appeared on countless radio and TV programs to address the situation. During each appearance, after a brief and unequivocal apology, he immediately directed everyone's attention to a "customer bill of rights" that the airline had just created and was going to implement immediately. It paid off: JetBlue's popularity hardly suffered.[25]

If this technique—a rapid admission followed by an immediate return to optimism—is able to make a difference in the case of genuine catastrophes, then it will certainly be able to help with bad news like the delay of a product launch or an email that was sent to the wrong recipient. Communications consultant Suzanne Bates put it this way: "Bad news is bad news, but it's also good news if you know how to handle it. Managing the tough questions can actually make your organization look better than before. . . . Someone has to be in charge. If you see those moments as leadership opportunities, it will change your attitude and help you when you're under pressure."[26]

The Primacy Effect

What should you do if you have both good and bad news to report? This question is not theoretical: Whether you are meeting with a customer or your boss or have to give a presentation, you will normally have a mixed bag of news to deliver. So, in what order should you present the information?

When I ask this question at lectures or seminars, the answer I receive is almost always wrong. To illustrate the point, let's have a look at this now-classic experiment from 1946 from the Polish-American psychologist Solomon Asch:[27]

Imagine that you are asked to judge the character of somebody based on the following list of adjectives: **intelligent, impulsive, industrious, critical, stubborn, envious.** Would your verdict more likely be negative or positive?

Now, what if you were given the following list of adjectives to describe the person: **envious, stubborn, critical, impulsive, industrious, intelligent.** Would your verdict have turned out differently?

You will have noticed that both lists contain the same six adjectives and the only difference is in their order of appearance. In the experiment, participants only received one of the two lists. Those who were given the first list typically rated the (nonexistent) individual as "competent," and those who received the second were more likely to describe the person as "problematic." The order of the adjectives had a decisive influence on the verdict. At this point, the relevance of the first line of this chapter, the juxtaposition of "yes" and "no," should be clear. If you bet that "yes" occurs more often, you belong to the majority. Most people have this impression because the list starts with "yes," although "yes" and "no" occur with equal frequency.

This is the "primacy effect" at work: The first words used in describing a person, place, or situation are decisive, because the subsequent words are not seen in isolation—they are only experienced in the context of the preceding words. In the case of the first list of adjectives, one gets the impression of a person who is "intelligent," and any words that follow are considered in this light, improving the effect of the characteristics that are not unconditionally positive.

"Intelligent and critical," for example, seems like a good combination. If the list begins with "envious," however, the adjectives that follow are seen in a completely different light. "Envious and critical" is not a very favorable combination. In fact, even "envious and intelligent" now comes across as negative, as it implies deceitfulness.

The first impression creates a sort of "form," and the halo effect of that first impression causes everything that follows to be seen in its light. The Austrian-British philosopher Karl Popper summed it up in his "searchlight theory," according to which humans see the world in the light of whatever thoughts are present in their minds.[28] Very similar relationships are discussed in the previous chapter in the context of the confirmation of high expectations: People try to confirm their first impressions. Behavior that deviates from the first impression will be partly ignored, and ambiguous behavior will be interpreted as though it confirms the initial impression.

For example, when colleagues whom we regard as very intelligent make rather unintelligent statements in a particular situation, we do not immediately revise our impression of them. Rather, we will subconsciously seek a plausible explanation, such as that they are often preoccupied by deep thoughts and therefore were not concentrating when they said something foolish. It would take quite a lot to change our original opinion of someone.

In fact, judgments made about individuals in the first 30 seconds of meeting them are not very different from those made after five minutes, even if completely new information about them comes to light in that time.[29] Unfortunately, this does not mean that we all have an unerring intuition about other people. Our assessments are not especially accurate, but it is hard for us to revise them. In fact, we tend to make our first assessment of someone even before our first encounter with that person, solely based on what we have heard from others or what information we have received about that person. For example, in a job interview, interviewers have already formed an opinion about you before you've walked in the door based on your application, cover letter, and resume.[30]

As the saying goes, "There's no second chance to make a first impression," and understanding the psychological mechanisms behind the primacy effect will help you ensure that your first impression is a success. In the same way an omelet actually tastes better when it is prepared by a chef who truly understands how eggs interact with milk—a phenomenon the Harvard professor Gerard Zaltman refers to as "implementable validity"—when you grasp the principles of perception, you can rest assured that you'll put your best foot forward.[31]

Therefore, when you first interact with someone, put particular focus on optimizing the perception of your competence. One way to do so is by following automotive executive Daniel Goeudevert's "Theory of 20." After studying literature at the Sorbonne in Paris, Goeudevert started selling cars and quickly rose to the board of Volkswagen. He developed his method as a young car salesman and was convinced that placing special emphasis on the "first 20"—the first 20 seconds, the first 20 words, the first 20 steps—was the key to his tremendous success.[32] The first 20 are decisive for establishing a positive impression in the mind of your conversation partner—if the first 20 don't do the job, everything else will be in vain.

The US psychologist Robert Cialdini was so interested in the mysterious techniques used by car salespeople that he took a job in a car dealership without letting anyone know that he was there to study their methods.[33] He found out about a classic sales tactic he experienced called "low balling," which also uses the principle of the first impression: The salesperson starts by offering a very favorable price and then goes with the customer for a test drive, at which time they discuss the details of the purchase. By the time they return, the customer's decision has been made and he is ready to buy the car. The purchase contract is on the table, waiting to be signed, but, suddenly, the salesperson "discovers" a mistake.

She runs to the sales manager, presumably to plead the customer's case, but the manager is unwilling to compromise— they would be losing money on the deal. Suddenly, the car is just as expensive as the competitor's and the salesperson can't budge because the manager has refused. What to do? The customer looks over at the new car: The children are playing in the back seat, his wife is looking forward to going out for a ride, and he knows his colleagues will gape in awe at his new vehicle . . . sure, he decides, the car is no longer a bargain, but the decision has been made.

Low balling, also called "bait and switch," aims to concentrate your interlocutor's attention on the benefits of the product until the decision is made. Only then are the disadvantages of the product revealed. However, due to the primacy effect, these downsides will not have the same weight and they will be more easily accepted. The amateur who wants to sell her car goes about making the sale in exactly the opposite way. She starts by mentioning the small dent in the fender or some other defect before the potential customer has even gotten near the car. After that, everything will be seen in the light of the car's defects, however minor.

So when facing good and bad news, it should be obvious by now where to begin: the positive aspects should be explained first so the audience starts forming an opinion based on these, not on any negative ones. Afterward, you can mention the negative points, knowing that they will now have a significantly smaller impact. Don't make the mistake of trying to get the negative part out of the way first. So, with every report, every presentation, every message, don't start by asking, "Do you want to hear the good news or the bad news first?"—start with the positive!

In discussing how to handle first impressions, I'd be amiss if I did not discuss the last impression as well, which is also of great importance. Indeed, the final impression remains the strongest memory that the other party takes with them, a phenomenon known as the "recency effect."[34] Jurors, for example, tend to best remember the witness who was questioned last. Does that mean that the final impression is more important than the first? Not at all—the first impression still influences everything that comes subsequently. Think of it like the headline of a news article compared to its last sentence.

If you want to sell a house, for example, you certainly want to present it to potential buyers in the most favorable light possible. Therefore, you should start your tour of the house with the most attractive room and finish the tour with the second-best room, showing the others in between. By using this order, you have a terrific beginning and a positive ending. If, however, you start with a bunch of messy storage rooms, the damage will have already been done by the time you finish up with the wonderful conservatory. The negative impression has been established, and even the greatest view will hardly change it.

The same idea can be applied to arguments: Start with your strongest point, one that will immediately be convincing. Then end with your second-strongest point (which can be more complicated than the first one because your listener will have time to think about it after you've stated it).

Just remember, when it comes to good news and bad news, start with the best, let the less positive items follow in its slipstream, and then shine at the end with the second best. This combination of the primacy effect and recency effect not only will soften any blow but will help you maintain your perception of competence no matter the information you're delivering.

Conclusion

When you buy a new television, you are delighted by its razor-sharp image and its refined remote. With a new car, you take pleasure in looking at the elegant lines of its silhouette and the beautiful interior. When it comes to services, however, you're typically employing them to deal with a problem that you'd rather not have. Your heating is not working, you have a toothache, you want to sue someone—all necessary evils. In contrast to high-tech gadgets or a pair of designer shoes, services are rarely a source of daily pleasure.

In fact, you barely notice these services until something goes wrong: the tax consultant misses a deadline, the alteration tailor makes your pants too short, or the cabinetmaker does a bad job repairing your shelves. If you are a service provider, it is much easier to look like a failure in the eyes of the customer than a success, since the customer is already bent out of shape about having to deal with whatever issue you are there to remedy in the first place. To control this negative imbalance, you must make the presentation of your success as palpable as possible and cushion any mistakes that could have a negative effect on the client's perception of your expertise.

With the help of the halo effect, you can use good news to get the most positive effect on your perceived expertise by making your presence as noticeable as possible during your presentation through physical presence, good lighting and a lot of movement, and anything else that will draw people's attention to you. With bad news, the opposite is true, as you must avoid being associated with it as much as possible. If you cannot avoid being present when the news is announced, be as inconspicuous as possible in your behavior, and position yourself at the edge of the conversation or room, almost in a shadow. Keeping that in mind, when you cannot frame a negative situation in a good light, admit to your every mistake immediately and then shift your presentation to positive details and the productive outcomes that can be learned from any mistakes made.

The halo effect also explains why the first impression is of crucial importance. Therefore, always begin with the good news rather than the bad news. The primacy effect will make a positive beginning shine on everything that follows. And, since the final communication, according to the recency effect, will remain the strongest point in your interlocutor's memory, you should end the presentation with the second-best piece of news. Seen in this light, it should not be very surprising that even gigantic mistakes do not necessarily have to have a negative effect on your perceived competence.

Competence Compendium
Good News, Bad News

◈ When delivering good news, be present and direct all attention toward you.

◈ When bearing bad news, utilize inconspicuous behavior.

◈ Deliver bad news in an angry tone (if you are a high-status male) or in a neutral tone (if you are a low-status male or a female).

◈ When bad news cannot be reframed, admit mistakes but focus on optimism.

◈ Primacy effect: always start with the good news.

◈ Recency effect: conclude with the second-best news.

CHAPTER 4

THE COMPETENCE FORMULA

FRAMING YOUR COMPETENCE

Smart and hard-working—doesn't exist
Smart and lazy—that's what I am
Stupid and lazy—for entertainment
Stupid and hard-working—heaven help us!

—CHARLES DE TALLEYRAND

The Amazing Fitzjames

British author Stephen Potter wrote a serious of humorous self-help books on how to gain an advantage in life. In one of them, he described one of the stories of a legendary Harvard student with the name Fitzjames.[1] Toward the end of his second semester, only a few weeks before the all-important final exams, Fitzjames suddenly disappeared. No one saw him at any lecture, seminar, or study group. His fellow students feverishly worked toward the final exams and were hanging on every word their professors said, but Fitzjames was nowhere to be found. On the day of the final, however, he walked into the exam room a few minutes late, sporting a heavy suntan and wearing a Palm Beach jacket. He slowly wrote his exam—and aced it!

This chapter is about how the Fitzjameses of this world accomplish such feats, and how you can use their ingenuity to display your own expertise. Fitzjames's careless attitude and seemingly effortless success caused him to radiate genius. Was he just a highly intelligent person with an off-the-chart IQ? Did he somehow cheat on the exam? How much did his "competence" truly come into play?

In principle, it's not so easy to figure out how big of a part an individual's competence will have in finding a successful solution to a given problem. The result of a team's price negotiations or a successful treatment by a physician, for example, appears clear at first glance. However, the factors that are significant for the achievement of these outcomes are entwined in the result and difficult to unravel—since factors other than mere competence will play a role. But which factors? The American psychologists John Darley and George Goethals examined this question and summarized these relationships in a formula:

$$P = [(A + A') * (M + M')] + (D + D') + L$$

P = performance
A = stable ability factors
A' = temporary ability constraints
M = stable motivational factors
M' = temporary motivational factors
D = usual difficulty level
D' = temporary factors affecting difficulty
L = luck

Simply put, there are three factors that the observer, when evaluating an outcome, concentrates on:[2]

- motivation
- difficulty level (ease)
- luck

According to this formula, the more difficult the task, the more bad luck experienced, and the less effort the individual put into the task, then the greater the role that the individual's competence will have played in the successful result.

These relationships are obvious and also explain why the lawyers I mentioned in chapter 1 needed almost 10 years to decide whether a new employee had the qualities necessary to become a partner in the firm. They needed to unravel an entanglement of competence, the task's degree of difficulty, luck, and motivation to make an evaluation of an employee's competence separate from the other factors.

Understanding the interactions of these factors will enable you to control the perception of your own competence.

Tough and Unlucky

In his famous Stanford commencement speech from 2005, the legendary Apple founder Steve Jobs said about his beginnings, "I didn't have a dorm room, so I slept on the floor in friends' rooms, I returned Coke bottles for the 5¢ deposits to buy food with, and I would walk the 7 miles across town every Sunday night to get one good meal a week at the Hare Krishna temple."[3]

If you read a biography of any great captain of industry, you should always have enough tissues at hand. Almost all of these heroes had to overcome the greatest difficulties and the most unfortunate circumstances; the poor fellows were spared nothing—and, like Jobs, in spite of these obstacles, they made it to the absolute top. How? Can there be any explanation other than that they were simply magnificent individuals?

Former US president Bill Clinton told the story of his undeniably hard start in life again and again: his father died in a car crash before his birth, and he grew up with a step father, who was a heavy gambler and alcoholic, and who regularly abused his mother and half-brother.

Such stories provide a rich texture to a person's life, while also showing his or her humble beginnings, but there is also a practical lesson here. Now don't worry if you're not able to dish up a sob story like Clinton's. Even those who can't claim to have started from the very bottom will almost certainly have had to overcome some difficulty before they could reach their goals, or at least their present intermediate goals. Such stories not only helped these people become more likable, they also helped them to manifest their competence. This idea can be applied to any daily task and subsequent accomplishment— without dramatic tearjerkers.

The method here is to draw attention to the high level of difficulty and the complex circumstances of the upcoming task. Just as athletes will refer to bad weather conditions or to their history of injuries before a game, you can, as a salesperson, for example, point to unusually volatile market conditions or, as a lawyer, point to the special trickiness of current case law. The more difficult the situation, the more competent you will seem. When you, first, have been unlucky, and second, have had to meet a truly herculean challenge, there are two good reasons— unrelated to your competence—why you might fail. Explaining these reasons in advance will make them more credible than if you bring them up after the task is completed—like most people do. In the latter case, especially after failure, they just sound like a bad excuse.

It is crucial to mention these obstacles even when you are successful, instead of saying something like, "Ah well, I was just lucky." You want to highlight, not downplay, your success. By pointing out the difficulty even in the case of success, your performance will be attributed to your exceptional level of competence rather than to external factors.

You might be asking, "Doesn't this suggestion contradict the previous chapter, in which the motto was 'show optimism'?" No, because you should certainly still make a point of spreading optimism—only now you are doing so in spite of all the obstacles that you have listed. Your motto should thus not be "No problem!" but rather "Despite all the obstacles, no problem for me!"

And while you're at it, even if you're overwhelmed, make sure to keep your cool. You want your performance, and the following success, to come across as effortless.

Effortless Superiority

In 1917, the German composer Hans Pfitzner was sitting with his colleague Richard Strauss at the premiere of Pfitzner's opera *Palestine* at the Munich Prinzregenten Theater.[4] Before the curtain went up, Pfitzner whispered proudly to Strauss, "This piece is the result of 10 years' hard work." The mischievous Strauss replied, "Why, then, do you compose, if it is so difficult for you?" To an audience of classical music lovers, Strauss's name remains well known—Pfitzner's, not so much.

Giving the impression of excessive effort has a negative impact on the perceived level of competence. If you give the impression that you had to make a considerable effort to achieve a particular goal, your perceived competence will suffer. In other words, the same result can be reached either with great effort and a low level of competence or with small effort and a high level of competence.

Everything is easy for true experts—they just have it in their blood. When he was working on his opera *La gazza ladra* (*The Thieving Magpie*), Italian composer Gioachino Rossini is said to not have retrieved pages of the scores that had fallen from his desk while he was composing. Rather, he preferred to write the pages again—it required less effort for him.[5] In the 16th century, the Italian aristocrat Baldassare Castiglione described the most important characteristic of a nobleman as *Sprezzatura,* which was "to have a certain air of nonchalance that concealed the skills involved, and seemed to demonstrate that whatever he did or said was achieved effortlessly, and almost without thinking."[6] Concealing all effort is actually the cornerstone of one of Oxford University's colleges, whose unofficial motto is "Effortless superiority."

Natural talent is more prized than acquired skills. For example, why do parents like to hear the teacher say that their child, although highly intelligent, only got a B– in calculus because he was so lazy? Because no parents want to hear that it was almost a miracle their child got a B– and that he only received it because, although dim-witted, he was very hard working. We see an identical outcome, yet two completely opposite perceptions of the child.

Perceived effort must be minimized to maximize perceived competence. So should you present yourself as lazy? A tricky question. Doing so would be an advantage for your perceived competence, but it could make a bad impression regarding your level of dedication to your job, company, or performance. You therefore need to maintain a delicate balance. Give people the feeling that the task in front of you—despite the adverse circumstances—does not worry you at all. You were born to meet this challenge. This does not mean that you will take care of the entire task before breakfast, otherwise you will end up getting too much work pushed your way. You will certainly have to exert some time and resources on the task at hand, but it won't give you a headache, because you are a natural.

Especially when mentioning earlier successes, you should give the impression that you've never had to exert yourself very much in the past, such as during your college days. I still remember well the time I met Edzard Reuter, the former chairman of the board of Daimler (the producer of Mercedes cars), shortly before I started working on my law degree. He explained to me that law school had been so easy for him, he spent most of his time on the tennis court. While I was at law school—just child's play, of course—my respect for Mr. Reuter grew with every exam into a thing of vast proportions. You should, therefore, never say that you had to work harder for your degree than anyone else. Rather, you should make the individual you are talking to believe that you were born for your field and have always had an affinity for your line of work, just like anyone else who has a natural gift for something.

You should never mention that numbers repelled you before you became an accountant; or that advertisements gave you cold chills before you started work in the advertising industry. A genius is chosen by destiny and loves his or her profession. Do you think Ludwig van Beethoven actually wanted to be a gardener or Pablo Picasso a doctor?

Anne-Sophie Mutter, one of the world's leading violin players, has said in many interviews that she never practiced very much—about 2 hours a day. Studies that have been conducted about musicians' practice times, however, show that the best violinists will normally practice 30 hours per week, starting at the age of 12. With that stat in mind, Mutter's story seems rather doubtful; it seems more likely that such natural talent, of the kind that directly leads to being a world-class musician, does not exist and only through practice could one achieve such mastery of an instrument.[7] Even having read research supporting this and having talked to many musicians who confirmed it, I cannot help but think that Mutter just might be one out of a billion. Indeed, it isn't the grim overachiever who is esteemed the most, but the gifted—Mutter doesn't enjoy her immense level of respect for nothing.

Melvin Reich had a small shop in New York for decades whose only business consisted of making buttonholes in clothing: "We do buttonholes and buttonholes and buttonholes. I am specialized, like the doctors. The one who takes care of the throat does not take care of the eyes. I take care of the buttonholes." When Reich was asked once if he also did zippers, he replied, almost outraged, "Zippers are a totally different field. It's a different game. A man can only do so much."[8] So, who would you go to if you needed a buttonhole for your favorite jacket?

The master knows that he is absolutely right for his present position and has never doubted his choice of profession—his path was predestined. For him, the only possibility was to land where he is now. And that is how it should look for you, too: your personal development has inevitably led you to your present profession. A glance at the biographies of famous personalities will also help here: they generally speak of a straight path, according to the motto "Fate has chosen me." This idea is also touched on in the previously mentioned speech that Steve Jobs gave at Stanford University:

> Because I had dropped out of the university and no longer attended any classes, I decided to go to a course in calligraphy and learn something about it. There I learned about typefaces with and without serifs, and about the different spacing between different letter combinations. I learned what is great about great typography. . . . None of this had even a hope of any practical application in my life. But 10 years later, when we were designing the first Macintosh computer, it all came back to me. And we designed it all into the Mac. It was the first computer with beautiful typography. . . . And since Windows just copied the Mac, it's likely that no personal computer would have them. If I had never dropped out, I would have never dropped in on this calligraphy class, and personal computers might not have the wonderful typography that they do. Of course, it was impossible to imagine that when I was in college. But it was very, very clear in hindsight, 10 years later.

You should think about how to describe the path that led you to your present position as a straight line; your hero's journey. With Jobs, though he dropped out of school and took what he thought was a useless calligraphy class, both of those events led him directly to his destined position. So even if you've taken some turns in your life and career, you can tailor how you present them so they appear as direct stepping-stones to your current profession.

Once, in one of my training courses, one of the participants was the head of customer support at a blue-chip company. He told me how he had worked as a bouncer in a club when he was a student. He didn't see any connection to his current job at first, but then he drew this straight line: he had always cared about providing safe environments and worked hands on to ensure a smooth flow of events. By first examining and then sharing two or three experiences like that, you will also make the course of your personal career development appear preordained.

Another way to signal effortlessness through perceived natural talent can be found in the use of stereotypes. We all have a picture in our minds of how the ideal specialist in a certain field should look: a physicist like Albert Einstein, a journalist like Larry King. They have become archetypes. The typical scientist is considered absent-minded, odd, and doubtless a genius, while the star attorney is suave, smooth, and well spoken. How do others imagine an exemplary representative of your field? How would he or she dress and talk, and what kind of a general impression would he or she make?

I know a successful doctor who is not all that interested in the details of his profession but who understands very well how to convince his patients of his high level of expertise. When he is on the job, he always wears a stethoscope around his neck. Though he almost never uses the instrument, he is aware of its effect—this is simply how a doctor should look.

One of his colleagues, a family practitioner who was born in China, performs acupuncture in a small German city—the demand is enormous. He learned the discipline of acupuncture exclusively in advanced training courses in traditional Chinese medicine in Germany from German practitioners. Nevertheless, he is regarded, far beyond the city limits, as *the* undisputed expert in his field. When he talks about it, he gives a knowing smile: a Chinese acupuncturist must be especially good, better than others—or so the patients believe, anyway.

And yet so many people purposely avoid seeming like the ideal, typical representation of their profession! It reminds me of the story of the donkey who wanted to be a lapdog.[9] The donkey worked hard for its master all day long and stood in the stall all night. The farmer's dog, in contrast, slept in the house, didn't have to do anything, and was constantly fed treats. Then the donkey got an idea: Why not act like the dog? He ran up to his master, wagged his tail, and tried to jump into his lap. What happened?

The donkey was tied up in the barn and beaten.

Your customer or boss will not, hopefully, tie you up and beat you, but it is better for you, in any case, to represent yourself appropriately. The world does not appreciate biotech executives who act like laid-back musicians or tax consultants who prattle on about philosophy.

To fit the stereotype, those with true natural talent love and live their profession. They draw on a great store of knowledge and know their job like the back of their hand. The architect should be an expert on the history of the landmark buildings in her city, the lawyer should be able to talk about the first contracts in ancient Rome, and the salesperson should know about trading practices on the Silk Road. The natural talent also lives his or her area of expertise in daily life. The engineer will have a technically advanced chronometer on his wrist and make his notes on the newest smart device.

It doesn't take a lot of effort to seem effortless. Remember to always give the impression that you didn't have to try very hard to achieve your earlier successes—as a natural talent, born for your profession, everything is easy for you, from training to climbing the career ladder. Speak about your progression through life as if it was predetermined. With only a few reference points on hand, you should be able to illustrate this journey as a straight path. Also make the stereotype work for you, living out the ideal image of a specialist in your profession in your body and soul.

Last, when you let your colleagues, manager, or boss know that you will throw yourself 100 percent into the job they have for you, then you are unbeatable. There is nothing better than a natural talent who applies all his or her powers to meeting the challenge at hand.

Conclusion

Many luminaries describe their lives as a quest to where destiny (not effort) lead them. This Hero's Journey is, in fact, an archetypical motive.[10] It was described by the Swiss psychoanalyst Carl Jung and elaborated by American mythologist Joseph Campbell, whose work would become the template for hundreds of Hollywood blockbusters—from Star Wars to the Lion King.[11] The Hero's Journey consists of three main parts:

1. Departure (call of adventure with initial refusal to the call).
2. Initiation (road of trials, meeting with the goddess).
3. Return, after which neither the world nor the hero is the same.

From professional athletes to politicians, luminaries regularly describe how they had to overcome difficult obstacles, such as poverty or family issues, to get to where they are today. They most definitely weren't dealt a lucky hand and yet made it to the very top. What factors other than mind-boggling abilities could explain their success?

As you've seen in this chapter, in the best-case scenario, success will be exclusively attributed to exceptionally high competence and nothing else. It is equally advantageous if a failure can be attributed to external factors rather than a lack of competence. Especially in the case of failure, the so-called fundamental attribution error must be observed: individuals prefer to explain the behavior of others by their character traits rather than external factors.[12] If your neighbor greets you in an unfriendly way, you will be more inclined to attribute this to his solitary nature than to the possibility that some unpleasant event had shaken him up badly that day. We tend to attribute the behavior of others to internal causes because we prefer others to be responsible for their actions, and because we only see the person and not the conditions that caused the actions. However, with our own behavior it is the other way around: we tend to explain our own behavior with external factors, because we do not see ourselves but the world around us.

The effect of the fundamental attribution error—that is, the fact that individuals will be held personally responsible for the results they produce—is advantageous when you have completed a task successfully. The success then seems to clearly be a result of your own abilities and competence, not any external circumstances. You should enhance this perception through your own efforts as much as possible. With failures, however, you should eliminate the fundamental attribution error. Make sure that the external circumstances—difficulties and bad luck—are brought strongly into focus so that your (deficient) competence will recede into the background. In both cases, your competence must be *isolated*, either as a decisive factor—after success—or as a factor to be ignored in the larger context— after a failure.

How do you most effectively frame competence? A story of a gunslinger from the old Wild West can answer that question.[13] Once upon a time, a stranger walked into a small, dusty Texan town and could not believe his eyes. On the siding of a number of houses, there were painted targets riddled with bullet holes, but whoever had been shooting must have had superb aim, as they had hit the bull's-eye every time. A man with a revolver was leaning up against a nearby wall. The stranger asked him who had fired all the shots. The man looked up and replied, "Well, it was me." Naturally, the stranger was very impressed.

"How do you always hit the bull's-eye in the exact center?" he wanted to know.

"It's quite simple," said the gunslinger. "First, I shoot. Then I paint the target."

If you establish the right frame, any result can make your competence shine.

And now, to return to the legendary Harvard student Fitzjames: despite skipping lectures and showing up to the test with a fresh tan and in a beach outfit, he aced his exam and became top of his class. However, he hadn't been seen in the weeks leading up to the finals not because he was partying or chilling at the beach but because he had been holed up in his room that entire time cramming for the test. While he studied, he sat beneath a shining sun lamp to disguise his hard work with an impressive tan. Well, I have no idea whether the story of Fitzjames really happened, but this is the stuff of legends.

Competence Compendium
The Competence Formula

✧ Emphasize the role "competence" plays in your success
  by
  ❖ directing attention to the difficulties of the task
  ❖ pointing out unfortunate circumstances
  ❖ showing no effort.
✧ Act like earlier successes, training, and education were
  easy for you (*Sprezzatura*).
✧ You were born for your job: your path to it was predetermined (display a hero's journey).
✧ Use the stereotype of the ideal specialists in your field
  who love and live their profession.

CHAPTER 5

VERBAL COMMUNICATION

HOW TO SPEAK LIKE AN EXPERT

In my youth, I was also slow to speak and quick to act; but in the school of life, I learned that words, and not actions, rule the world everywhere.

—HOMER

As Seen on TV

Without thinking about the question for too long, how would you assess the competence of the ladies and gentlemen who explain the world for us every evening on the nightly news? Few people would doubt their competence.[1] In fact, news commentators are widely regarded as very competent, although they do nothing more than read what is put in front of them on the teleprompter (unless they also belong to the editorial group).

The way people speak—loudly or softly, slowly or quickly—has a significant influence on our perception of their competence. When evaluating the intelligence of another person, we prefer to use verbal indications rather than body language.[2] In the interplay between these two, verbal and physical, the effect of verbal evidence is the dominant factor. Even when individuals can only be seen and not heard—like when you mute your TV—verbal factors will still carry the most weight. How is this possible when nothing is heard? Because competence killers, such as stuttering, can be perceived through visual observation alone and will, even without sound, have disastrous consequences for the perceived competence of the person speaking.

In fact, the manner of speaking seems to be even more important than the actual content of what is said. Therefore, to increase the level of perceived competence, you should scrutinize the way you speak. In addition to the flow of your words and how you emphasize specific ones, there are several different decisive factors that signal your expertise through verbal communication.

Pronunciation

Pronunciation has a significant impact on a person's perceived level of competence.[3] Consider how the tempo of speech has an effect. If your goal is to seem as competent as possible, how quickly should you speak? Will you stand out if you speak slowly? All-knowing oracles customarily state their prophecies very deliberately—and who can compete with the competence of an oracle?

Research provides unequivocal results: it is, in fact, not slow but *fast* talking that leads to a significantly increased perceived level of competence.[4] The unconscious hypothesis behind that perception seems to be that the speed of speaking mirrors the speed of thinking, following the rationale that a fast talker is also a quick thinker.

However, you must also clearly articulate your words in spite of your tempo. There is hardly anything that has as negative an effect on the perceived level of competence as mumbling or incorrect pronunciation.[5] Therefore, be sure to practice speaking not only quickly but also clearly and precisely. A helpful exercise is to repeat a classic tongue twister like "Peter Piper picked a peck of pickled peppers" or to practice monologues from a play (I usually recite Macbeth's dagger monologue that I learned as a high school thespian).

In addition to clarity and speed, the tone of your voice is of vital importance. Speaking in a shrill-sounding voice or constantly clearing your throat not only irritates the listener but also results in a lower level of perceived competence. Using a pleasant voice, without unnecessary interruptions, leads to a higher level of perceived competence.[6]

Employing a steady voice, with a smooth flow, is particularly effective. If you avoid stammering, you will seem *even* more competent.[7] It is also helpful to speak in a somewhat deeper voice, as a lower voice pitch (of men and women!) leads to a higher perceived competence.[8] But make sure to avoid speaking in a monotone as a large vocal range, incorporating both high and low tones, will seem considerably more competent.

Loudness also has an effect: a higher volume level (somewhat louder than "normal") also leads to a higher level of perceived competence.[9] But be careful—your volume level should only be *slightly* higher than average, especially when dealing with other cultures. Asians as well as Europeans habitually perceive US-Americans to be too loud and speaking too loudly actually reduces the perceived competence.[10]

A faster tempo, a clear articulation, a smooth flow, a deeper tone, and a higher volume are only the beginning of mastering verbal communication.

Standard English

In one study, participants listened to recordings of actors and were then asked to identify which of them were experts in the material discussed.[11] Only those who spoke standard English were judged to be experts, while regional accents and dialects caused a negative impact and were almost stigmatizing. Accents or dialects typically lead to an array of negative attributions: low-status, a lower level of persuasiveness and credibility, and, quite directly, perceived competence.[12]

If you speak in a dialect or with an accent, a listener will automatically assign you to a specific social or cultural group. Whatever preconceived notions the listener has about this group will then be applied to you and your status.[13] In the spectrum of dialects, there is, therefore, a ranking of the associated status: the more prestigious, the higher the perceived competence. In a study with 60 US students, individuals speaking British English were regarded to have a higher status than those speaking American English—even by other Americans.[14]

But wouldn't there be an advantage to speaking in the same dialect as the individual you are talking to? If you speak in a Brooklyn accent in Williamsburg, for example, isn't there a resulting sense of community that would be beneficial to your perceived competence? It's true that by speaking in a similar dialect as others, you will seem more likable to them.[15] Even so, you will still be considered less competent, including by individuals from the same region speaking the same dialect.[16]

Of course, dialects and accents are part of an individual's identity, and they can certainly have positive effects.[17] In a number of studies, speaking in a dialect led to others having a higher opinion of the speaker's loyalty and integrity.[18] Still, the language resulting in the highest assessment of social status is typically completely free from any dialect: an individual who correctly speaks standard language will come across as the most competent.[19]

A similar effect exists with foreign accents. Correct, standard English will normally be rated highest, but there are differences between accents in the associated status ranking: linguistic hints of nationalities that are normally considered to have high social status will result in a higher level of perceived competence.[20]

So foreign accents and even regional dialects can in fact increase the level of perceived competence when they mirror a cliché that signals expertise. It is advantageous for a moonshiner to speak with a Southern drawl and a beer brewer to speak with a German accent.

I once heard of a French restaurant in Los Angeles that, for a short time, had an excellent reputation based on its enormous authenticity. A contributing factor to this reputation was that all the waiters spoke with a strong French accent. That is, until one day a French tourist ate there and attempted to speak with the messieurs in his mother tongue—not one of them could speak even one word of French. In fact, they were struggling actors and the owner was Mexican.

Using a false dialect or accent is not wise. If you have a choice, speak standard English. In the United States, standard US English is preferred, while in the United Kingdom, the "standard accent" is the "BBC accent"—speaking the "Queen's English" would come across as pompous and fake if you are not part of the British upper class.

But be honest with yourself and do not overestimate your abilities in this area. A study showed that most individuals believe that they speak a standard version of their language, but that most of them are mistaken.[21] When the participants heard themselves on a recording, they refused to acknowledge that they were speaking in a dialect, even though the people with whom they were speaking could easily hear it.

When talking to old friends and family, you may be more comfortable speaking in your natural accent; however, when you're in a professional situation where you want to exhibit your expertise, make sure to tone it down as much as possible. Though an accent or dialect is hard to break, consciously paying attention to it during your conversations, presentations, or speeches will help you scale it back.

Effective Speech

Whether in a one-on-one conversation, during a meeting, or at a Q&A session, how long should you talk for? Is it better to make your contributions short but speak more often? Or should you make your contributions longer but speak with less frequency? The so-called productivity during a conversation actually has a considerable influence on your perceived level of intelligence:[22] it has been found that speaking *often* for a *medium length of time* is most effective. You should contribute to the conversation at regular intervals, but be careful that your input is a suitable length—not too long and not too short. When giving your two cents, use many different words, since a large vocabulary indicates higher intelligence and thus higher competence.[23] Don't repeat yourself. Unnecessary repetitions cast a negative light on the speaker and may be seen as an indication of a lack of intelligence.[24]

It is also important to pause briefly between sentences.[25] In this way, you avoid rushing through your point or explanation, giving your audience the opportunity to process what is being said and providing yourself with enough time to formulate the next sentence. Above all, put in a pause before your most important arguments—think of it like a drum roll. By doing so, you ensure that your best arguments do not get lost but instead come in loud and clear. You have certainly had the experience of one of your excellent points not getting the attention it deserved, that your thoughts were not truly heard when you presented them. In such a situation, you then have to try, laboriously, to sell your idea to the group, but it's already too late—once it has subsided into insignificance, you will be unable to resurrect it.

One final factor to consider in regard to your effectiveness is more than a matter of etiquette: Is it OK to interrupt another speaker? What if you have something crucial to say? Is it possible to exhibit dominance during the conversation by cutting someone off? Do you demonstrate a special commitment by frequently speaking over others while they are in the middle of making a point? The answer to all of these questions is simple: absolutely not. Quite apart from the fact that in Western cultures it is considered rude to interrupt, it also has a negative effect on your perceived competence.

As shown, it's important to know when to speak and how to do so effectively. The frequency and amount of time are paramount—don't overdo it. It's not just a matter of etiquette, but if you're long-winded, repeating yourself, and interrupting others, you'll seem more like a babbling buffoon than a competent professional.[26] Even if you have these skills down pat, you can still run into issues. That's where the concept of "power talking" comes into play.

Power Talking

In her much discussed work "Language and Woman's Place," American linguist Robin Lakoff argues that the social disparities between men and women in our society are reflected in linguistic differences.[27] Lakoff observes that women typically use "powerless" speech patterns containing what are considered certain low-status elements. Meanwhile, masculine language displays higher status and greater power by dispensing with unnecessary ballast, including the specific following types:

- tagging questions (for example, "That is an interesting field, *isn't it?*")

- peculiar intonational patterns in which a statement ends on a high note as though it were a question, even when it's not (for example, "The results are *in?*" compared to "The results are in.")

- hesitation (for example, "My daughter . . . *uh* . . . was never there.")

- trivializing phrases (for example, "you know" or "pretty good")[28]

- excessive politeness (for example, instead of "Close the door," "Will you please close the door?" or even "Won't you please close the door?")

Lakoff's findings can be summarized as follows: "powerless speech" does not impose a point on others and thus appears overly polite and weak. For example, she argues that a sentence beginning with "Won't you please" is characteristic of women's speech and unconvincing. The powerless speaker does not expect to be taken seriously and will therefore not be taken seriously. Perceived status plays a major role here: Powerless language is associated with low social status and thus with low education and incompetence. Power talking, however, is seen as an indication of high social rank, indicating a high standard of education and thus a higher level of competence.[29] These conclusions about status ranking are, in fact, a reflection of reality. Lakoff assumed that powerless speech is mostly used by women. However, analyses of courtroom cases and particularly witnesses' speech showed that speech is in fact a question of social status: the lower the actual social status, the more frequently the test individual will use powerless speech— regardless of the person's sex.[30]

It is therefore important to avoid these types of mistakes and use language that is commanding and devoid of any clutter. Most importantly, concentrate on avoiding stammering in any form. You will be judged as more competent if you do not hesitate, if you refrain from putting "uhs" into your sentences, and if you avoid correcting and repeating yourself.[31]

There is possibly no other technique that will allow you, with such relatively simple means, to effectively raise your perceived level of competence to be more convincing than employing power talking. Strong, self-confident language will get you very far. Maintaining clarity in your style of speech is key in this regard—though, surprisingly, the clarity of your content is another story.

Unnecessary Complications (Skip This Section!)

A scientist who had revised one of her articles several times decided it was the absolute best it could be and sent it off to a prestigious magazine in her field.[32] It was rejected. She then submitted the first version she had written, a draft that she believed was totally incomprehensible. To her chagrin, this time, it was accepted. It is sad but true: incomprehensibility is often valued more highly than clarity.

The 19th-century philosopher Arthur Schopenhauer invented the mocking term "Hegeling" to describe the pompous philosophy of his colleague Georg Wilhelm Friedrich Hegel. Schopenhauer explained the term in this way: "One reads and reads, without ever taking possession of even one single thought, while the writer, who has nothing meaningful or specific in mind himself, piles word upon word, phrase upon phrase, and, in spite of that, says nothing because he has nothing to say, knows nothing, thinks nothing, and still wishes to speak, and, therefore, does not choose his words so that they give a suitable expression of his thoughts, but rather so they better can disguise his own lack of any."[33]

Even though this criticism of Hegel may be justified, Hegel was, in his time, considered *the* philosopher, much to the annoyance of the less successful Schopenhauer, who, however, wrote in a crystal-clear style.

In this vein, the psychologist J. Scott Armstrong examined 10 management periodicals thoroughly and found, to his disappointment, that those written in a complicated style were perceived as better.[34] Articles containing identical content but written more clearly were judged to be less competent pieces of research—even by experts. The consequences are, according to Armstrong, startling but clear: "Researchers who want to impress their colleagues should write less intelligible papers. Journals seeking respectability should publish less intelligible papers. Academic meetings should feature speakers who make little sense."

That assertion may be going too far, but the results, unfortunately, speak for themselves: artificially complicated content has a positive impact on the perceived level of competence.

An excellent, as well as simple, application of this principle leads to an increased use of numerical symbols over alphabetical ones or, according to Armstrong, to trading intelligible for unintelligible semantics and to the syntheses of fewer sentences from more.[35] Sounds quite competent, doesn't it?

It is also possible to express the first sentence in the preceding paragraph in a much more understandable way: "The application of this idea is fairly simple: you can either use as many numbers as possible or, as Armstrong suggests, change every understandable word to one that is incomprehensible and merge several sentences into one long one." Get the point?

Above all, numbers serve to substantiate your arguments effectively and increase your level of perceived competence. In one study, two accounting recommendations were to be evaluated by highly qualified participants. One of them was full of numbers, and the other one contained all the important numerical values but was otherwise rather text heavy. The outcome was unequivocal: more numbers led to a higher level of perceived expertise for the individual.[36]

They are not only effective on individual decision makers either; entire financial markets are more likely to react to company information if it contains numbers.[37]

This research result is one of the few that I really don't like putting down on paper (and why I asked you to skip this section). The finding is in opposition to the advancement of scientific knowledge and even to a company culture that promotes thoughtful discussion and transparency. But I feel it is my obligation to give you the unfiltered results of research.

So, then . . . if you want to achieve a high level of perceived competence, clarity of content does not need to be your highest priority.[38] Sometimes it absolutely makes sense not to completely make sense.

Conclusion

Admittedly, the advice of this chapter reads almost like the operating instructions for a lawnmower. This chapter is more a list than a combination of concepts, but don't be fooled by the simplicity and brevity of this topic: we stand on the shoulders of giants—a number of prominent scientists have come up with these findings during decades of laborious work.[39]

You do not have to be a news commentator, pose in front of a green background, hold a batch of notes in your hand, or stare at a teleprompter to catapult your communication abilities into a new dimension. The impact of verbal communication is such that you can fundamentally increase your level of perceived competence by the use of power talking alone. And one more thing: yes, the techniques discussed here also work on the telephone.[40]

Competence Compendium
Verbal Communication

✧ Speak a little faster than usual, but clearly and smoothly.
✧ Speak somewhat deeper and louder than you usually would.
✧ Do not talk in a monotone but rather cover a large scale of tones.
✧ Use clear pronunciation and precise articulation.
✧ Dialects and accents are only advantageous if they match a fitting stereotype.
✧ Speak frequently and for a medium period of time.
✧ Insert pauses into your speech, particularly right before your key arguments.
✧ Use a wide vocabulary.
✧ Avoid redundancies.
✧ Do not interrupt the person to whom you're speaking.
✧ Use power talking, avoid over-politeness, and speak with confidence.
✧ It can be helpful to complicate your arguments and use numbers.

CHAPTER 6

NONVERBAL COMMUNICATION

HOW TO MOVE LIKE AN EXPERT

It might be possible to distinguish from behind a blockhead, a fool, and a man of intellect. The blockhead would be characterized by a leaden sluggishness of all his movements; folly is stamped on every gesture; so too are intellect and a studious nature.

—ARTHUR SCHOPENHAUER

The Effects of Nonverbal Communication

When I give a talk on nonverbal communication, I begin with the following words: "Put your left hand in front of you, your right hand above it. As soon as I say so, clap your hands together." Without pausing, I clap, and almost the entire audience does so as well—even though I haven't given them the command yet. This little demonstration quickly and clearly illustrates my point to the crowd: what you say is less important than what you actually do. To prove the point, having done this little exercise is much more impressive than just reading about it.

Even though verbal communication and the manner of speaking is of crucial importance, the effect of body language is usually stronger on our subconscious than that of the spoken word.[1] We see this idea play out in how people consume news. Those of us who watch television end up drawing conclusions about a story or report that are often contrary to the conclusions

of those of us who listen to the radio, even though the content
of the two mediums is identical.[2] When pictures speak a different language from words, the images prevail. In fact, some
psychologists consider nonverbal communication to be the
decisive key to influencing others.[3]

We also consider body language—with the exception of
facial expressions—to be authentic, exhibiting how a person
truly feels about a given situation, conversation, or task.[4] We
all know how easy it is to deceive others with our words, and
how empty and dishonest they can be. It's less common to
fake nonverbal communication, our bodies' cues and movements.

Despite all this, we underestimate the role of nonverbal
communication in terms of our own external impact and, as a
rule, focus more on our words.[5] However, if we deliberately
use our nonverbal communication skills, we can strongly influence the specific impressions we make on people and present ourselves in a certain light. Luckily, decades of research—based
on years of comparing nuances in body language—provides
us with deep insight and findings that you can implement
almost immediately. A huge potential slumbers here, just
waiting to be awoken to contribute to your perceived competence.

Near and Far
In 1972's unforgettable The Godfather, Don Corleone, played
by Marlon Brando, always places himself very close to the
people he speaks with—especially if they are responsible for
his bad mood. The godfather thus did not stand or sit out of
consideration to others so they could better understand him,
despite his chronic mumbling. Rather, he wanted to intimidate
his opponents.

The US psychologists Stuart Albert and James Dabbs conducted an experiment in which they closely examined the effect of physical distance between people.[6] Ninety subjects each listened individually to students who told them something about two subjects for five minutes—overpopulation and openness in personal relationships.

Afterward, the subjects had to evaluate the students according to various criteria, including their perceived competence. Albert and Dabbs came to the following conclusions: A distance of only 1–2 feet (30–60 centimeters) between the subjects and students actually caused nervousness and tension in the conversation partner—many people, and Americans in particular, find such a closeness to be downright invasive.[7] At the same time, this intrusion of personal space led to a defensive response by the subjects and thus to a reduction in the students' perceived competence.[8] Therefore, outside the world of gangsters on the silver screen, such an awkward position is not recommended.

A distance of 14–15 feet (2–4 meters) from the person you are talking to also reduces the impression of competence. This amount of space leads to a more negative attitude and a more hostile mood in both people involved, which may be due to the fact that it is difficult to create a rapport or real connection with someone over a wider distance.[9]

The most competent way to place yourself is to keep a distance of 4–5 feet (1.20–1.50 meters) from the person you are talking to. This research result is easy to translate into everyday life, whether standing or sitting. If you are giving a presentation, for example, don't position yourself too far away from the audience. When you have visitors at your desk during a meeting or other formal discussion, make sure that the chairs are optimally placed for this distance. In casual standing conversations, a distance of about two steps from the person you're speaking with is best.

Of course, you can't carry around a measuring tape. As a rule of thumb, try to place yourself close to the other person without intruding their personal space. This rule, however, can be difficult to follow around the globe, as massive cultural differences exist between some countries. For example, in Latin America and Asia—especially in India—people tend to keep less distance from each other.[10] Therefore, it makes sense in these cultural circles to move a little closer to your conversation partner. Where personal space begins is a question of tact and sensitivity that plays a role in all of the techniques described throughout this book.

By the way, the question of the right distance comes down to a beautiful "win-win" situation: if you are 4–5 feet away from your interlocutor, then, lo and behold, he or she is also 4–5 feet away from you—neither of you is nervous or awkward due to proximity, and you will both look good!

Stand Properly, Sit Properly

In addition to knowing where to stand, it's also imperative to know specifically *how* to stand, and also to sit, when trying to convey competence. One major rule that you most likely heard from your grandmother is that an upright posture works like a charm—she was right! Unlike some other body language discussed later, such poise applies to both men and women alike and influences perceived competence.[11] You may also recall your parents chiding you not to fidget—once again, they were right! Nervous, superfluous movements have a negative effect on a person's perceived intelligence and thus on one's perceived competence.

The ways in which men and women position themselves during a conversation do not always have the same effect. For example, when men speak to an individual or group of people, the angle at which they face their audience considerably influences their perceived competence—not so with women.[12] Generally speaking, men should stand facing their audience head on or slightly averted. They are perceived to be considerably more competent if there is a 30-degree angle between their own body alignment and that of their listeners. If you're a man, you don't have to walk around with a set square and compass— the rule of thumb here is quite simple: stand slightly at an angle to the person opposite you.

This basic rule should be observed in presentations and in conversations, but also when being photographed, especially for important photos in the professional context, such as an accompanying picture in a magazine article or the company's website. This small turn is just a little something extra to create a considerable effect. However, for one reason or another, this angled body language does not translate into increased perceived competence for women.

To summarize, always stand calmly upright and, if you're a man, make sure to position yourself at an optimum, 30-degree angle to the person opposite you.

In addition to the way you compose yourself while standing, how you sit also influences your appearance and sends a message to those around you. In a study investigating the effect of sitting on persuasiveness, researchers examined different styles of sitting, specifically looking at how relaxed a subject appeared—stiff and formal, for example, as compared to a more casual posture.[13] A *slightly relaxed* posture was found to provide, by far, the most beneficial effect for men, whereas for women the *slightly tense* posture was proved more advantageous.

The *slightly tense* posture that makes women appear competent and confident has the following characteristics:

- leaning the body slightly forward, approximately at an angle of 10 degrees to the chair backrest
- keeping the back straight, without any tension
- resting feet flat on the floor
- positioning hands, arms, and legs symmetrically

The men's *slightly relaxed* posture looks like this:

- tilting the body about 10 degrees forward
- making the body's back visible but not strongly curved
- resting hands in an asymmetrical position on the lap (for example, one hand on the knee, the other on a thigh)
- tilting arms and legs slightly forward, with one foot always closer to the front than the other

Such a manual on how to sit may seem strange at first glance. Just try it out, it may come easy to you!

In addition to how you compose yourself while sitting, you can also increase your persuasiveness by placing yourself at the head of the table whenever possible.[14]

In a study on the power of seating placement, four test subjects argued over how much compensation an accident victim should be awarded, and they all came to a substantial average sum. A fifth person, who had been planted by the researchers, joined the group, chose to sit down at the head of the table, and argued in favor of a much lower sum. In light of the fifth person's argument, the rest of the group also lowered their suggested compensation, reducing the total by almost 30 percent.

When researchers assigned chairs, however, the head seat did not exert a greater influence. The fifth person's effectiveness was therefore caused not by merely sitting at the head of the table but by the fact that he had selected that very chair. What is even more astounding is that the process of choosing seats took barely five seconds, while the discussion lasted 40 minutes, showing that if you take the initiative—even for just that brief moment—to sit at the head of the table, you will be overwhelmed with positive associations. You appear independent, self-confident, and stable, and the rest of the people at the table even regard you as a leader.

But isn't it somewhat rude or presumptuous to just snag the head seat? During the experiment, there was no evidence to indicate this, presumably because people simply underestimate the considerable importance of choosing a seat—they just don't think much about it. Surely there are cultural differences. In countries where the seating arrangements are based on hierarchies that have to be strictly adhered to, one should exercise restraint. At a business dinner in Tokyo, for example, the most prominent seat—usually the head seat or the most comfortable one—is called *kamiza*. It is strictly reserved for the person with the highest status. Be careful about choosing the *kamiza*, as you could insult others—and end up getting the bill!

Eye Contact

Grigory Yefimovich Rasputin—a miracle healer, monk, mystic, and secret lover of Alexandra Feodorovna, the tsarina of Russia in the late 1800s and early 1900s—knew how to captivate people. There is hardly another historical figure surrounded by so many fascinating stories. One of many accounts about the cryptic "Strannik," the mysterious pilgrim—as he was referred to—reads as follows:[15]

> Rasputin took a step forward and stared at the people
> with his forehead frowned. Shivers came upon the men
> and women. It was as if he pierced them with his
> sparkling, hard, little eyes. He reached out his arm.

"You there—you on the stool," he commanded. "Come here!"

The fat little man looked horrified. "I can't . . ." he stuttered. "I haven't been able to stand for two years. The doctors say—they say the muscles of my back are paralyzed. Help me, Strannik! Help me! I will give you . . ."

Rasputin's glowing eyes stared at the man. "Stand up," he said. His voice was soft and hoarse. It was quiet in the small group. From far away, the noise of the market was heard. The man on the stool had turned pale as death. The sweat droplets were on his forehead. Slowly, staggeringly, he rose from his stool. He stood. He took a hesitant step—and then one more. A third one. And then he stood in front of Strannik, the miracle man—trembling, covered with sweat . . .

"A miracle," whispered the young woman wearing the colorful headscarf and crossed herself. The little man was still standing in front of Rasputin. For a moment he swayed, then he stood still.

"You're going home now!" he was told by Strannik. "You'll go, and you won't have any more pain in your back."

A haggard woman fell to her knees. She kissed the miracle man's hand. She whispered, "Thank you!"

Perhaps it was Rasputin's clairvoyant powers that helped him anticipate the findings of modern psychology—eye contact plays a major role in communication. Frequent eye contact makes you appear stronger, which has a significant effect on your persuasive power and, in extreme cases, makes suggestions possible, such as the one just described. Research has also shown that eye contact actually influences perceived competence directly.[16]

But be careful: making eye contact while your interlocutor is speaking actually harms your perceived competence![17] Direct eye contact with the speaker is associated with a low status, possibly because it is interpreted as a submissive gesture—servants look at their masters while they take their commands. And yet, as a rule, we tend to look at our interlocutors when we listen and not when we ourselves speak.[18] A balancing act develops here: you don't want to appear rude by demonstratively looking away, but you also shouldn't look at your conversation partner in a servile manner.

When thinking about eye contact, the so-called Nixon effect should also be taken into account. Named after the former US president Richard Nixon, who blinked dozens of times during his resignation speech after the Watergate scandal, the Nixon effect refers to excessive blinking, which is perceived as a sign of anxiousness and nervousness. It is therefore not surprising that in US presidential campaigns, the candidates who blink least usually win the election.[19]

To sum it all up, look your conversation partners in the eyes as often as possible when you are speaking, but not when you are listening to them. Also, don't blink too much. To come back to Rasputin: he looked at the old man masterfully when he told him that he could walk. He didn't blink or divert his attention but rather kept the man fully engaged, causing him to pull together all his strength and stand. But when the old man talked about his suffering, Rasputin turned his gaze away. In doing so, he maintained a position of superiority and awe—and thus became the miracle man we still talk about.

Smile Please?

Legendary defense attorney Gerry Spence relays his thoughts about smiling with the following:[20]

> Does it work? If you attend a cocktail party and look around, you will see nice smiles stamped on nearly all the faces. One thinks: "What a great time everyone

must be having! And how nice everyone is!" Yet we know that the room is not filled with nice people but with a mix of bastards, fakes, wife beaters, child abusers, not to mention a few decent people. If you watch the couples walk from the party to their cars, you would see that they have now taken off their smile masks. Some are bitching about the party. Some are mad at their boyfriend for not having shown them enough attention or for having shown too much attention to someone else's.

Is smiling really that bad?

Well, it is a complex matter, as the active research on this subject shows. On the one hand, you increase your own popularity and radiate motivation by smiling.[21] Both are definitely conducive to making a good impression.

On the other hand, there are a number of disadvantages.[22] Those who grin all the time are perceived as less intelligent. Frequent smiles are also associated with low social status: it isn't the peer who is eager to please but the subordinate. Especially when smiling seems inappropriate, such as in an unpleasant situation—when you have missed a deadline or shipped the wrong goods—you run the risk of coming across as the cliché of a used-car dealer. A serious expression is not an immediate sign of competence, but in critical conversations it is at least a sign of higher status and dominance. The idea is quite similar to nodding: in itself, it appears likable, but if used too often or at the wrong time, nodding communicates a lower status and thus lower competence.[23]

In women, the effect of a serious expression is even more pronounced. When a woman's eyebrows are pulled down as in anger or displeasure and her head is slightly lowered, displaying an exceedingly serious impression, her perceived status is even further increased.[24]

Constant smiling not only is strenuous but can also come across as out of place and even harmful. The important thing is not to succumb to the silly notion that we constantly have to grin. You should therefore smile when you feel like it—but only then.

In summary, permanent smiles are in no way appropriate, and a misplaced grin even has a negative effect on your perceived competence. As a woman, you can reinforce the effect of a serious expression with lowered eyebrows and lowered head to increase your social status and receive greater respect. But during appropriate moments, an authentic smile can have a positive effect and instill feelings of personal happiness to boot.

Body Contact

US president Lyndon B. Johnson was a master of the art of the tactical touch.[25] He is said to have squeezed his conversation partners' knees or shoulders and even pounded his fingers on their stomachs in a way that put them at ease and ingratiated himself toward them.

Particularly today, you (and me, too) *truly* need a good sense of tact here—perhaps more than with any of the other techniques discussed in this chapter—since touching another person can appear inappropriate and could lead to a highly negative reaction.

However, we all have an innate need for human touch—even babies who do not get enough physical contact become anxious and restless. Doctors, for example, touch their patients to signal protection and care. Some psychologists consider touch to be the most important nonverbal signal of all.[26] Touching the person you're speaking with not only increases your own status but also gives them a feeling of security, which, thanks to the halo effect, contributes directly to your perceived competence.

Try patting your conversation partners on their shoulder or place a hand on their upper arm while talking. We regular see this type of interaction when watching politicians meet. They often appear to be in a competition of who can touch whom more often.

If you feel uncomfortable in employing this technique, you can at least still use this knowledge on the one occasion when you have to touch another person for better or worse: the handshake. Make a habit of placing your free, left hand on the other person's upper right arm to maximize touch at that moment. Again, we can learn from top politicians: take a look at the photos of political summits and the attendants' high-contact handshakes, underpinning their authority and competence.

Height

When it comes to physical height's influence on perceived competence, the research can more or less be summarized clearly and quickly: the bigger, the better.[27] This is especially the case for men.

Even in ancient Egypt, the higher men's status, the taller they were depicted in pictures. It works both ways: the higher a person's status, the taller others perceive him or her to be.[28] Students, for example, regularly estimate that their professors are taller than they actually are. And how amazed are people when they find out their favorite Hollywood star only measures five feet two?

In an experiment about how physical height affects perception, participants were presented with photographs of a man.[29] One group received a picture of him in which he appeared tall, while another group received one in which he appeared short. Indeed, participants looking at the photo in which the man appeared tall were much more likely to consider him a leader. Taller men are perceived as dominant and healthier, probably a result dating back to prehistoric times and Charles Darwin's theory of natural selection. This effect is more pronounced in men than women. Due to the halo effect, this perception translates to other factors such as competence.[30]

In fact, taller men are privileged in almost all walks of life.[31] For example, men over six feet (1.83 meters) receive a 12 percent higher starting salary than those who are shorter than six feet.[32] The data on all US presidential elections show that taller candidates received significantly more popular votes and had a higher chance to be reelected.[33] Height has even increased in significance, since presidential campaigns now take place mainly on television, where body height is quite obvious. It is therefore hardly surprising that shorter candidates' campaign teams usually go out of their way to cover up the difference in size between their candidates and their opponents.

If you don't happen to be taller than average, you may be thinking this information is all fine and well (or not), but how can you benefit from knowing it? Luckily, you don't have to stretch yourself out on the rack—the perception of size can be manipulated to increase your perceived competence.

First of all, only a few inches decide whether people see you as tall or short: a five feet ten (1.79 meters) man is considered to be rather short, while one who is only a few inches taller (that is, six feet) appears rather tall.[34] Every inch counts! Shoes with heels, for example, can unobtrusively increase your height by up to 4 inches (10 centimeters). There even are shoes that come with invisible heels or lifts, so no one can tell that you're "boosting." You may think wearing such footwear is preposterous or vain, but in reality it is an astute calculation. Another option, if you work behind a sales counter, for example, is to simply add height to the floor where you regularly stand. Pinstripes and a uniformly colored suit, which does not visually divide the body into two halves, also make you look taller.

However, it may also suffice to adopt the optimal posture. You can gain a few inches with a mere upright posture. Try the following: Stand with your back against a wall and press completely against it so that not even a sheet of paper fits between you and the wall. If you then take a step forward, you will feel somewhat stiff at first—you have now reached your maximum height. Never forget that a few inches make the difference. Before important conversations, you should get used to taking this detour by the next wall, as it only takes a few seconds. Just make sure that it's not just a whitewashed wall that will rub off on your entire back—I'm talking from experience.

It is also important to act tactically, depending on the situation. If the people around you are shorter than you, remain standing as long as possible: try to perform any introductions or initial conversations while everyone is standing and get everyone to remain standing as long as possible. Position yourself as close to them as you can to emphasize the difference in your height, especially if you are in a meeting or at an event with competitors. When you are around taller people, however, make sure not to be in their immediate vicinity in order to avoid direct comparison. Then try to get everyone to sit. When you take your seat, maybe even place a pillow down first. You can also always offer your partner the comfortable, but *low*, sofa while you sit on the hard, but *high*, chair. Or you can attempt to be the only person standing in a room of seated people, as long as it doesn't come off as awkward. Regardless of how you approach the given situation, once you are literally towering over everyone else in the room, you will notice how much more convincing you seem.[35]

Enthusiasm

The effect of nonverbal communication has rarely been illustrated in such an astonishing way as it was in the "Dr. Fox experiment."[36] Psychologists sent an actor to give a lecture at an education conference. They presented him as "Dr. Myron L. Fox," created an impressive biography for him, and gave his lecture the promising title "Mathematical Game Theory as Applied to Physician Education." Though the actor knew nothing about his lecture's subject matter, his talk went on for an hour. The audience, which included psychologists, psychiatrists, and social workers, stayed for the entire presentation. Was the content of the speech that great? Not at all—according to the authors, the material consisted of "an excessive use of double talk, neologisms, non sequiturs, and contradictory statements." And yet, the audience of experts gave the presentation an overwhelmingly positive rating. Not a single listener noticed that what the actor said during the lecture was pure nonsense.

Though the manufactured doctoral degree and an impressive CV certainly played a role in the audience's buying into the presentation, it was found that the actor's enthusiastic body language made the decisive difference. When "Dr. Fox" received high evaluations he was full of enthusiasm, expressed through his lively body language. But when he presented the same speech to a different but similarly composed audience in a motionless and monotonous way, his evaluations dropped sharply.

A similar study, in which a professor taught the same course twice, once enthusiastically and once somberly, also found that the enthusiastic appearance had a more positive effect—even though the content was absolutely identical.[37] I have personally observed these results when giving presentations. If I limit my movements and focus solely on the content, it is much harder to reach and connect with the audience.

To infuse enthusiasm into your talks or speeches—whether during a presentation or product launch—keep moving, instead of allowing the lecture to degenerate into a dialogue with the first row. Try to get a good feel for the entire room so your behavior can adapt to the audience's expectations and emotions. Instead of constantly looking in the same direction or at the same people in the crowd, make sure to look around, selecting different individuals or areas in the room. Your facial expression as you speak to the audience should also match your words—you want people to read in your face the emotion you're trying to express.

It is also important to gesticulate with your hands, not in a choreographed way but spontaneously and in harmony with the content you're discussing. You can also take a lesson from former US president Barack Obama: even when sitting behind his desk reading from the teleprompter, he would address all those present through many cameras from different angles, making an animated, lively, and thus enthusiastic impression on the viewers.

Whether you're speaking to a large audience or small one, using a teleprompter or no technology at all, or presenting material you're familiar with or content that you've never even heard of before, it is good advice to stick with what acting coach Hal Persons preached to generations of students: Imagine that you are a lightbulb, pressing energy up through your body and into your head. Let that light turn on.

Conclusion

Imagine this: You want to get your finances in order at the end of the year before the dreaded tax season, so you head to a financial adviser a friend recommended for some guidance. He welcomes you into his office, where you sit in a chair about two feet away from him. When he speaks to you, he looks you straight in the eye. You ask him a question, and he thoughtfully turns his gaze away. Although he is friendly, when push comes to shove, he puts on a serious face. When he gets up, he stands at a slight angle from you, and when you tell him about your greatest worries concerning your financial situation, he puts his hand on your shoulder while giving you advice. When he invites you to a meeting of other clients, he seems to tower over everyone else in the room, places himself at the head of the table, and sits there looking relaxed. However, when he talks about his work, he is full of enthusiasm and verve. Wouldn't you feel great about him?

As you can see, all of these techniques can be implemented easily without changing your personality. And yet these nuances have a considerable influence on the perception of your person and therefore your competence.

One final note on the subject: You may have heard of the 55/38/7 formula, which goes back to a study by the Armenian American psychologist Albert Mehrabian.[38] In the 1960s, Mehrabian studied the effects of nonverbal communication. In one study, he filmed students speaking in different ways: emotionally positive, negative, or neutral. Afterward, test subjects who viewed this footage indicated how likable they thought the people were on the film. The actual words spoken played hardly any role in the viewers' impressions. Much more important for the evaluation were the people's voices and facial expressions. From this experiment, Mehrabian developed the following "formula":

Total Liking = 7% Verbal Liking + 38% Vocal Liking
+ 55% Facial Liking

Since then, there has hardly been a book or training seminar on body language that does not depict this formula as if it were carved in stone—after all, it catapults body language to the top of the Mount Olympus of significance. Mehrabian, however, was surprised by the spread of his formula, which he limits to the specific context of his investigation.[39] So even though body language is essential indeed, it is only one of several steps on your road to perceived competence.

Competence Compendium
Nonverbal Communication

✧ Keep a distance of 4–5 feet from the person you're speaking with.
✧ Maintain eye contact when you talk, but break it when you listen.
✧ Don't blink excessively.
✧ Do not smile constantly.
✧ Touch others when it is appropriate.
✧ Stand at a slight angle from the person you're speaking to.
✧ If you're a woman, sit in a slightly tense manner; if you're a man, sit in a slightly relaxed one.
✧ Always select the seat at the head of the table.
✧ Height is crucial for men and should be remembered in any formal setting.
✧ Show enthusiasm during presentations by moving around and using large gestures.

CHAPTER 7

BEAUTIFUL AND POPULAR

HOW TO INCREASE YOUR POPULARITY AND ATTRACTIVENESS

I choose my friends for their good looks, my acquaintances for their good characters, and my enemies for their good intellects.

—OSCAR WILDE

The Constant Error in Psychological Ratings

More than 100 years ago, US psychologist Edward Lee Thorndike conducted an experiment that seemed quite unimpressive at first glance but turned out to be revolutionary. He asked military officers to evaluate their subordinates based on such diverse aspects as fitness, intellect, orderliness, leadership, loyalty, and reliability.[1]

Thorndike noted that the officers' individual evaluations of a person, in most cases, showed surprisingly similar positive or negative correlations among totally different, unrelated qualities. For example, those considered neat were also considered loyal. Those rated as intelligent were also seen as physically fit. This finding made no sense to Thorndike: neatness and loyalty should have no bearing on one another, nor should intelligence have a direct influence on fitness. Thorndike described this phenomenon as "constant error in psychological ratings." With this study, he instituted the term "halo effect," the key phenomenon discussed throughout chapter 3. As a reminder, the halo effect shows that positive news radiates positively over every other aspect of a person or event, and bad news does so negatively. Starting with only a few points of reference, this halo effect therefore applies to the entire assessment of a person.

Surely there were top students at your school who received excellent grades in almost all subjects, even if they had not particularly excelled in them for virtually an entire semester— they still got As. Then there were the "blockheads," who, regardless of their actual performance, were simply unable to rise above the impression their teachers had of them—or even of any of their siblings whom the teachers had previously taught.

Teachers are usually not deliberately unfair, but they are victims of this common error, a mistake that also undermines experienced executives whose employee assessments are usually based on very few factors.[2]

As discussed, positive or negative aspects influence the overall picture people have of you, which, of course, also affects your perceived competence. If you have done a good job in one area, this impression will color other areas as well.[3] In other words, completely irrelevant factors—such as friendliness or a well-groomed appearance—can influence your perceived competence and contribute to positive developments in your career.

Consequently, creating an overall positive impression is of decisive importance. You must therefore make sure to always come across as friendly, polite, attentive, educated, and so on— the list can be expanded by any number of positive aspects. As discussed in chapter 2 regarding high expectations, people's observations are heavily influenced by their first impressions.[4] Whether a positive or negative impression exists, it will be unconsciously strengthened by your actions. Supervisors who are well disposed toward employees tend to perceive their positive behavior and remember it better than negative behavior. The opposite is true if the employee is perceived negatively.[5]

Unfortunately, this effect is most pronounced when a negative feeling prevails. During a job interview, an applicant's tasteless tie has a stronger negative effect than the positive effect that would have been created had he worn a particularly nice tie. Therefore, any positive impressions you make have a matching effect on your competence, and this effect is even stronger with negative impressions. So try to make a good overall impression and, even more importantly, do not attract negative attention!

With this wisdom, one could, in principle, conclude this chapter, were there not two decisive aspects to assessing people, both of which have a particularly high impact on perceived competence: popularity and attractiveness.

Some people appear likable—others do not. Some are considered attractive, while others aren't. The main factors that lead to a particular judgment on your likability and attractiveness are not as obvious as they may first seem. With the following findings, however, you can enhance those factors, while increasing others' assessment of your competence in the process.

Popularity

What could be more human than the desire to be liked?

This is how Edward E. Jones, one of the most influential social psychologists of the 20th century, explained his reason for spending decades researching how to get other people to like you.[6] And, as explained earlier, due to the halo effect, popularity strengthens the impression of competence.[7]

Even the simplest technique for increasing your own popularity, classic ingratiation—in which a person deliberately tries to place himself or herself in good favor with another individual—is generally successful.[8] Job applicants who ingratiate themselves during an interview are perceived as more qualified and tend to be hired more often. Those who ingratiate themselves to their bosses or managers receive better assessments, are promoted more often, and get bigger raises. The effect isn't only observed from the bottom up either. Managers who ingratiate themselves with their colleagues and employees are also more convincing and can more easily implement changes at work. So flattery does in fact get you pretty far.

Am I therefore recommending that you tell your coworker how great he looks, how brilliant his ideas are, and what a terrific guy he is? Not quite. Instead, I want to show you the results of research and give you an understanding of specific techniques to increase your popularity that work. Surprisingly, although the practical relevance of this research is paramount, these results are barely known or discussed outside the scientific community.

The three methods that are decisive for achieving our goals in this area are ingratiation (enhancement of others), opinion conformity, and self-presentation (enhancement of self).[9] Let's begin by taking a deeper look at the one aspect already mentioned: ingratiation.

Ingratiation

Joe Girard has received a number of entries in the Guinness World Records as being the most successful car salesman in the world. Born in the United States in the late 1920s to poor Sicilian immigrants, as a child, Girard contributed to his family's income by shining shoes after school. It wasn't until the age of 35, when he began working at a Chevrolet car dealership in Michigan, that his incredible knack for sales revealed itself. On day one of the job, Girard sold his first car. Soon after, he would start selling up to 18 cars per day, averaging nearly 1,000 per year—enough to win him four world records in all.

Girard's recipe for success? He simply showed customers that he liked them—and hardly in a subtle way.[10] Every month, he would send his customers—former or prospective ones—a card with nothing on the front but the words "I like you." Girard clearly knew that his customers were aware these cards were nothing more than part of his sales pitch. Still, it worked.

Research on the subject reaffirms Girard's approach: if you give someone a compliment only because you need that person's help, regardless of whether the compliment is in earnest, your popularity increases, even if the attempt to flatter that person is obvious.[11] The transparency of flattery seems not to bother us to a certain extent, as we human beings seem to simply have a very strong need to be pleased with ourselves.

This approach works even better when our dependency on the other person is less obvious.[12] Such would be the case, for example, if you said something kind, even though you have nothing immediate to gain from it, on an innocuous company outing away from the workplace. Jones speaks of this as a "reservoir of good will" that should be built up as early as possible in any professional relationship.[13] The best way to ingratiate yourself to people is for them to find out about your compliments from a third person. If others tell them about your public praise of them, it is all the more powerful.

When directly giving someone a compliment, though, presentation is key. For example, a good introduction to a compliment is, "You might not want to hear this, but . . . ," or, "I don't want to make you uncomfortable, but . . . ."[14] Then you follow the statement with the compliment. In this way, you conceal your praise at first through your supposed expectation of the person's resistance. In doing so, you will pleasantly surprise him or her and, at the same time, come across as humble.

When giving any praise, make sure that it is not too general—the more specific, the more effective. A colleague patting your back and giving you a brisk "good job" is nice but certainly less effective than a more detailed compliment, such as, "I'm impressed by how you were able to bring everyone to the table and convince them of the new sales initiative with such crystal-clear arguments."

Despite the importance of complimenting others to ingratiate yourself, never make far-fetched compliments that have no basis in truth. Respect and sincere interest in the other person is sufficient. As the American writer Ralph Waldo Emerson knew, "In my walks, every man I meet is my superior in some way, in that I learn from him."[15] Point being, you can typically find a way to sincerely compliment another person. To do so, figure out where your fellow human beings' special talents lie. Even if that skill ends up being a somewhat unusual hobby like collecting butterflies, your respect for that person will grow as soon as you recognize the passion with which he or she is pursuing it.[16] And, in turn, that person will tend to like you.

In many ways it comes down to a sense of respect for the person you're speaking with. The term "respect" comes from the Latin re-, meaning "once again," and spectare, which means "to look." If at first glance you don't see anything special about the person to whom you're trying to ingratiate yourself, look again, and this time look closer—you will find something.[17]

The pinnacle of showing respect toward others is asking them for their advice. Rather than praising their intelligence, ask them what to do in a certain situation.[18] For example, say, "This one employee is always late to work, but I don't know what to do to get him to start coming in on time. Do you have any experience with that?" Whatever their response, they will be pleased that you approached them, as it indicates that you respect them and take their opinions seriously.

In Dale Carnegie's famous 1936 book, *How to Win Friends and Influence People*, the author explained how Theodore Roosevelt amazed and amused his guests with his versatile knowledge. Whether he was talking to a diplomat or a cowboy, President Roosevelt always knew his way around the particular conversation. He had a little secret: on the eve of such meetings, he read books on subjects that he knew were of interest to his guests.

Carnegie wrote, "For Roosevelt knew, as all leaders know, that the royal road to a person's heart is to talk about the things he or she treasures most. . . . You can make more friends in two months by being interested in other people than in two years of trying to get people interested in you."[19] According to Carnegie, you must recognize that the person you are speaking with may be much more concerned about his own toothache than a famine in India. Therefore, make sure the people you talk to understand that you are truly interested in them, their concerns, and their interests.

You don't always have to signal this interest through words—you can let your actions speak instead. Doing others favors or even giving them small gifts not only makes them feel obliged to respond in kind, but due to a sense of gratitude, they'll want to return the good will.[20] If you give someone something freely, with no strings attached, you will be treated as helpful and friendly—and, of course, your popularity increases.

One last way to ingratiate yourself with others is by employing the *mirroring* technique.[21] In mirroring, you copy or imitate the person you're speaking with, causing the two of you to resemble each other within a few minutes. This idea is also referred to as the "chameleon effect." During the conversation, your posture, word choice, rate of speech, facial expressions, and even accent become more and more similar to one another.

This mirroring can be used deliberately, in moderation, to gain affinity. Mirroring is surprisingly undetectable, especially when a few moments lie between it and the other's original behavior.[22] As the Irish author Oscar Wilde knew, "Imitation is the sincerest form of flattery."

Opinion Conformity

In spite of the high value we put on the diversity of opinions, it has been shown time and again that we especially like people who agree with us.[23] Having the same opinion as other people in a given group greatly contributes to your popularity among them. However, as with all methods of influencing others, you cannot proceed clumsily, especially when people are well aware of possible manipulation. For this reason, research on the topic is particularly focused on how people conceal their deliberate use of opinion conformity. If you overdo it and agree with everything others say, you can quickly land on the opposite side of the intended result—no one likes a bootlicker.

So what can you do that is less obvious than just agreeing with everyone on everything? One way is to reflect the opinion of the particular person you're trying to influence on a certain subject publicly, before he or she expresses it.[24] Jones recommends researching that person's opinion and discussing it with a third party that has some insight on it. He then suggests that in the next public situation, such as a meeting or presentation, you take the floor and immediately open the discussion with that like-minded opinion, thus appearing sincere.[25]

When it comes to your boss, do you need to agree with her or him on everything? No—but you should on important topics.[26] Sharing fundamental values has a positive effect on everything else in regard to your popularity and perceived competence. In regard to unimportant topics, having a different opinion does little harm. It is imperative, however, that you show absolute certainty in your shared opinion and remain ambiguous about points where you two disagree.

On a related note, instead of immediately agreeing with the other person, it is sometimes more effective to start with a different opinion. After a few minutes of discussion, however, say, "Well, you have convinced me." Now you are not only signaling agreement, but you have also created an impression of reflection and openness to arguments.[27] But beware of "deception detection" tactics. For example, if you are in full agreement with a person's opinion and you make an argument for his case, but then that person pulls a 180—taking the opposite point of view—and you quickly follow suit, you may be unmasked as a flatterer.[28]

American physics professor Alan Sokal played with the impact of opinion conformity when he published an article titled "Transgressing the Boundaries: Towards a Transformative Hermeneutics of Quantum Gravity" in the respected journal *Social Text*.[29] On the day of publication, Sokal revealed that the piece was a prank: the article was nonsensical and consisted of nothing but hollow phrases, but it was peppered with sentences that apparently gave away his leftist attitude.[30] With what is now known as the "Sokal Hoax," Alan Sokal wanted to prove his point that you can make just about any argument as long as you seem to be of the same (political) opinion as the people you're addressing, which in this case were the left-leaning magazine readers—a beautiful illustration of the impact of opinion conformity.

Self-Presentation
Though ingratiation and opinion conformity are important for popularity, and perceived competence, if you go around constantly handing out compliments, you may end up looking like

a mere apple-polisher. So though praise plays a major role in your relationship with others, it is also of vital importance to put yourself in the right light.[31] The good news is that humans are intuitively good at this type of self-marketing.

In one experiment, subjects were asked to make a positive impression on their conversation partners; nearly all of them succeeded in doing so without any instructions.[32] In general, we know how to make others like us, through kindness, courtesy, and modesty (the last, however, as discussed earlier, should be used only with regard to trivial matters—you don't want to come across as incompetent!).

Perhaps not quite so obvious is the colossal importance of highlighting similarities between you and another person, also known as the "similarity attraction theory."[33] When you go out on a first date, for example, do you look for differences or for similarities between you and your potential partner? Precisely. When US psychologist Robert Cialdini worked undercover at a car dealership to learn its legendary sales techniques firsthand, as mentioned in chapter 3, he reported that salespeople were trained to pay close attention to anything they may have in common with the customers—or could appear to have in common with them. For example, if they spotted golf balls in their customer's trunk, they were supposed to mention that they hoped for better weather so they could soon get out on the fairway and hit a few balls.

Research and practice agree: similarities in terms of age, religion, political opinion, or other minimal commonalities increase mutual fondness and, ultimately, influence one another.[34] This shared feeling created by commonalities has deep roots in ancient tribal logic, which placed an emphasis on the group as a whole. Keeping our legacy in mind, always show your interlocutor that you are on the same side—for example, use "we" as appropriate during a conversation rather than "I." Above all, seek out and emphasize the things you have in common, such as where you were born, what schools and universities you attended, your birthday, and any mutual friends or colleagues you may have.[35]

Openness is also an important factor for likability and credibility, so it's good to share something about yourself during every conversation.[36] Talk about where you want to travel next, which country you would most like to visit, or what book you are currently reading. Share things about yourself that are personal, but nothing intimate—if you talk about your sexual preferences too early, for example, you will make yourself unpopular (and come across as a creep). And, of course, the information you provide should not cast you in a bad light— who wants to work with a loser?[37] Openness has yet another advantage: because your conversation partners unconsciously imitate you, you will learn more from them, helping you better assess your personality and recognize commonalities with them, further increasing the possibilities for positive self-presentation and influence.[38]

Self-confident people tend to open up more about themselves, but unfortunately, this type of openness is difficult for many of us.[39] In addition, there is a gender-specific difference: women open up more to people they like, while men are more likely to share information about themselves with others whom they trust.[40] To a certain degree, when trying to influence peoples' perception of you, you should open up to both those you like and those you trust, not just because you might gain a friend or two but also because your popularity will grow among the intended group and your perceived competence will therefore increase.

Summary: The Three Keys to Popularity

The results of research about popularity are largely in harmony with common sense: First, occasionally drop a compliment or two, and always show others respect and an interest in what they're saying. Second, express the same opinions as the person you're speaking with—at least on important issues. And finally, appear likable through openness and elaboration of similarities. Though they are commonsense, by being fully aware of these techniques, you will gain a better understanding of the dynamics of interpersonal relations.

Today, it is not enough just to be popular with the boss. In the age of flat hierarchies, it is more important than ever to be positively perceived by colleagues on your level, or even lower ones. Keep in mind that assessments from all levels are taken seriously nowadays, and you never know who may cause you trouble or give you praise. The good news is that the techniques described here are all the more effective with subordinates, as they aren't expecting you to deliberately garner favor with them. However, ingratiation, opinion conformity, and self-presentation should be used with everyone you encounter, no matter their position or role—you want your popularity to extend as far as possible.

Apart from being likeable, there is one other aspect that has a key impact on the overall impression you make: your physical attractiveness. Although not as easy to influence as likeability, there are many ways you can utilize the insights of current research to your benefit.

Attractiveness

Our fascination with beauty is as old as humankind.[41] In the Stone Age, black eye shadow, mixed with lead sulfide and charcoal, made its first appearance. Way back in ancient Greece, the ruler Solon forbade the excessive selling of cosmetic ointments—apparently, even then, too many people were caking on makeup. According to the Bible (Exodus 2:2), Moses was exceptionally beautiful as a baby, an important distinction for a man who would one day be known for parting the Red Sea. Anthropologists regard the urge to increase our attractiveness as one of the earliest signs of civilization, while some even consider it an instinct.[42]

Hardly anyone doubts that physical attractiveness can be helpful in certain situations, but its true power in all areas of our lives is hard to imagine. Just ask someone to tell you about a particular person—almost without fail, they will first describe the person's appearance.[43] Appearance is an obvious feature, and unlike other facets of communication, it is constantly visible throughout any in-person interaction. In fact, attractiveness is a crucial part of any first impression, as it leads to conclusions about other factors in regard to your personality and capabilities.[44]

Physical attractiveness is just as important in business relationships as it is in romantic ones. Although this factor plays an even greater role in its effect on the opposite sex—dependent on sexual orientation, of course—attractiveness is still the central variable in nonintimate relationships, such as a friendship between heterosexual men.[45]

These assumptions begin early in life: children prefer to play with more attractive playmates.[46] Shockingly, parents even feel greater affection toward an attractive infant.[47] The more attractive a high school teacher or college professor, the higher his or her competency ratings are across the students.[48] Teachers also rate attractive pupils as more competent.[49] Attractive people are also more likely to be praised for success, while unattractive people are blamed for failure.[50] Employees who are considered attractive receive up to 10 percent higher wages and are more likely to be promoted.[51] More attractive politicians receive significantly more votes than their less attractive counterparts—all over the world.[52] And the list goes on.[53] Altogether, the evidence clearly suggests that attractive people are generally more convincing.[54]

But when people are asked whether external beauty influences their judgment, they likely dispute it. Yet, in experimental situations, those same people will reveal how attractiveness influences them. Even when people interact for a longer time and already know a lot about each other, the relevance of attractiveness does not decrease.[55]

Attractive people are thus seen to have much more positive qualities. They are perceived as more intelligent, nicer, and funnier.[56] And, what is important to our cause, they are perceived as being more convincing and more competent.[57]

Unattractive people, however, are associated with negative characteristics[58] (unattractive men are penalized even more than unattractive women).[59] The effect of the phenomenon can be reduced to a short, simplistic statement: what is beautiful is good.[60] But not too beautiful!

Fortunately, we do not have to look like supermodels to truly convince others of our skills and capabilities. In one experiment, the competence and trustworthiness of dentists was assessed.[61] As expected, the comparatively more attractive dentist was rated as more competent and trustworthy. However, the *most* attractive dentist in the group received lower ratings than the merely rather attractive one. How come? Once someone is *too* beautiful, the observer becomes aware of the rating error and an alarm bell shrills. This finding shows that the effect of attractiveness actually appears only if the observer is not aware of it.[62] In this respect, attractiveness has a positive effect on perceived competence, but this only applies up to a certain, very high degree of attractiveness.[63] Therefore, if you are already on the threshold of becoming a top model, you don't need to worry about the following techniques to increase your attractiveness.

The rest of us can be advised on how to enhance it. Not surprisingly, billions are spent every year on cosmetics and plastic surgery. Yet hardly anyone knows the truly relevant factors—not even the surgeons themselves, which explains a lot of the faces you encounter even at high profile events. If you know what really matters to others, however, you can immediately increase your attractiveness and boost your perceived competence.

The Factors of Attractiveness

In an experiment, for just one second, students were shown pictures of two US Senate candidates.[64] They then had to select the one that seemed most competent to them. In 70 percent of the cases, the person judged more competent by the students was indeed the one to win the actual election. Whether after a month of campaigning or after only a few seconds, the assessments are frighteningly alike. People judge the competency of others fairly uniformly, on the basis of physical appearance, with lightning speed. Competence or even beauty is therefore not in the eye of the beholder.[65] Instead, it seems that the factors of beauty are shared almost universally.

In the case of men, the face is the central factor of attractiveness, followed by physique (weight in combination with proportions).[66] In women the opposite is true: the figure has priority over the face. This finding alone is of vital significance when you want to improve your appearance—body or face. Let us first consider the attractiveness of the face and how it plays into people's conception of beauty and competence.

The Face

For Leonardo da Vinci, beauty was a matter of proportions. Da Vinci divided the face into sevenths—for example, the nose should occupy two-sevenths of the face's length—and meticulously adhered to this rule in his work.[67] Current attractiveness research came up with a few more complex formulas.

In modern research, there are three main theories that try to explain the essence of beauty: sexual dimorphism, symmetry, and averageness. Let's have a closer look at these ideas.

According to the theory of sexual dimorphism, women's faces are attractive when they are typically feminine, and men's faces when they are typically masculine.[68] And indeed, women's faces are perceived as more attractive when they have typically feminine facial features such as full lips, big eyes, and a small nose. This theory does not hold true for men, though. A male face with typical masculine traits—including narrow lips and eyes and a receding hairline—does not appear more attractive to observers. On the contrary, even in men, feminine facial features are considered more attractive.[69] Think of male models with their rather big eyes, full hair, small noses, and full lips—not necessarily traditionally masculine, but attractive nonetheless. Very closely related is the *kindchenschema*, or "baby face," identified by the Austrian zoologist Konrad Lorenz, which has typical female features in a superimposed form, characterized by a relatively large head, round cheeks, and a small nose—think of Disney characters.[70] Indeed, women with baby faces are rated more attractive, unlike men.[71]

So is the world filled with covert pedophiles? Not quite: research has shown that the attraction of the baby face comes not from the childlike elements—such as a small mouth, and round eyes—but from the youthful ones.[72] Thus, in contrast to the term "baby face," it is actually *youthfulness* that leads to increased attractiveness among women.[73] And youthfulness is not attractive because men seek women who appear to be easier to oppress—as feminist theories postulate.[74] The reason rather lies in the fact rather that the phase of fertility in women is relatively short and that younger women can potentially pro-duce more offspring.[75] This argument is supported by the fact that in cultures, in which lifelong relationships are the norm, younger women are preferred even more.[76] The exact positive features of youthfulness are not yet fully discovered.

The second main theory regards facial symmetry as a key to attractiveness. Recent research, however, has shown that sym-metry is almost irrelevant to the question of whether a person is perceived as attractive.[77] Though particularly asymmetrical faces are perceived as unattractive, our tolerance of this feature is relatively high, as the right side of the face, on average, is larger than the left (check the mirror!); we are therefore accus-tomed to asymmetry.[78] If symmetry were *the* decisive feature of attractiveness, we'd all be better off parting our hair in the middle than on the side—a curious idea, particularly for men not living in the 1920s.

The third and most prevalent theory of attractiveness, which considers averageness to be attractive, has its roots in the 19th century. Victorian explorer Francis Galton combined sev-eral faces on a photographic plate to find what was considered the most attractive average face.[79] This combined face was rated higher in attractiveness than any of the individual faces. In a modern experiment, two US psychologists, Judith Langlois and Lori Roggman, merged multiple faces into a single one using a computer to evaluate the individual faces—again, the combined or "average" face was rated higher than any individ-ual face. These experiments led to the widespread view that "average is beautiful."[80]

Indeed, "average types" seem to be free from harmful mu-tations or abnormalities, which on an evolutionary level makes people with average facial features good candidates for repro-duction.[81] Also, we may like "typical" faces because they sim-ply reduce complexity in a complex world and we are thankful for anything that looks familiar.[82] Furthermore, the combination of several individual faces makes the average face more symmetrical, which may be a decisive factor for increased attractiveness.[83] Finally, combined faces, as in the experiments just discussed, feature flawless skin, because impurities and bumps neutralize each other.[84]

In a groundbreaking (and so far unpublished!) research project, German psychologist Martin Gründl identified flawless skin as the decisive factor in the determination of the attractiveness of average faces. Gründl also found that the average face is not seen as *very* attractive but merely perceived as "passable." In other words, averageness protects against "ugliness," but it won't catapult you into the upper echelons of beauty. Particularly attractive people have a number of different characteristics—just think of Julia Roberts's expressive mouth or George Clooney's distinctive chin. In Gründl's studies, those composite faces that were rated the most attractive were composed of only eight faces, all which were rated as attractive per se, not by combining dozens of average faces. Gründl called this result the "Raphael effect," after the celebrated Italian painter's depiction of Galatea, which captured the essence of several beautiful women.[85] So true beauty is a combination of attractive, not average, features.

Then what makes our faces attractive? In trying to answer this question, we must consider that the three "great" attractiveness theories are flawed. As shown in this brief overview of decades of attractiveness research, neither symmetry, nor sexual dimorphism, nor average appearance has a significant effect.[86] And the effect of the "baby face" on female attractiveness cannot be precisely measured.

Gründl summarizes these findings as well as possible: "A face is attractive when it has the features typical of attractive faces and unattractive when it has the features typical of unattractive faces."[87] In other words, several attractive factors result in an overall attractive picture.[88] The details of this idea were examined in greater depth by Gründl. In fact, he was able to come up with the following factors to describe what facial attributes people find attractive, which are surprisingly similar for men and women.[89]

WOMEN

- fuller, well-maintained lips
- darker, thinner eyebrows
- thicker, longer, darker eyelashes
- no dark circles under the eyes
- higher cheekbones
- narrower face/little fat
- narrow neck
- narrower nose
- smooth, flawless skin
- tanned skin

MEN

- symmetrical mouth
- fuller lips
- smaller folds between the nose and corners of the mouth (nasolabial folds)
- darker eyebrows
- numerous and darker lashes
- narrow face/less fat
- upper facial hemisphere wider in proportion to the lower
- higher cheekbones

- prominent lower jaw and chin
- narrower neck
- no receding hairline
- smooth, flawless skin
- tanned skin

In addition to Gründl's findings, there are other details to consider: people look at your entire face first, then home in on your eyes and mouth—the nose is relatively unimportant.[90] Have a look at stars who are considered particularly good looking: many have especially attractive mouths and eyes, but not particularly beautiful noses.

Hair color also plays a major role: women with blond hair are classified as attractive, but those with dark hair are perceived as more intelligent, which is even more important for perceived competence[91] In the case of men, the situation is different: men with blond hair are considered to be nicer, but also less attractive, while dark-haired men—like dark-haired women—are considered both more intelligent and more attractive.

Certainly some factors are subject to the fashion of the times. In the middle of the 20th century, higher eyebrows were considered to be attractive, typified by Swedish-born American actress Greta Garbo, but today, lower ones are favored.[92] Facial hair has also been evaluated quite differently over the years—at least in men.[93] Bearded men, however, are generally perceived as mentally stronger no matter the time period.

Wearing glasses usually reduces attractiveness,[94] but the effect of glasses adds 14 points to a person's perceived IQ, as an experiment from the 1940s showed.[95] The people who wore glasses in this experiment, however, were judged only using photographs. In direct interaction, the effect of glasses is only short-lived: after only a few minutes, glasses no longer play any role in the assessment of a person's intelligence.[96] Wearing glasses is therefore only recommended for short interactions because after a while it only decreases your attractiveness.

What you can and will do with all this information is of course at your discretion. In any case, many of these factors can be relatively easily influenced. Darker eyebrows and eyelashes and tanned skin, for example, can usually be created with little effort. In men, small cosmetic procedures, such as removal of the nasolabial folds, have a measurable benefit, while women can easily mask rings under their eyes with makeup and also give their cheekbones the desired highlight. It is therefore no surprise that women who use makeup are definitely perceived as being more attractive.[97]

Whether or not we believe people should be judged on a "pretty face," the fact of the matter is that they typically are. Thanks to this overview of the facial factors that really count, though, you now know what you can focus on to increase your attractiveness, whether you're a man or a woman. Of course, as mentioned, even though your face plays a major role in perceived attractiveness, your physique does too—especially if you are a woman.

The Body

Body fat has long been seen as a sign of prosperity, but today this trend has practically been reversed, at least here in the Western world, where obesity is often associated with poverty.[98] In poorer countries, however, larger physical figures are preferred. Swedish psychologist Malte Andersson investigated 62 cultures around the world and found that slimness is considered the beauty ideal above all others, but only in countries where there are no food shortages.[99]

There are a number of methods for measuring the human body, including the body mass index (BMI), the waist-to-hip ratio (WHR), and the waist-to-chest ratio (WCR), all of which correlate with one another.[100] The WCR, for example, directly relates to the attractiveness of men, which is mainly decided by the upper body.[101] The famous V shape—wide shoulders combined with a narrow waist—is still considered very attractive. The "classical," typical male body has therefore in no way lost its attractiveness, while the trend toward more muscle mass has actually grown.[102] However, here, too, influences of time period and culture must be observed.[103] In Taiwan, intelligence is a key feature of masculinity, so the male physical ideal is less muscular than the one in the United States.[104] Greek beauty ideals, for example, actually involve more muscle than English ones.[105] And the Portuguese focus on muscle-packed men and women who tend to have curves.[106]

Men's BMI, the index of general slenderness, follows in second place behind the WCR. Here the average lean man is more attractive than the overweight one, but the very slim man is also worse off.[107]

In women, the BMI and the slenderness of the whole body are the most important factors when it comes to physical attractiveness.[108] However, the WHR also plays a major role. The Indo-American psychologist Devendra Singh analyzed the winners of the Miss America competition from the 1920s through the 1980s and found that the ideal body types for this contest were virtually unchanged over generations. You can calculate your exact WHR by dividing your waist circumference by your hip circumference. So, for instance, a 25-inch (63-centimeter) waist circumference divided by a 35-inch (90-centimeter) hip circumference results in a WHR of 0.7. The WHR of Singh's ideal type has always been between 0.72 and 0.69 (with Playboy models having a WHR between 0.71 and 0.68). Therefore, the WHR ideal appears to be 0.7. Singh has demonstrated this phenomenon through such different "beauties" as Marilyn Monroe, Sophia Loren, Twiggy, and Kate Moss, all of whom have a WHR of about 0.7.[109] Whether it is exactly 0.7 or not, one thing is clear: a relatively narrow waist, in combination with medium-wide hips, is attractive.

Overall, it can be said that the right proportions in men are more important than mere slenderness. In other words, as a man, if you have a wide waist, you do not have to lose weight to increase your attractiveness. You could also work out to increase your chest circumference, which is therefore more important to attractiveness than building muscle in your arms or legs. For women, slenderness is the most important factor, followed by "classical" female proportions.

Summary: The Benefits of Attractiveness

Now you know about the outrageously great importance of attractiveness in almost every life situation. It follows that it is not only a symptom of vanity to care for your appearance. In addition, you now know which factors actually determine attractiveness, and also that the face is more important in men, the figure in women. Many of the factors that affect attractiveness are relatively easy to influence. It is crucial, however, that you do not ignorantly invest time and effort in aspects of your physical appearance that will have little outcome.

Interestingly, our standards are higher than reality: Gründl discovered in his experiments that even top international models and finalists in beauty pageants barely exceeded the rating level of "somewhat attractive" (a rating of 5 out of 7). The best ratings were received by computer-generated figures—those that did not exist in real life.[110]

And if you feel, whether rightly or wrongly, that you are fighting a lost cause when it comes to your physical appearance, there are two consolation prizes. First, in one study, it turned out that women who were considered extremely attractive in their college days were less happy in their 40s than those who had been considered less attractive during college.[111] Since personal happiness is usually dependent on the comparison of your current life situation with an earlier one, formerly attractive people almost inevitably sink into a low point as they age—women as well as men.

The second consolation prize for less attractive people is that they are more likely to be hired by a person who believes they are likely to compete with the applicant sooner or later within that company. Here, the person hiring prefers the unattractive candidate.[112]

Overall, however, as stated at the outset of this discussion, it has been found that, to a certain extent, people presume that "what is beautiful is good." And in fact, there is also a link between attractiveness and actual—not perceived—competence.[113] For starters, given all the advantages, you already demonstrate a certain practical intelligence by paying attention to your appearance. According to US psychologist Leslie Zebrowitz, intelligence therefore leads to increased attractiveness.[114] In addition, more attractive people are generally treated better: others are more likely to encourage and trust them.[115] Through this treatment, it is also likely that attractive people then develop greater self-assurance over the course of their lives—whoever is treated better develops more positively.[116] Due to all these benefits, a positive impact on perceived competence is created.

Some scientists consider more beautiful people to actually be more intelligent. They justify this by pointing to the fact that smarter men tend to be more successful and marry more beautiful partners. The result are children who are even more beautiful and intelligent, as attractiveness and intelligence are hereditary.[117] A witty but also controversial hypothesis![118]

Conclusion

The findings presented in this chapter are by no means as obvious as they appear at first glance. For a long time, for example, there was a widespread view that competence and human warmth were counterpoles.[119] According to this theory, competence was valued as useful and warmth as likable, and as a consequence, those people who were not likable were perceived as more competent and the nice ones as incompetent.[120] In other words, competence and affection were mutually exclusive. However, more recent research has concluded that the halo effect is much stronger: affection has a positive effect on perceived competence.[121] So when we like someone, we tend to regard him or her as more competent. Conversely, competence also has a positive effect on affection.[122] This means that when we consider someone to be competent, we tend to like him or her more. Just think of any of your favorite comedies: we like the brilliant nerd, even if he is somewhat weird.

Would you hire someone you find abominable, disagreeable, or disgustingly unattractive? Maybe. But only if you considered that person to be really, really brilliant. In case you are not a genius, you should exploit the effects of popularity and attractiveness: they can be extremely useful to you, because according to the halo effect, every positive impression shines on all other factors related to your personality, including competence. And there are, as shown, many indications that popularity and attractiveness are the most important factors in creating a universal "good impression."

We like to be persuaded by people who are attractive and popular,[123] even if we know that they are acting in their own interests, such as sales people.[124] When we deal with unattractive, unpopular people, however, we build up a subconscious resistance to their attempts to convince us.

Apart from the fact that you can use the information in this chapter to increase your popularity and attractiveness in order to be perceived as more competent, you can also indirectly capitalize on this knowledge: make yourself aware, day by day, as to what extent popularity and attractiveness distort your judgment of others. You don't have to go so far as to avoid looking at a person's photo when you receive a job application or avert your gaze when speaking with someone, because the effects of niceness and attraction have a universal impact on almost anyone who will meet the job seekers, from the customer to the receptionist. It is therefore better to place particularly likable and attractive employees where they can have the greatest impact, typically "out front." We see this idea play out all the time in visual media, such as on TV and the Internet, where the benefits of popularity and attraction are reinforced. This media should be used in a targeted manner and with the right representatives for your company.[125]

The power of positioning attractive, pleasant staff members in the proper place is especially useful when your employees have to deal with customers with little knowledge of the product or service you're selling. An interesting study showed that, above all, poorly informed voters were more heavily influenced by the attractiveness of politicians.[126] The less they were concerned with the politicians' ideas, the stronger the attraction was. The authors of the study recommended that political parties run attractive candidates, especially for relatively small local elections, where the voters tend not to deal with content in detail.

The universal impact of the halo effect discovered by Edward Thorndike is always astonishing: once a restaurant is classified as "healthy," such as the fast-food chain Subway, people tend to underestimate the calorie content of all dishes on the menu.[127]

And if you are perceived as popular and attractive, everything else that you do will be positively affected, including your perceived competence.

Competence Compendium
Popularity and Attractiveness

Create a positive overall impression, especially regarding your popularity and attractiveness.

Popularity
Ingratiation
- Build a reservoir of goodwill early on.
- Make compliments specifically and reluctantly (for example, "You don't want to hear this but . . .").
- Show respect and sincere interest and ask for advice.
- Talk about things that are important to the other person.
- Do favors for others or give them presents.
- Mirror the other person: align your body posture, choice of words, and tempo of speech.

Opinion Conformity
- In important matters, publicly express the other person's opinion before he or she does.
- If you agree with someone, act decisively; otherwise, show uncertainty.
- Let the other person convince you of his or her position or argument.

Self-Presentation
- Point out similarities between you and the other person.
- Provide personal but not intimate information.

Attractiveness

Face

Focus on developing decisive features, including darker eyebrows and eyelashes and smooth, flawless, and tanned skin.

Body

For men (men's faces are more important than their figures):

✧ The upper body and the WCR are key (classic V shape).

✧ The average slim figure is the most attractive, but proportions are even more important.

For women (women's figures are more important than their faces):

✧ The BMI, and thus the slimness of the entire body, is decisive.

✧ Observe the ideal WHR.

CHAPTER 8

STATUS

THE POWER OF SYMBOLS

The world more often rewards the appearances of merit than merit itself.

—FRANÇOIS DE LA ROCHEFOUCAULD

Image Consultancy for Consultants

You can become a management consultant right after elementary school—even if you didn't graduate. In contrast to auditors, doctors, or lawyers, consultants don't need any formal training. Specialized knowledge plays practically no role in their services—not the ideal condition to be taken seriously and justify high fees. To avoid this impression, the "world's newest profession," as Oxford researcher Chris McKenna refers to management consulting, has deliberately copied the language and symbols of other professions that already have a high status.[1] From the outset, these consultants appeared as "Doctors of Management," describing their activities through medical analogies. By doing so, they added a coating of scientific character to their "expert knowledge" and assured their clients that they would act conscientiously and discreetly, just like an actual doctor.

However, Marvin Bower, a lawyer and the long-standing head of McKinsey & Company, felt that this analogy, and the accompanying portrayal of his clients as "sick enterprises," had a negative ring. So when he became the company's managing director in 1950, he drew parallels between his profession and other fields: the scientific excellence of engineers, the numerical accuracy of economists, and—most importantly—the high status of lawyers. He thought this elevated status would create a perception of professional qualification, which would in turn justify astronomical fees and also grant access to the highest levels of companies' hierarchies. McKinsey praised itself at the time: "We serve business concerns on management problems in much the same way that the larger law firms serve them on legal problems." Bower's strategy worked, and McKinsey's success radiated out to the whole profession—consultants today enjoy a stature similar to lawyers.

Status is not an invention of business and not even of civilization, but it is deeply rooted in nature. Just think of chickens and their "pecking order." Canadian psychologist Jordan Peterson draws attention to lobsters, which have occupied the bottom of the ocean for over 300 million years.[2] Once a lobster is defeated in combat by another lobster, its chances to win the next fight diminish significantly—even against previously defeated lobsters. In fact, the lobster's brain dissolves, developing a new, subordinate brain. Peterson adds: "Anyone who has experienced a painful transformation after a serious defeat in romance or career may feel some sense of kinship with the once successful crustacean."

When you are low in the status hierarchy—male or female— you have, as Peterson aptly describes, "nowhere to live (or nowhere good). Your food is terrible, when you're not going hungry. You're in poor physical and mental condition. You're of minimal romantic interest to anyone, unless they are as desperate as you. You are more likely to fall ill, age rapidly, and die young, with few, if any, to mourn you." Peterson points out, "When the aristocracy catches a cold, as it is said, the working class dies of pneumonia." The same is true in the animal kingdom: when there is an avian disease, it is the birds lowest in the pecking order that die first.

However, if you are of high status, your life will be a success: "If you're male, you have preferential access to the best places to live and the highest-quality food. People compete to do you favors. You have limitless opportunity for romantic and sexual contact. You are a successful lobster, and the most desirable females line up and vie for your attention. . . . If you're female, you have access to many high-quality suitors: tall, strong and symmetrical; creative, reliable, honest and generous." Indeed, female animals typically choose the male with the highest status, as this is the most efficient way to identify the best man around. And, in today's world, women seek status of their own.

Displaying status is of crucial, archaic relevance to our lives. One of the ways to do so is to have the right posture, which has already been discussed in the chapter on high expectations. When we are defeated, we do, according to Peterson, resemble lobsters who have just lost a fight: "Our posture droops. We face the ground. We feel threatened, hurt, anxious, and weak. If things do not improve, we become chronically depressed. Under such conditions, we can't easily put up the kind of fight that life demands, and we become easy targets for harder-shelled bullies." The confident posture, however, reflects status.

This chapter will look at more effective ways to fundamentally increase your status.

Status and Competence

The American psychologists Anthony Doob and Alan Gross conducted a remarkable experiment in 1968. They had a man wait in a car at a red traffic light, and when it turned green, instead of moving forward, he simply remained there.[3] Doob and Gross tried the experiment both with a luxury limousine and then with a worn-down compact to observe whether the type of car affected the other drivers' reactions—you bet it did!

When waiting for the small car to move, the drivers behind it became aggravated. Almost all of them honked, some several times, and a couple even drove into the car's rear bumper. With the expensive car, only half of the drivers honked and more or less all of them waited patiently until the car eventually rolled away, just before the light turned red again.

When another group of subjects were asked how they would behave in such a situation, however, the vast majority said they would honk at the expensive car before honking at the small one. They weren't lying; status just works subconsciously. Doob's and Gross's study impressively demonstrated how strongly status symbols work and how they unconsciously affect our thoughts and actions.

The extent to which we are influenced by people who are considered to have a high status has also been shown by the notorious Milgram experiment. During the experiment, subjects gave supposedly excruciating electric shocks to other people—who were in fact actors—when they gave a wrong answer to a test question.[4] Why would people like you or me cause so much pain to others? Because, as they later reported, an academic with a prestigious title wearing a white lab coat told them to do so.

Perceived status has an effect in all areas of life—a mechanism known as "status-generalization."[5] Our status places us in a particular hierarchical level not only at work but also in society as a whole.[6] Therefore, the opinions of individuals with a high professional status carry weight in discussions about totally unrelated areas: when your family practitioner talks about politics, chances are she is taken rather seriously, even if she isn't particularly knowledgeable in this field. People with higher status exert a greater influence and are more likely to be followed.[7] This status level leads to higher authority, greater respect, and increased trust. Across all cultures, higher status also directly leads to an increase in perceived competence.[8]

It's not just a person's job that contributes to this perception, either—mere status symbols directly affect perceived competence as well.[9] In one study, the following ranking of status symbols, sorted by their significance, was determined:[10]

1. Company car
2. Assistant
3. Title on business card
4. Expenses budget
5. Frequent flyer card
6. Corporate credit card
7. Office art

Other relevant symbols included a company apartment, employee discounts for purchases within the company, spots at the company kindergarten, gym membership, and a parking space directly by the building.

By knowing which status symbols really count, you can aim for what really matters and really increase our perceived competence. Apart from such tangible factors, there are more subtle ways to strengthen our status.

Habitus

When I'm in the lobby of a grand hotel, I like to watch people enter. Some are immediately eyed with suspicion by the staff, while others are greeted with the widest of smiles. It's not that they are celebrities; they are probably not even staying at the hotel. The crucial factor lies in their *habitus*. Habitus, described by the French sociologist Pierre Bourdieu, is a person's behavior and appearance, including his or her clothing, language, and apparent lifestyle.[11] Whether fair or not, by observing a person's habitus, we can assess his or her status within moments.

If, as already discussed, you use an accent that suggests a lower social standing or if you act in a way that suggests a lower level of education, your status will be almost irretrievably diminished. Certain behaviors can be fatal to your appearance. And a high-status habitus can open doors to just about anywhere. Why are the offspring of high-status families usually doing so well, even if not much of the family's tangible legacy is left? Because—apart from probably a good education—they act in a way that is instantly recognizable as a high-status habitus.

I am convinced that no other factor has such a massive impact on our perceived competence, and thus on our persuasive power, as habitus. An English proverb says, "It takes three generations to bring forth a gentleman." But don't worry, it can be accomplished much faster than that. Recognizing your own habitus, and developing the ability to interpret others', is the first step to understanding and utilizing status to increase your perceived competence. One of the most important aspects in this process is realizing the power of something you likely take for granted every day: your clothes.

Clothing and Accessories: The Classic Status Symbols

In an experiment, a man crossed a street despite a Do Not Walk signal. He first did so wearing typical work clothes, and then again while dressed in an elegant suit and a shirt and tie.[12] Behold! As many as three and a half times more people followed the man when he was elegantly dressed. In another experiment, it was found that people using a telephone booth (yes, the experiment took place many years ago . . .) were much more willing to hand over change to a well-dressed actor who had "forgotten" his quarters to make a call than to someone who was poorly dressed.[13]

Clothing as a status symbol has a remarkably strong effect. All clothes signal a certain status, though some more than others, such as a military uniform covered in medals or pins. It is true that today, in an era of democratic attire, it is no longer possible to detect people's "rank" by quickly glancing at their clothing, but it provides clues nonetheless. Doctors' white coats cement their status, just like Ferragamo ties do on Manhattan's Wall Street and Hermes ties do in Frankfurt's banking world.[14] Clothing directly influences a person's perceived credibility, reliability, and competence.[15]

No doubt most people are aware that if you are "well dressed," you will be perceived more positively.[16] And yes, depending on the occasion, we certainly use clothing more consciously than any other status symbol: if we want to portray a sense of professionalism, we dress formally, and if we want to appear likable, we go for casual attire. People appear competent when dressed formally and likable when dressed casually.[17]

And yet people place remarkably little emphasis on their clothes in everyday life. What are you wearing right now? Have you chosen your clothing wisely? When an interviewer questioned passersby on why they were wearing the particular clothes they had on that day, it became evident that there was hardly any connection between their preferred style and the clothes they actually wore.[18] Their attire was chosen for supposedly practical reasons, such as comfort or weather, totally neglecting the effects it had on perception.

Even though attractiveness can influence perceived competence, as discussed in the previous chapter, status is more important when it comes to clothing.[19] For women, "sexy" clothing leads to a lower perceived competence.[20] Higher status is therefore more important than attractiveness when selecting clothing. High quality with a classic fit is therefore better than modern, super-slim-fit outfits. When choosing what to wear, it is important that your clothes reflect the status you desire, according to the saying "Don't dress for the job you have but for the one you want." That being said, you must have some tact in making sure your clothes don't cause you to appear pretentious.

Note that style is not a question of money. A well-fitting suit does not cost more than a poor-fitting one, just as a crisp white shirt is no more expensive than a rumpled purple one. In this era of industrial mass production, you can purchase a sizable wardrobe for less than ever and even have it customized or altered by a tailor without having to spend much. However, it is always better to have two excellent suits or dresses than a wardrobe full of discount garments.

It's important to choose not only your clothes wisely but also any other object that surrounds you. A smart sales representative knows that she should sign a contract with an elegant Montblanc pen instead of a cheap plastic one. Private bankers know to place brochures offering their services in elegant leather cases instead of plain manila folders.[21] Look around your workstation at the stationary, lamp, pictures, and any other objects. Were these items deliberately placed together, or are you sitting in the midst of a collection of haphazardly combined clutter?

Imagine that you call a handyman to come fix your heater and he shows up with a tattered wicker basket, a few shabby tools, and some old lightbulbs clanking against each other—are you going to trust this guy?[22] Likewise, whatever "tools" you use or display provide people with clues about your competence.

As early as 1959, Bower explained to his consultants at McKinsey, "The attitudes of top executives toward us as people often carry more weight in the shaping of firm reputation than even the major recommendations we develop for them. And those attitudes—whether favourable or unfavourable—are fashioned from an accumulation of little things. Example: one top-management Englishman, asked by another how our consultants get along with his people, said: 'Fine. They even wear conservative neckties.'"

What constitutes a status symbol certainly depends on the environment, but you will find them everywhere, whether in a conservative bank or in a tech start-up. No matter the setting, there will be a certain inventory of unwritten social norms with which you must abide in order to be accepted by the group and to improve your status within it.[23] Some creatives, for example, forgo ties but stand in line for five hours for the latest Adidas sneakers. In Maoist China, the most zealous communists ran around in inconspicuous smocks, but they were tailored out of fine Italian fabric.

All that said, there is an exception to the rule: there are some among us who break away from norms and standards and by doing so further elevate their status.

The Effects of Nonconformity

What about luminaries like Steve Jobs or Mark Zuckerberg? Did Zuckerberg not climb on stage at the World Economic Forum in Davos, sporting shorts and flip-flops in a room packed with people all clad in suits? What happened when Jobs addressed the whole world wearing jeans and a black turtleneck? Weren't they admired even more precisely because they were wearing these apparently low-status outfits?[24]

The answer is yes. People who already enjoy a high status can increase it by abandoning traditional status symbols.[25] This concept is known as the "red-sneaker effect," a term that refers to the idea that some people wear regular red sneakers when elegant shoes would be more appropriate.[26] Particularly in Western culture, individualism and independence are appreciated, so ostentatious nonconformity can result in increased status and a higher perceived competency.

However, the decisive prerequisite for this approach is that people already have a high degree of respect for you, such as if you're an undisputed expert in your field or a cofounder of a successful company. It must also be clear that you *deliberately* violate the norms. Only then is nonconformity interpreted as a self-confident gesture, rather than a merely awkward or even embarrassing act.

If such unconventionality is merely a glitch, or if it is overdone, then it will fail, in accordance with the old Latin motto *Quod licet Jovi, non licet bovi*, "What is allowed to Jupiter is not allowed to an ox." So if an intern wears a tie as a scarf for a formal occasion, he will be considered a jerk, but if a multibillionaire founder of a start-up decides to do so, he demonstrates his independence from petty conventions.

Nonconformity is therefore only effective on rare occasions, when your status is already high. Under most circumstances, it is better to play it safe: the way you dress—whether conforming to the norms or not—is a matter of respect. I wouldn't recommend approaching a client in a T-shirt, nor should you go to a wedding wearing a hoodie. With your clothes, you demonstrate the respect you pay to the occasion and the individual in front of you. It is therefore not surprising that there is an actual correlation between clothing and work ethic: a more relaxed dress code leads to an increase in lateness and absences.[27] Incidentally, reactions to tattoos—once a major sign of nonconformity—were also investigated in this context: they appear to have lost their shock value, and therefore only have relatively weak influence on the perceived competence. This influence, however, is still rather negative, especially when dealing with older people.[28]

To sum up, nonconformity can be very effective when you already are very respected in your field. However, your status is not just related to how you dress. The way you interact with the people around you has an outsize effect on your status and, as a consequence, also on your perceived competence.

High-Status Interaction

Our status also expresses itself through how we communicate with one another. As mentioned in the chapter on nonverbal communication, body language and even body size have a direct impact on your perceived status. And a particularly simple tactic is to select the head seat in order to present yourself as leader of the group.[29]

As also discussed in the chapter on verbal communication, power talking has a positive effect on your social rank, while hesitant, uncertain language undermines your status. If you start a sentence with, "One might perhaps think that . . . ," it is unlikely you will be able to convince anyone of your point, and your status will be diminished. You shouldn't downgrade a self-assured statement to a meek opinion.

But should you therefore only speak in statements, not letting anyone reply or provide their own input? Not at all—by asking questions, you can direct the conversation to wherever you want it to go. Especially by using open-ended questions— those that require more than a yes or no response—you can quickly lead the person you're speaking with into a terrain you're familiar with and subsequently cement your own status by discussing a topic you know intimately.

After asking a question, it is good to be silent for a moment— silence is an excellent means of demonstrating power. By letting in the silence, you demonstrate control and self-confidence— unlike an incessantly babbling jester. Another beneficial effect of remaining silent is that you may provoke the person you're talking with into sharing information that she or he would have otherwise never disclosed, simply because many people just cannot stand silence during a conversation.

Just as a king does not interfere in the bickering of the politics of the day, you should also keep away from any petty trench warfare. Build bridges instead. If your colleagues start arguing during a meeting, propose a compromise. Next, have them shake hands, just like Bill Clinton did when Shimon Peres and Yasser Arafat closed ranks between their factions—the subsequent photograph is possibly the most famous of his tenure and a cornerstone of Clinton's status as a world leader.

Another wise tactic during any interaction is to give a positive appraisal of someone's work or personality. Praise is usually delivered from top to bottom and therefore bolsters your status in a pleasant way. About medals, the physical version of praise, Napoleon once said, "Toys and Tinsel! . . . But with such tinsel, people are led."[30] Try telling your customers what you like about their office design; praise your colleagues for their commitment during the most recent meeting.

But only praise what is worth praising; let the others work for your approval. A remarkable experiment from the 1950s illustrated the startling effect that sacrifices have on us. In the experiment, women who wanted to participate in a discussion about sex had to pass a so-called embarrassment test beforehand. They were asked to read obscene passages from a book aloud without hesitating or blushing—and in the 1950s, this was no trifling matter.[31] The test was given under the pretext of ensuring that the potential test subjects had no problem with talking openly about sex. Next, the subjects sat in on a discussion group that was designed to be as trivial and boring as possible. Surprisingly, they assessed the group and the discussion favorably. An interesting correlation became clear: the more obscene, and therefore embarrassing, the "embarrassment test" was, the more positively the women evaluated the discussion.

A similar experiment was carried out almost 10 years later. By then the Woodstock era was in full swing and the "sex test" had lost its horror, so instead the subjects had to endure electric shocks before becoming a member of the discussion group.[32] It was found that the strength of the electric shocks directly correlated with the perceived value of the membership; the stronger the shock, the more interesting and desirable it became to belong to the group. The same idea can be seen with initiation rites in fraternities or army units, which are more than mere savagery. The members of a group with tough admission criteria will appreciate the membership much more and therefore serve the group more actively and loyally.[33]

So people value what they gain through a certain amount of effort. Therefore, you should indeed praise others, but only for something remarkable. Make them work for your esteem. But what about your customers? You can hardly treat them with electric shocks. However, the title of a *Harvard Business Review* article suggests a somewhat evil idea: "Torment Your Customers (They'll Love It)." In the article, the author recommends not to chum up to them too much.[34] With prospective clients, don't immediately squeeze your business card into their hands, especially not an overly busy one that includes your email address, landline office number, landline private number, and three cell numbers, along with an additional one scribbled on with a pen. If you have made a good impression on them, rest assured, they will find you. Also, don't immediately return calls or answer every email two minutes after you've received it—you are not a servant. And even in the case that you are one, stick to the credo of the Ritz Carlton hotel group that its employees carry with them on a laminated card: "We are ladies and gentlemen serving ladies and gentlemen."

When you're meeting people face to face, have them come to you, as is the case with any good negotiation. Simply put, whoever is sought out gains a higher status. Think about a bartender as compared to a waiter: you have to wave the bartender down and compete for her attention, whereas the waiter acts more like a lackey, coming to your table at your beck and call to take orders.

Of course, there is an invisible barrier between the hurdles we can expect others to accept and just terrible service. You don't want to seem too distant, unfriendly, or arrogant. As with many of the lessons throughout this book, understanding where that line is, and making sure not to cross it, takes tact that can only be gained through real-life experiences.

Playing the Educational Game

In many countries, such as Germany and Austria, doctoral titles are rather common among management and professional services providers. Similarly, in the United States, the master of business administration (MBA) plays a major role.

Research agrees. It doesn't even matter in which discipline a graduate degree was acquired: such a title conveys universal competence. Even if person who earned an MA is employed as a used-car salesman, due to that MA distinction alone his status is automatically increased and he is perceived as more competent.[35] And, as every university advertises, there are indeed significant differences in starting salaries between those people with a postgraduate degree and those without.[36]

Diplomas and certificates are also considered to be objective evidence of expertise.[37] Americans are not squeamish here and often receive beautiful diplomas for little more than just showing up—I've seen an elementary school graduation certificate in a mahogany frame with golden trim. Pride in such accolades may be going overboard, but in contrast to Americans,

Europeans can be unnecessarily reticent. A friend of mine even punched two holes into her Cambridge University diploma right after the graduation ceremony and then stuffed the piece of paper into a ringed binder.

In addition to academic titles, the position held within the company also counts in regard to one's status. In countries where titles of rank play a vital role, such as in China, bilingual business cards have become common. On one side of the card, a person's English title may be "PR department manager"; on the other side, in Chinese, the title may be much more flowery, something like "Director of Public Communications."[38] Personally, I am surprised that so few companies give credence to such titles: giving employees important-sounding titles costs nothing, but they influence outside perceptions considerably. Those companies that do understand this concept actively support their employees by awarding titles, such as a global PR agency, which calls their junior employees "executives" rather than "assistants." This title lets them shine in front of any audience and also makes them more loyal to the company, in accordance with Napoleon's thoughts on medals.

When it comes to establishing your status, do you want your business partners to have to blindly guess what educational or professional qualifications you have acquired? Of course not. You therefore need "objective" clues so others can easily assess your skills, as mentioned in the chapter on high expectations. So don't be afraid to decorate your office with diplomas, certificates, or other awards. When your visitors enter the room, they will be looking for signals about your competence and status, just as your opinion on a restaurant would likely be affected when you discover a Zagat seal indicating a top rating at its front door.

If you really want to acquire the reputation and status of an expert, publications are the best possible way, as the written word still has an immensely strong effect.[39] As they say in academia: publish or perish. A book, newspaper column, or even your own blog turns you into a connoisseur in the eyes of the audience. In this information age, we can express ourselves easier than ever on any topic. As an architect, you can give advice on building your dream house or, as a gardener, you can provide tips on growing small, edible plants on a balcony.

In whatever way you display your education and expertise, it is not only a matter of having a specific proficiency in one topic; it is more about playfully showing your knowledge in what the German literary scholar Dietrich Schwanitz calls the "educational game."[40] Interestingly, the natural sciences play no part when it comes to your perceived education; you can in fact freely admit that you know nothing about chemistry or physics and your authority will not be undermined whatsoever (unless, of course, you are a chemist or a physicist). When it comes to liberal arts, the situation is different, especially with literature, philosophy, and politics—the pillars of the educational game.

Demonstrating an uncultured habitus and an ignorance of these pillars will hardly convince others of your high educational aptitude or achievements. Even if you buy the collected works of Shakespeare and put them next to your TV, you're not fooling anyone (though they may look impressive). If you actually read Shakespeare, however, you gain insight into the language and thoughts of the educational milieu—and you will be one of the few people who have read the great poet and thinker outside the classroom.

According to Schwanitz, by even reading a single great novel, one crosses "the boundary between literary education and ignorance." The scholar recommends, though not without a slight wink, that the budding literary expert begin by reading a work that is considered one of the great novels, but also one which hardly anyone has read. James Joyce's *Ulysses* would be an ideal choice. This one book can then be used as a castle from which one can, as Schwanitz writes, "attack, and arbitrarily make a comment on any unknown writer, but to which you can retreat to immediately, if it was getting dangerous." If the conversation then turns to Henry David Thoreau, for example, you could continue to take part, with a remark such as, "Joyce makes it difficult for the reader, whereas Thoreau is very, very effective in his wording." Such a statement, according to Schwanitz, "just can't be wrong."

BIRGing: Using Indirect Status

Some years back, while still a student, I ran into the movie director Quentin Tarantino—the man behind masterpieces such as *Pulp Fiction* and *Django Unchained*—and asked to take a picture with him. Not a digital selfie but an actual photo that I later had developed. This photo, which was quickly worn out, brought me more respect from my friends than any other thing I had done in my life so far—which probably says more about me than about the picture.

However, in a similar manner, the US psychologist Robert Cialdini reports how much his reputation rose among architects because of the mere fact that he was born in the same city as the famed 19th-century architect Frank Lloyd Wright.[41] The German psychologist Hans-Dieter Mummendey recalls that at a psychological symposium in New York years ago, he was appreciated not so much for his contribution on stage but because of the fact that he ran into the actor and filmmaker Woody Allen on his way to the conference hotel, a story he told to his colleagues' delight.[42]

Did these brief encounters or thin connections really impart some of the luminaries' genius on Cialdini and Mummendey? Certainly not—no rational person would argue that their competence had even increased by a whit. And yet you can profit from other peoples' status by mere association with them, as status and the halo effect work together here. Cialdini calls this "Basking in Reflected Glory," or BIRGing.[43] Simply put, any connection with a person of high status, even if vague, directly affects your status as well.

If you mention your acquaintances to other people in an effort to boost your status by association, make sure to do so in an appropriate manner and at the right time—you don't want people to think you're just namedropping to impress them. There are subtle ways to use BIRGing, for example, by highlighting the smallest, slightest similarities you share with a particularly high-status individual.

From his Woody Allen experience, Mummendey learned that these similarities can be quite broad: "common origin, common place of residence or work place, common political or religious beliefs, same sport or other leisure activities, sameness or similarities in any appearance, in relation to clothing or similar things. To mention this or that politician or athlete came from the same hometown as ones-self, this or that actor with whom you attended the same school or met him/her in the elevator."[44]

Indeed, you can even associate yourself with the positive qualities of another person if you share the same birthday or with the positive qualities of a holiday that might fall on your birthday.[45] The American psychologist Al Harrison went through thousands of biographies in the *Who's Who* encyclopedia and found that many celebrities were presumably born on holidays such as New Year, Christmas, or Independence Day.[46] Louis Armstrong, for example, claimed to be born on July 4, although he was actually born on August 4. Especially prominent theologians claim to celebrate their birthday on Christmas Eve—just like Jesus Christ himself.

So don't be afraid to draw attention to true parallels with icons, even those who are not in your own area of expertise. Such similarities may appear incidental; nonetheless, these tiny parallels actually have great effects—even on exceptionally intelligent people.[47]

Of course, don't start ridiculously bragging about whom you know or how you're connected in some tiny way to a famous or well-respected person. There is certainly a threshold that must not be exceeded. In most situations, it is therefore sensible to highlight the desired association in an incidental way. For example, it is quite inconspicuous to have your friend with the highest status in the room introduce you to the other people present. Think about it this way: if a CEO presents you to someone, you will always be associated with the high status of that chief executive. The same applies when you're giving a presentation or other talk—always ask the person with the highest status to make your announcement.

Moreover, your alleged relationship to certain luminaries does not necessarily have to be verbalized—images suffice. I experienced how effective this tactic is firsthand when I sat in the office of the film producer Arnon Milchan at the 20th Century Fox Studios in Los Angeles. Milchan has produced several great movies, including *Once upon a Time in America*, *Pretty Woman*, and *12 Years a Slave*. As I sat alone in Milchan's office waiting for our meeting, I gazed at the photographs adorning his wall: Milchan with various movie stars, presidents, and even at the side of the UN secretary-general. With each picture, my respect for him increased immensely and tangibly.

In order to utilize the benefits of BIRGing, it is not even necessary to have actually met the person you're associating yourself with.[48] Priests and other holy people have a high status because of their close relationship with a god, while American politicians regularly speak about the nation's almost mythical Founding Fathers, subtly drawing a connection between themselves and these revered men. In Mongolia, the warlord Genghis Khan is stylized as a half god; in Tajikistan, the poet Rudaki is hailed as a saint. Why? Because the glorification of historical figures directly shines on their heirs. What about you? Do you have luminaries in your field to which you can create a connection? The more you think about this idea, the more people will come to mind, and it will be quite reasonable to refer to them at the right time. Drawing a connection to institutions can also work accordingly in raising your status: a university or a well-known employer, for example.

People tend not to think about how this association works both ways: I have seen it all too often when people complain about their former employer or school. What is the consequence? Their status suffers, because they create a negative association. Instead, you should praise everything that is linked to you.[49] Instead of praising your own accomplishments or performance, praise others—doing so is far less suspicious and has the same desired effect. For example, if you talk about how grandiose you found your first job many years ago because the company was well organized and immensely innovative in strategic planning, this directly radiates to you and your expertise. By saying only good things about these companies or institutions—which you are associated with whether you like it or not—your status increases, and with it your perceived competence.

Conclusion

The late Oxford professor Sir Alfred Ayer was once a guest at an illustrious party in New York City in the late 1980s, when suddenly a quarrel broke out: a dangerous-looking man began pestering a young model named Naomi Campbell, and the other guests did not dare to intervene.[50]

Only the frail, 77-year-old Sir Alfred took a stand for the girl and spoke up—but the aggressor did not retreat.

"Don't you know who I am?" he snapped at Sir Alfred. "I'm Mike Tyson, the heavyweight champion of the world!"

"Well," replied Sir Alfred. "And I am the former Wykeham professor of logic at Oxford University. Now that we both know that we have reached the top of our respective professions, we can talk like gentlemen." And so, the legend claims, he calmed things down and the party went on.

Whether you like it or not, across the board, hardly anything convinces other people of your competence as effectively as the perception of high status: if you get a steak served under a silver bell at the Le Bristol hotel in Paris, it will taste better than a similar piece of meat on a plastic plate in a bar next door.

Consider quotations: it is a good thing for an uneducated man to read books of quotations. How impressive did you find the sentence you just read? Did you think of it as particularly wise or interesting? I doubt it. And yet that line is a quote from the eminent British statesman Winston Churchill. Had I made the sentence immediately identifiable as his quote and placed it prominently at the beginning of the chapter, I am sure it would have had a totally different, more profound effect on you. Quotations are only appreciated when they are recognizable as such, elevated from a banal remark to the pinnacle of world wisdom. Such is the power of status.

Even margarine benefited from the effects of status: it was not until the butter substitute started being wrapped in golden foil bearing a crown that it began to gain popularity.[51]

Monarchs have forever known about the importance of status, and they literally set it in stone with monuments, statues, and buildings. Think of the giant skyscraper banks and glitzy company headquarters that create a sense of awe in those who pass by or walk through the grand entrance.

As early as 1899, US economist Thorstein Veblen described how people buy certain things only to increase their status, a theory he called "conspicuous consumption." The *Veblen Effect* was later named after him, which describes the phenomenon of increasing—not diminishing—demand for a good despite raising its price.

Though the whole world knows about these mechanisms, status symbols work nonetheless, even in the Western Hemisphere, where status supposedly doesn't play a major role anymore, and of course, even more so in status-oriented cultures.[52] However, the habitus of a person with a high status cannot be reduced to simply wearing a Rolex—although this is part of it. In addition to mere objects, the corresponding communication and interaction are also required. Combining all these factors directly leads to a higher perceived level of competence.[53]

With a higher status you make it easier for your client or customer to decide in your favor. The manager of one company breaks it down in this way: "You know, I could get this [legal expertise] somewhere else. I can use a medium-size firm in Kentucky, and they're fine. But I'd like to be able to tell my directors I got Baker MacKenzie—a high-status firm. There's less to justify before the deal and after the fact if something goes wrong."[54]

And there is yet another advantage. Have you ever seen a very prominent speaker, a president, or a movie star live on stage? In the past, when I saw the magnificent actor Kevin Spacey deliver a talk at the height of his fame and glory, I was amazed at the wave of euphoria that welcomed him on his way to the podium. The slightest trace of a joke made the audience roar with laughter, because we were flattered that such a luminary would even deign to make us laugh. Had a janitor gotten up on stage and made the same joke, the audience would have stared at us silently. Even the same exact speech delivered by the same speaker, Kevin Spacey, now, after his tragic fall from glory, would most likely have an entirely different effect. As a matter of fact, people with a high status are just more popular.[55] Mind you, status differences become less relevant when we know each other well,[56] but for a first impression, their relevance can hardly be overestimated.

Are there gender differences when it comes to status? Yes, there are. As compared to men, women prefer fewer status differences and structures, such as can be seen in flat hierarchies.[57] Women are also less eager than men to aim for status and tend to be more modest—a mistake, as status is a key aspect to win people over. Therefore, women should particularly embrace the aforementioned methods.

However, the world has changed tremendously in this area: In an experiment in 1971, award-winning paintings were rated of equally high artistic value, whether by women or men.[58] Non-award-winning paintings, however, were rated higher if they had been created by men. In other words, both men and women artists were only rated equally when they were both at a very high level—below that level, male artists were considered to be more competent. Fortunately, things have changed: more recent studies have shown that there are no more differences between the status of men and women, at least in the Western Hemisphere.[59]

Back to McKinsey, where we started this chapter: the only men who walked around in dark suits in Los Angeles in the late 1960s were employees of either McKinsey or the FBI, which actually led to some confusion once in a while.[60] But the success of consultants today speaks for itself. A reporter for *Business Week* was startled by the fact that in 1965 there was one consultant for every 100 managers—by 1995, there was one for every 13 managers.[61] Since then, the number of consultants has continued to mushroom. It doesn't seem too far-fetched to postulate that one day soon all managers will have their own consultants at their side—this is possibly one of the explanations for the large increase in the number of "coaches" who regularly work one on one. Of course, to join these consultants' ranks, you don't have to be an expert, as Oxford researcher Chris McKenna sums it up: "Behaving like a professional would serve just as well as becoming one."[62]

Competence Compendium
Status

High status has a direct impact on perceived competence and popularity.

Habitus
✧ The habitus includes your entire appearance and conduct.
✧ Choose your clothes, and any items that surround you, wisely.
✧ Failure to conform only has a positive effect if you already have a high status.

Interaction
✧ Select the seat at the head of the table.
✧ Use power talking.
✧ Use questions and silence.
✧ Avoid trench warfare and reconcile quarrels.
✧ Praise others but let them work for your approval.
✧ Don't chum up!

Education
✧ Titles and job titles are seen as "objective criteria" of status.
✧ Display diplomas, certificates, or awards.

◇ Publish articles, books, or blogs.

◇ Play the "educational game" to demonstrate your high level of education.

BIRGing: Indirect Status

◇ Establish associations with high-status people or institutions.

◇ Mention any similarities with authorities.

◇ Praise people and institutions that are linked to you.

WHAT NOW?

There will come a time when you believe everything is
finished. Yet that will be the beginning.

—LOUIS L'AMOUR

Having read through these chapters, you have studied the condensed results of hundreds of studies, essays, and books. But what remains when the dust has finally settled?

"Well, well," you might tell yourself, "very interesting"—and then continue about your day, taking the same approaches you've always taken and doing the same things you've always done. Chances are you will continue working on becoming even more competent in your area of expertise. Good, but not enough. Don't forget that competence alone isn't enough—you must also focus on the perception of your competence. Think about this book as a personal reference library and guide to help you show your competence, and work on internalizing the advice given throughout.

You are likely wondering how in the world you will be able to remember all of this advice. Another question to consider: How in the world are you able to drive a car in the age before self-driving cars? Imagine that you had no idea what a car is,[1] and so I explained that it is something made out of a couple of tons of steel or aluminum that, after a few days of practice, you'd be able to drive around alone. Then I told you that with only the slightest effort, you will be able to steer this colossus through narrow streets that have no clear boundaries and are defined by simple white lines that you can only see, more or less, in the daytime.

And then I continued to describe how, while driving, you must always keep an eye on these white lines, even though you must also look straight ahead at the same time. And, of course, you need to look not only in front and to the side of you but also behind you using your mirrors—rear view, left, and right (and don't forget that objects in the mirror are closer than they appear!). And you have to shift gears using both feet and your right hand. But, after shifting, please get both hands back on the steering wheel immediately. Now and then, you must signal for turns. Turn on the windshield wipers. Choose the best route to your destination. And watch out! If you drift over the left white line even if just for a half second, your trip could end fatally, or—if you are luckier—in a wheelchair for the rest of your life. And please do not forget to look over your shoulder.

Of course, even if *you* do everything flawlessly, you are not alone on the road. Every day, there are thousands of others who drive past you, among whom are, potentially, drunk drivers, confused people going the wrong direction down a one-way street, and those with a death wish. If a driver coming toward you falls asleep for just a second, be prepared to live out the remainder of your days as a patient in an assisted-living facility.

How would you react to this description? You would refuse to even set your foot in such an infernal machine, and you would find it unthinkable that an ordinary human being could drive such a monster at all—let alone that billions of people do it every day.

Given the foregoing, compared to the daily drive to work, the effort to translate the methods described in this book into behavior in your daily life is not too great. And it will take you a long way, much further than any car.

Think of it in another way: How are the big four accounting firms, PricewaterhouseCoopers, KPMG, Deloitte, and Ernst & Young, different from one another? Or big law firms such as Latham & Watkins and Freshfields? Or consulting firms like Bain and the Boston Consulting Group? Are there any differences between them? If you ask around among their employees, you will probably hear a lot about gigantic differences in company culture and social interaction levels—things that you would hardly notice as an outsider.

The Swedish business thinkers Jonas Ridderstråle and Kjell Nordström have described this situation aptly: "The 'surplus society' has a surplus of similar companies, employing similar people, with similar educational backgrounds, working in similar jobs, coming up with similar ideas, producing similar things, with similar prices and similar quality."[2]

The good news is that even when the services and products your competitors and you are offering resemble one another, it is still possible to differentiate yourself. Just look at products that are virtually identical in chemical composition regardless of the producer. For example, even with sugar or flour there are certain brands that customers trust the most and are willing to pay more for. That is what this book is all about: explaining this kind of differentiation, this inexplicable advantage over others who can deliver a similar quality, and all the other techniques that will enhance your level of perceived competence.

Do you, however, still secretly think that it is somehow objectionable to actively seek to establish a better impression of your own competence? Do you feel that it is somehow disgraceful to want to shine more brightly? Then have a look around you:[3] You go to the hair stylist so that your hair will look better than it actually does. You spray yourself with deodorant and perfume to smell better than you actually do. As a woman, you probably wear heels to appear taller than you actually are. You wear lipstick and nail polish to make your lips and nails a different color from what they actually are. Do you find any of these actions objectionable?

We all have only one life at our disposal, and there is nothing wrong if we want to achieve our personal best while we're here. This book is not supposed to be a summons to deceive others with trickery. Your credibility, composed of a mixture of competence and trust, is in the long run even more important than competence alone.[4] Trust, in turn, is based on factors such as fairness, reliability, loyalty, and integrity.[5] Within these, boundaries, there is nothing wrong with putting yourself in the right light. To take an example from the world of the human, or all-too-human, efforts to present an attractive appearance: the idea is not to fill up the bra with socks to create the illusion of a huge bust but to find a bra with a perfect fit—a little push up is fine!

This view, that exceptionally positive effects can be achieved for everyone involved by the conscious use of these impression management techniques, is supported by research.[6] For one thing, your audience receives information about you that they otherwise could have missed, and for another, employers, especially, will consider it very valuable that their employees present the best possible appearance and thereby represent the company in the best possible way.[7] Therefore, do not hesitate to apply the techniques outlined here in this book.

But of course, as has been stated here again and again, you do need a certain amount of tact or situational awareness to judge the correct dosage for some of these techniques. If others notice an attempt at conscious manipulation, they will react defensively.[8]

And all of this advice applies to men and women alike. In the individual chapters, gender-specific mechanisms are pointed out repeatedly, but in general, the following can be said: while men, even a few decades ago, were generally seen as more competent, today's research shows no differences between the sexes—at least in the Western world.[9]

With many of these techniques, I am talking about small details, but it is precisely these that make the difference, especially today, when the competition is harder than ever before because you compete with the entire world. As mentioned in chapter 1, your customers will compare you not only to your competition a few blocks away, like they did in the past, but they will use the best in the world as their benchmark. The American economist Sherwin Rosen speaks of the "economy of superstars":[10] only a tiny lead, a sprint that is one-hundredth of a second faster; a certain feel in the pianist's "attack" that sounds just a tad more elegant; or a single technique that increases our perceived competence could make the difference in determining whether you will be celebrated as a master or ignored as a loser. Winner takes all! Would you prefer to buy a track by a no-name violinist for two dollars or pay 50 cents more for one by the violin talent of the century, Joshua Bell?

One more example with Joshua Bell, the great violin virtuoso, who played his Stradivarius with barely any audience in the metro station in Washington, DC. Gene Weingarten, the *Washington Post* journalist who conceived the experiment, described the amazing result by using the concept of "art without framing": even a major painting, which we would marvel at in a museum, would hardly be noticed if it were displayed at a restaurant, outside its normal museum context, and could be bought for a couple of dollars.

The British artist Banksy, whose works are otherwise sold for millions of dollars, delivered a powerful illustration of this hypothesis when he or she (Banksy's identity is still a mystery) let his or her pictures be sold anonymously for several hours in New York's Central Park.[11] Banksy had the same experience as Joshua Bell: after one hour, the first customer purchased two pictures for the price of one—for a total of 60 dollars. The pieces could have gone for millions, but they didn't because they lacked the right "framing."

What else did Joshua Bell have to say about his experiment? "When you play for ticket-holders, you are already validated. I have no sense that I need to be accepted. I'm already accepted." That is the purpose of the methods described here: justified recognition. Without anyone having to buy a ticket.

SCIENCE AND THE WORLD

In the end everything will be fine, and if it isn't, it is not yet the end.

—OSCAR WILDE

I magine that someone politely approaches you on the street and briefly describes some of the techniques I have covered here in these pages. He then asks if you think you would be influenced by them in any way if they were used on you. What would your answer be? I bet you'd say no—most people would deny that such techniques or tools would influence how they perceive any given person.

These people wouldn't be lying, but they would be missing a major point essential to understanding how these techniques work: the process of perception takes place almost solely in our subconscious.[1] This fact shouldn't be that surprising since our brains consist of over 100 billion neurons. The cerebral cortex alone contains up to 30 billion neurons—the cornerstones of our thinking processes—that are linked to each other. The possible neural connections therefore amount to a number that can be expressed as 10 followed by more than one million zeros. For comparison, if you calculate the total number of particles in our universe (grab a comfortable chair and snacks), the number will only be a 10 with 79 zeros after it. Our different neurons have countless "conversations" with one another, and we only very seldom take part in them.

The insights gathered in this book derive mainly from psychology and sociology, specifically social psychology, which deals with the experiences and behavior of individuals in social contexts. In 1934, the American philosopher George Herbert Mead postulated that our identities are formed only through interaction with others.[2] The Canadian sociologist Erving Goffman regarded every interpersonal encounter as theater and the participating individuals as actors.[3]

In the field of social psychology, I am especially interested in the subfield of *person perception*.[4] The purpose of this discipline is to accurately analyze the naive, everyday psychology that all of us use all the time.[5] In this subfield, I am, above all, concerned with the field of *impression management* (also called *self-presentation*), which is the conscious control of our effect on others.[6] As mentioned in chapter 7, thorough analyses of what we can do to improve our popularity already exist and popularity can have an influence on perceived competence.[7] However, the interactional purpose of increasing the level of perceived competence has, strangely enough, never been dealt with systematically.

From Detail to Overview

If you take a look at the table of contents of this book, you will note many differences in the determinants of perceived competence. You may find yourself asking whether some of the methods described throughout these chapters might conflict with one another. There is, therefore, the question of possible interdependencies. More generally: How do the many individual parts make up a whole?

According to the so-called summation model, an overall impression emerges from a summing up of partial impressions.[8] According to this view, the overall impression (in this case, the perception of competence) is a result of $a + b + c + d$ and on down the line. In this manner, high status increases the level of influence, and if a high level of attractiveness is added to that, the level of influence will rise even more.[9] The overall impression is, in this view, simply the sum of its parts, and the more the individual factors increase perceived competence, the more they will count as a group. Interdependencies would, according to this line of thought, only play a subordinate role.

However, let's examine the other extreme, an approach that consistently subordinates the individual elements to the whole: *Gestalt perception*.[10] According to this approach, an image of the person being interacted with emerges that is much more complex than it would be if you only looked at the individual, observable qualities. Why is that? We draw on visual factors such as appearance, or specific behavioral patterns, to arrive at conclusions about things that are not visible; when doing so, our brain is able to automatically weave all the new, incoming information into concepts that are already present. Here, the much-cited halo effect comes into play again, according to which every impression is processed on the basis of already-existing impressions. With negative contextual information, the individual will be judged more negatively; with positive contextual clues, the person will be considered more positively.

Gestalt perception, however, goes even further: Different properties are considered clusters, connected to one another like bunches of grapes and put into the appropriate "drawers" together. These "drawers" function as narrowly defined, naive, theories of personality called "implicit personality theories,"[11] or "consensus maps" when the subjects are not solely people. We also put objects or even ideas into these drawers, something that comes into play, for instance, in market research (for example, when Ikea wants to know what belongs to the "home" cluster, or if Chrysler wants to know what is associated with Jeeps).[12] Many neurologists and psychologists work to decipher the maps (for example, via analyzing word clouds) that are at work in our brain, maps that play a growing role in product development and advertising decisions. These maps are highly irrational. We even link fruits and vegetables with certain personality properties: lemons are thought to be sympathetic, mushrooms are social climbers, and onions are supposedly stupid.[13] Candy companies use this to their advantage: Skittles, for example, all taste the same—they only have different colors. Why? As Brandeis researcher Don Katz says, "The Skittles people, being much smarter than most of us, recognized that it is cheaper to make things smell and look different than it is to make them actually taste different."[14] Our brain sees the different colors and we assume they are linked to the flavor: for example, yellow with lemon, or red with strawberry.

However, in this book, we are interested in people, and therefore in *implicit personality theories*—more specifically, in the contents of the "competence" drawer.

I have already mentioned the best example of how this drawer functions; here, we are talking about stereotypes, our overall set of assumptions about the properties of a certain type of person.[15] Looking like the cliché of an expert, purely in appearance, is very useful, precisely because your appearance alone will already open the desired drawer. If you are, as discussed, a doctor walking around with a stethoscope around your neck, or if, as an engineer, you always use the latest gadgets, you will make it easy for your audience to find the optimal drawer to place you in. But, apart from such occupation-specific clichés—which may very well achieve the desired effect—the other techniques described in this book will also direct attention specifically to the "competence" drawer.

These drawers are shared within cultures. Do you remember the study in chapter 7 in which a group of students, on the basis of photos showing two candidates for the same political office, were asked which candidate gave them the strongest impression of competence?[16] The students pointed to the winner of the election in about 70 percent of the cases: the winner had opened the correct drawer for the voters as well as for the students.

These drawers play a huge role, not least because the choice of which drawer to open depends very much on the interpretation of ambiguous information. As discussed in chapter 2, people tend to make choices that confirm their prejudices (confirmation bias). Our ability to create a coherent overall picture from very few clues is quite startling. Consider this drawing:

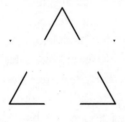

You recognize two triangles, even though one of them can be reduced to three dots and three empty spaces. Recent research has shown that our brains perceive the lines of the imaginary triangle as if they really existed.[17] The reason for this is the law of closure, according to which we will perceive a shape, even with very few reference points, as a coherent image.[18] In the same way, we are able to arrive at an overall "shape" for a person from a meager set of clues, which means that, in any context, we have created an unsustainable simplification. But we have no choice. If we had to analyze every stimulus carefully and thoroughly, we would simply collapse from the overload. For that reason, we use the few visible clues to deduce the properties that are not visible.

There is another advantage to fitting yourself perfectly into the "competence" drawer. Memories must be reconstructed each time they are recalled.[19] And gaps in our memories will be mended using pieces of information that fit the existing image. This process can easily lead to distortions.[20] When others remember you after a conversation, they will have afterthoughts that conform to their personal implicit personality theory—even if those things did not actually happen. People will trust their ideal images more than their own memories. If you have achieved the impression of competence, others will tend to remember aspects and occurrences that reinforce your perceived competence—even if they never happened.

Seen in this way, interdependencies represent not only dangers but also possibilities, because every positive factor confirms other positive factors and reinforces the effect of those—and, a little at a time, the desired drawer will be opened.

The Faulty Competence Detector

Conversely, the implicit personality theory also implies that other people can just as easily convince us to put them into the drawer they want. Consider this issue from the opposing perspective: in your professional life, as well as your private one, if you need to make a decision about, or perhaps the acquaintance of, someone new, there would be great value in the ability to accurately judge the competence of the person in question. But there is, as already described, one small problem.

We are frighteningly bad at making an accurate assessment of other people's competence, and the same is true for the closely related factor of intelligence.[21] In one experiment, only 20 percent of the people tested were able to assess the intelligence of others with higher accuracy than a random number generator.[22] It should be noted that women tended to be better than men at judging the intelligence of others after a short meeting; however, they were still far from being accurate.[23]

According to the two Israeli American psychologists Amos Tversky and Daniel Kahneman, we go through two stages when evaluating others. The so-called *System 1* comprises the first impression, a cursory assessment without conscious thought.[24] If we consciously decide to interact with the other person, *System 2* is activated: our powers of reason are then brought into play.

The problem with these systems is that in the case of assessing competence, even reason doesn't help. It is, as already noted, much more difficult to recognize true competence than to expose mere incompetence. Certainly, many Sunday drivers on the freeway often irritate you. But would you ever notice if the best driver in the world zoomed past you? Probably not.[25]

Well then, how do you properly assess other people's competence? Knowing who is competent and who isn't, is, of course, a skill of great significance—whether choosing a lawyer or hiring an employee. And yet I saved this information until this late point in the book, hidden at the very end of the epilogue in order to reward you for bearing with me to the very end.

There are several key factors that can help us correctly judge the competence of another person. During an analysis of the competence of doctors, it turned out that neither experience nor the reputation of an alma mater was decisive in determining the true level of competence. The highest level of correlation with the actual competence level was found in the doctors' final grades, their number of completed postdoctoral education programs, and, curiously, the number of subscriptions they had to professional periodicals.[26]

To assess intelligence, which is closely related to competence, there are, however, some generally valid factors. The following items are characteristics of an actual high intelligence:[27]

- speaking quickly
- using easily understandable speech and standard English
- making eye contact while talking
- displaying self-confident behavior
- reacting quickly and with little hesitation

All of these aspects have been discussed in previous chapters as a way to increase your perceived competence. Unlike many of the previously discussed points, however, these five items are also indicators of *actual* high intelligence. All of these points can rather easily be evaluated by mere observation. Interestingly, it is easier for us to make an accurate evaluation if we only hear people and do not see them—visual factors are often misleading.[28] Women also show their intelligence more openly than men, so intelligent women tend to be perceived as intelligent.[29]

Besides these behavioral clues, you can also test the intelligence of a person through these three quick assessments:[30]

1. Does he or she ask the right questions, and is he or she able to distinguish the important aspects from the unimportant aspects of a situation?
2. If you ask questions about the most essential part of the issue at hand and what the person's approach would be, do you receive logical answers that deal directly with the questions?
3. Does he or she describe all the alternative courses of action, as well as their concomitant advantages and disadvantages?

These clues will help you judge the person's intelligence with a relatively high level of accuracy and, with it, the nearly congruent competence level. By doing so, you will be able to make a smart decision about whether you will allow yourself to be convinced by this person, and to what extent. Only then will you be truly free to choose.

NOTES

Chapter 1

1. Weingarten (2007). This story was also used as an introduction to the book *The Invisible Gorilla and Other Ways Our Intuitions Deceive Us* by Christopher Chabris and Daniel Simons (2009). The authors, however, used it to illustrate "inattentional blindness"—that is, the phenomenon that people miss significant things right in front of their very eyes when focusing on something else, such as on their way to work. I doubt that it would have made a difference in their judgments if the people focused on Bell.
2. Litzmann (1927), p. 111.
3. See Bunderson (2003), p. 559; Murphy (2007), p. 326 with further references.
4. Tsui & Barry (1986), p. 586; Judge & Ferris (1993), p. 97; Ferris & Judge (1991).
5. Sugrue (1999).
6. For a more detailed analysis, see Morris (1999), p. 55.
7. Tetlock (2005). Further developed by Tetlock, Mellers, Rohrbaugh, & Chen (2014); Mellers et al. (2015).
8. Bunderson (2003), p. 559.
9. According to these results we are totally unable to assess others' abilities: Cook (1939); Gurnee (1934); Laird & Remmers (1924); Pintner (1918); according to them we are at least better than chance: Anderson (1921); Gaskill, Fenton & Porter (1927); even more optimistic: Ambady & Rosenthal (1992); for a good overview: Reynolds & Gifford (2001, p. 187–188) and Murphy et al. (2003, p. 486).

   Research mostly focused on whether we are able to properly assess our conversation partner's state, especially emotions such as fear (e.g. Hall & Bernieri, 2001). When traits were rated, the focus was more on aspects such as a tendency to depression or—closer to competence—credibility (e.g. Ambady & Rosenthal, 1992; see Murphy et al., 2003, for a discussion).
10. D. E. Rosenthal (1976), p. 260. Most leading law firms and consultancies use the "up-or-out" system, also known as the "Cravath System." The prestigious New York City law firm Cravath, Swaine, & Moore introduced this system in the early 20th century: young lawyers were hired with the clear option of either becoming a partner or being fired if they turned out to be less competent than expected.
11. See Fiske, Cuddy, Glick, & Xu (2002); Le Deist & Winterton (2005); Sandberg & Pinnington (2009).
12. Murphy (2007), p. 329, combined competence and intelligence (along with "smartness" and "brightness") to create a "composite perceived intelligence score." See also Reynolds & Gifford (2001).

13. Argyle, Ginsburg, Forgas, & Campbell (1981), p. 254; Wahrman & Pugh (1972). More recent studies show similar results: Judd, James-Hawkins, Yzerbyt, & Kashima (2005); Fiske, Cuddy, & Glick (2007); Rosenberg, Nelson, & Vivekananthan (1968); Wojciszke, Bazinska, & Jaworski (1998); Wojciszke (2005). Competence is also one of the three most important factors of leadership competence, in addition to administrative skills and human qualities (Mott, 1972; O'Driscoll, Humphries, & Larsen, 1991).

14. Judge & Ferris (1993), p. 80.

15. Lerner (1980).

16. Peter & Hull (1969). The previously discussed "up or out" system is one way of tackling this problem.

17. Clance & Imes (1978); see also Fast & Chen (2009).

18. J. Holt (2005).

19. Nesse & Williams (1994), p. 220; cf. Buss (2000), p. 16f.

20. Luhmann (1984).

21. T. Clark & Salaman (1998).

22. Godfrey, Jones, & Lord (1986).

23. See also Murphy (2007); S. P. Levine & Feldman (1997); J. B. Ellis & Wittenbaum (2000).

24. See Rosenfeld, Giacalone, & Riordan (1995).

25. J. Mayo, White, & Eysenck (1978); Eysenck & Nias (1988).

26. Frank (1961).

27. See Waber, Shiv, Carmon, & Ariely (2008); de Craen, Roos, de Vries, & Kleijnen (1996); Buckalew & Ross (1981).

28. Jamieson, Lydon, Stewart, & Zanna (1987).

29. Murphy (2007), p. 330.

30. Bromley (1993), p. 120. Typically, we try to demonstrate our competence in our CVs (Knouse, 1994; Metcalfe, 1992), in interviews (Ralston & Kirkwood, 1999), and on our websites (Connolly-Ahern & Broadway, 2007).

31. Littlepage, Robison, & Reddington (1997); Bottger (1984); and Shell & Moussa (2007), p. 13.

32. Waller & Younger (2017), p. 17.

33. About the effect on a company's reputation: Cravens, Oliver, & Ramamoorti (2003); Gaines-Ross (2000). About the effect on a company's actual performance: Rajagopalan & Datta (1996); Fanelli & Misangyi (2006); Waldmann, Ramirez, House, & Puranam (2001). Pollach and Kerbler (2011) also point out intercultural differences: in the United States, competent business leaders are expected to engage themselves much more in community matters than is the case in Europe.

Chapter 2

1. "Iconic Albuquerque" (2008).

2. "The Triumph of the Nerds" (1996).

3. There are several versions of this story; this one seems most likely. H. Evans (2004) based his story on Kildall's (never published) autobiography, which was completed shortly before Kildall's death in 1994 (Hamm & Greene, 2004).

4. Schuman (2008), p. 62.

5. Eagly & Acksen (1971).

6. Tedeschi, Schlenker, & Bonoma (1971).
7. Schlenker & Leary (1982).
8. Tversky & Kahneman (1991); Kahneman & Tversky (1979); see also Hogg & Abrams (1993).
9. Gross (1996), p. 182.
10. Raymond (2003).
11. Tsui & Barry (1986), p. 586.
12. For a good overview: Ansolabehere, Snowberg, & Snyder (2006).
13. The Center for Responsive Politics analyzed the years 1964–2014 ("Reelection rates," n.d.).
14. According to Hofstede (2001), there are certain differences among an aspect he refers to as "uncertainty avoidance" among cultures.
15. Oldmeadow, Platow, Foddy, & Anderson (2003), p. 148.
16. McGarty, Turner, Oakes, & Haslam (1993); Turner (1991); Turner & Oakes (1989); for an overview, cf. Oldmeadow et al. (2003), p. 148.
17. Ekman (2001), p. 228. In cases in which a lie detector is 80 percent accurate and 1,000 applicants are tested, if 10 of these are spies, then 8 of them would be exposed. However, 198 candidates (20 percent of the 990 honest ones) would be wrongly classified as dishonest. See also Vrij (2008), p. 31.
18. Judge & Ferris (1993), p. 84; for more specific information: Rowe (1989).
19. Plassmann, O'Doherty, Shiv, & Rangel (2008).
20. Swann & Ely (1984).
21. There are certainly differences between individuals, but in general, most people show a high level of trust in others. We therefore usually believe those to whom we are talking (G. R. Miller & Stiff, 1993, p. 35; see also McCornack & Levine, 1990; McCornack & Parks, 1986; Stiff, Kim, & Ramesh, 1992).
22. Snyder & Cantor (1979).
23. Elmar Stachels, former CEO of the German pharmaceutical company Bayer in China, comments, "Leadership in China means not forcing your point of view—not saying: 'I am the expert, I know everything'" (Fernández & Underwood, 2006, pp. 15, 85).
24. Wahrman & Pugh (1972). Although he was classified as unappealing, people preferred to work with him rather than with a nice but reserved person.
25. C. R. Berger & Bradac (1982); Cutler, Penrod, & Dexter (1990); Cutler, Penrod, & Stuve (1988); Lindsay (1994).
26. Bunderson (2003), p. 569; Bazil (2005), p. 42.
27. The corresponding quote is often incorrectly attributed to US poet Maya Angelou ("People will forget what you said, people will forget what you did, but people will never forget how you made them feel"); it is in fact much older (see R. Evans, 1971).
28. See also Hubbertz (2006).
29. Dutton & Aron (1974). See also White, Fishbein, & Rutstein (1981). Critical comment: Kenrick & Cialdini (1977).
30. Strack, Stepper, & Martin (1988). As early as 1974, Laird investigated the effects of facial muscle innervations, and Ekman, Levenson, and Friesen presented a landmark study in 1983. Lanzetta, Cartwright-Smith, & Kleck (1976) gave electric shocks to their subjects; some were asked to exaggerate their painful expressions, others were asked to suppress those expressions as much as possible—allegedly to deceive the audience. Subsequent questioning

revealed that those who increased the expression of pain felt the pain to be stronger and those who attenuated the expression of pain to be much weaker. For a critical discussion, see Stroebe, Hewstone, & Stephenson (1996), p. 326ff.

31. Joule & Beauvois (1998), p. 121f. The authors attribute this idea, which was systematized in the late 1960s, to the philosopher Baruch Spinoza.
32. Carney, Cuddy, & Yap (2010).
33. Peterson (2018), pp. 1–28; particularly pp. 25–27.
34. In the CBS broadcast *CBS Reports* on November 4, 1979.
35. Dijksterhuis & van Knippenberg (1998).
36. Bargh, Chen, & Burrows (1996).
37. After Grout & Perrin (2006).
38. Cf. Baumeister (1998); Baumeister, Smart, & Boden (1996); Kernis, Grannemann, & Barclay (1989).
39. Fast & Chen (2009); see also Carver, Lawrence, & Scheier (1999); Higgins (1987); Maner et al. (2005); Pyszczynski, Greenberg, & Goldenberg (2003); Stone & Cooper (2001).
40. Argyle (1979), p. 87.
41. D. J. Schneider (1981).
42. Culbert (1968); Vonk (1999).
43. E. E. Jones (1990), p. 181.
44. The study is cited from Beckwith (1997).
45. E. E. Jones (1990), p. 181.
46. Peters (2006).
47. Many thanks to Dr. Martin Gründl for pointing this out. See also Foster (2013); Hirschi & Jaensch (2015).
48. Weinraub (2000).
49. Hamm & Greene (2004).

Chapter 3

1. Forgas (1999), p. 68.
2. The first experiment on this was from Thorndike (1920).
3. Barrett (2005).
4. An excellent overview here: Rosenzweig (2007).
5. Bazil (2005), p. 40.
6. McArthur & Post (1977), p. 530f.
7. McArthur & Post (1977); cf. also Bierhoff (1989), p. 210.
8. Cialdini (1993), p. 190.
9. Judge & Ferris (1993), p. 88.
10. Bata & Sinclair (1990), p. 201.
11. Judge & Ferris (1993), p. 88.
12. Only later did it come out that he had, before his CEO post, when he was head of the Exploration and Production Division, known about the lower reserves for 18 months (Davis, Polk, & Wardwell, 2008).
13. See Schlenker & Darby (1981); Darby & Schlenker (1982); also Mummendey (1995), p. 158f.
14. McArthur & Post (1977).

'15. Tiedens, Ellsworth, & Mesquita (2000); Weiner (1986).
16. Hareli, Berkovitch, Livnat, & David (2013).
17. Livnat & David (2013); Tangney (1996); Rodriguez Mosquera, Fischer, Manstead, & Zaalberg (2008); Rodriguez Mosquera, Manstead, & Fischer (2002); Tiedens, Ellsworth, & Mesquita (2000); cf. Hareli et al. (2013).
18. Brescoll & Uhlmann (2008).
19. On assertiveness: Delamater & McNamara (1987); De Rivera (1977); on decisiveness: Rothman & Wiesenfeld (2007); Mikulincer (1998); on persistence: M. S. Clark, Pataki, & Carver (1996); Sinaceur & Tiedens (2006); also Hareli et al. (2013); on assertiveness and toughness: Delamater & McNamara (1987); De Rivera (1977); M. S. Clark, Pataki, & Carver (1996); Sinaceur & Tiedens (2006); Rothman & Wiesenfeld (2007).
20. See, for example, Cornelissen (2014), pp. 200–215; Argenti & Forman (2002), pp. 235–66.
21. Schlenker & Leary (1982).
22. Ulmer, Sellnow, & Seeger (2007).
23. See E. E. Jones & Pittman (1982); also Mummendey (1995), pp. 142, 148.
24. Bates (2005), p. 41f.
25. According to Salter (2007). After two weeks, at least 43 percent of their website users still chose JetBlue as their favorite airline; not the most representative measurement of their reputation but at least some sort of indicator.
26. Bates (2005), p. 42.
27. Asch, 1946.
28. Popper (1969), p. 127f.
29. Ambady and Rosenthal (1992); Ambady, Bernieri, & Richeson (2000).
30. Dipboye (1989); Phillips & Dipboye (1989).
31. Zaltman (2003), p. 24.
32. Goeudevert (1996).
33. Cialdini (1993).
34. Murdock (1962); Atkinson & Shiffrin (1968); Glanzer and Cunitz (1966).

Chapter 4

1. Potter, 1962, p. 287; from Jones, 1989, p. 484.
2. Darley & Goethals (1980). A similar result was found by Kernis & Grannemann (1990).
3. Jobs (2005).
4. Nöllke (2002), p. 314. I am much indebted to the German author Matthias Nöllke for his wonderful collection of stories, which I have liberally used in this chapter.
5. Nöllke (2002), p. 312.
6. Castiglione (1999).
7. Ericsson, Prietula, & Cokely (2007). Whether they are musicians, athletes, or chess players, it supposedly takes 10,000 hours of practice—from the performances of the Beatles to Bill Gates's programming work—to make a true expert.
8. Kleinfield (1993).
9. See Nöllke (2002), p. 99.

10. For a historical description, see Segal, Raglan, & Rank (1990).
11. Campbell (1949). Hollywood producer and writer Christopher Vogler created a highly influential seven-page memo for the Disney Company on Campbell's work, which was then turned into a book (Vogler, 1990).
12. L. Ross (1977).
13. See Nöllke (2002), p. 210.

Chapter 5

1. For example Powelz (2011) or Weibel, Wissmath, & Groner (2008).
2. Reynolds & Gifford (2001).
3. See Murphy, Hall, & Colvin (2003); Borkenau & Liebler (1995); Reynolds & Gifford (2001); Pancer & Meindl (1978); Behling & Williams (1991).
4. For example, N. Miller, Maruyama, Beaber, & Valone (1975); Murphy et al. (2003); and Reynolds & Gifford (2001).
5. See Addington (1971); Scherer (1979).
6. See Murphy et al. (2003); Zuckerman & Driver (1989).
7. See Mehrabian (1972); see also Sereno & Hawkins (1967).
8. Brown, Strong, & Rencher (1975); Klofstad, Anderson, & Nowicki (2015); Klofstad, Anderson, & Peters (2012); Tigue, Borak, O'Connor, Schandl, & Feinberg (2012).
9. Mehrabian (1972).
10. Scherer (1979) came to the conclusion that Germans are especially quick to react negatively to a volume that is *too high*. On the other hand, Americans are more likely to have a generally more positive assessment of a higher volume.
11. Wilkinson (1965).
12. On lower status: Giles & Powesland (1975); see Giles (1970); Riches & Foddy (1989). On lower persuasiveness: Giles (1973). On lower credibility: Dixon & Mahoney (2004); Lev-Ari & Keysar (2010). On lower perceived competence: Mulac & Rudd (1977). A measurement was carried out using the 'SDAS', the speech dialect attitudinal scale (Mulac, 1975, 1976).
13. See, for instance, Ng & Bradac (1993); Gluszek & Dovidio (2010); Ryan & Carranza (1975).
14. M. A. Stewart, Ryan, & Giles (1985); see also D. S. Ellis (1967).
15. Giles (1970).
16. See Cargile (2000). Yzerbyt, Provost, & Corneille (2005) found that French-speaking Belgians were thought to be less competent not only by Frenchmen but also by their French-speaking compatriots.
17. Taylor, Bassili, & Aboud (1973); Giles & Johnson (1981, 1987); Rakic, Steffens, & Mummendey (2011a, 2011b).
18. Fuertes, Potere, & Ramirez (2002); Giles (1971).
19. See Giles (1970). See also Brown (1969); Taylor and Gardner (1970); current: Reynolds & Gifford (2001).
20. See Giles (1970); Ryan & Sebastian (1976); Ryan (1979).
21. Wilkinson (1965).
22. Scherer (1979).
23. Murphy et al. (2003).
24. Berger & Bradac (1982).
25. See Murphy et al. (2003).

26. See Scherer (1979).
27. Lakoff (1973); although the term "power talking" was probably coined by Walther (1996).
28. Hosman & Wright (1987) and Hosman & Siltanen (1991) came to the conclusion that a small number of hedging attempts would increase the impression of competence, but this can be ignored because the overall effect of the powerless style is so negative that a differentiation here is not necessary. See Scherer (1979); Bradac, Hemphill, & Tardy (1981); Bradac & Mulac (1984).
29. See Scherer (1979); Bradac et al. (1981) and Bradac & Mulac (1984).
30. O'Barr & Atkins (1998).
31. G. R. Miller & Hewgill (1964); Hawkins (1967).
32. According to Armstrong (1980).
33. Schopenhauer (1913b), p. 182. Unless otherwise noted, all translations are my own.
34. Armstrong (1980).
35. Siegfried (1970); Armstrong (1980).
36. U. Anderson, Kadous, & Koonce (2004). The only exception: if the individual submitting the document had a high level of motivation for deception, then the test subject would examine the numbers thoroughly. Also see Kadous, Koonce, & Towry (2005); Porter (1995); Birdsell (1998).
37. Hutton, Miller, & Skinner (2003).
38. Mahoney & Finch (1976); R. G. Williams & Ware (1976).
39. The "social psychology of language" explores how cognitive factors affect the understanding and creation of language. See Giles & Coupland (1991), p. xi. Reynolds & Gifford (2001).
40. Gifford & Reynolds (2001).

Chapter 6

1. The expression "body language" was coined by the following early studies: Birdwhistell (1952, 1970); Efron (1941); Ekman & Friesen (1969); Exline & Winters (1965); E. T. Hall (1959, 1963, 1966); Kendon (1967); Mehrabian (1971, 1972); Scheflen (1964, 1965, 1966); Sommer (1969). However, the term is now used for such an array of situations that it has become almost useless (cf. R. P. Harrison, 1979, p. 218).
2. Hellweg, Pfau, & Brydon (1992); cf. Bugental, Kaswan, & Love (1970).
3. Cf. Argyle (1979), p. 127; Murphy (2007).
4. Especially in Western and Far Eastern cultures, strong conventions dictate that conversation partners have to face each other with friendly faces, hence the caveat regarding facial expressions (Argyle, Alkema, & Gilmour, 1972).
5. Cf. Mehrabian (1972), pp. 105, 189; Zaidel & Mehrabian (1969).
6. Albert & Dabbs (1970).
7. Davis (1971, p. 82) puts it nicely: "Puritan heritage could have something to do with US Americans being particularly careful not to intrude personal space: We equate physical closeness with sex, so that when we see two people standing close together we assume that they must be either courting or conspiring."
8. Cf. Brehm (1968). About personal space: Sommer (1969).
9. Pease & Pease (2004).

10. Watson (1972); Watson & Graves (1966); more generally: E. T. Hall (1966).
11. Murphy (2007), p. 327ff.; Murphy et al. (2001); Murphy et al. (2003).
12. Mehrabian (1972).
13. Mehrabian (1972), p. 72ff.
14. Hare & Bales (1963); Strodtbeck & Hook (1961); cf. Nemeth & Wachtler (1974), p. 532.
15. Liepman (1957), p. 11ff.
16. N. R. Anderson (1991).
17. Dovidio & Ellyson (1982).
18. Cf. Exline (1963); Exline, Gray, & Schuette (1965); Kendon (1967); Kleinke, Berger, & Staneski (1975).
19. Tecce (2004).
20. G. Spence (2006).
21. See N. R. Anderson (1991). Even smiling babies have a positive effect (Power, Hildebrandt, & Fitzgerald, 1982).
22. On the effect on perceived intelligence: Murphy et al. (2003). On the effect of low status: N. R. Anderson (1991); Mehrabian (1972), pp. 81–82. On the effect of serious expression on status and dominance: A. G. Halberstadt & Saitta (1987); Keating et al. (1981).
23. Mehrabian (1972).
24. Schmid Mast & Hall (2004).
25. See Mummendey (1995), p. 201.
26. Argyle (1979), pp. 126, 272; Henley (1973).
27. Feldman (1971); Henss (1989).
28. Cf. P. R. Wilson (1968).
29. Blaker et al. (2013).
30. Cf. Henss (1989); Roberts & Herman (1986), p. 134. On evolutionary psychology: Van Vugt, Hogan, & Kaiser (2008).
31. Argyle (1979).
32. Deck (1968).
33. Stulp, Buunk, Verhulst, & Pollet (2012).
34. Judge & Cable (2004).
35. Booher (2011), p. 16.
36. Naftulin, Ware, & Donnelly (1973).
37. W. M. Williams & Ceci (1997). Similar, Radmacher, & Martin (2001), who found out that the professor's extroversion was the most important factor investigated. Cf. also Riniolo, Johnson, Sherman, & Misso (2006); Pozo-Muñoz, Rebolloso-Pacheco, & Fernández-Ramírez (2000).
38. Mehrabian (1967).
39. Mehrabian (2009), p. 75ff.

Chapter 7

1. Thorndike (1920).
2. F. W. Schneider, Gruman, & Coutts (2012); Rosenzeig (2007).
3. Latham & Wexley (1981), p. 102. A term used is the "status characteristic framework"—e.g., by J. Berger, Fisek, Norman, & Zelditch (1977). For a good overview: Bunderson (2003), p. 562.

4. This mode of action of the halo effect corresponds to the prevailing opinion of Heider (1958) and Shelly (2001).

5. See in addition Bolino, Varela, Bande, & Turnley (2006); and also Ferris, Judge, Rowland, & Fitzgibbons (1994). The impact of the halo effect is all the more intense when the observer has an extreme feeling for the observed, whether positive or negative (Tsui & Barry, 1986). For a theoretical overview: Forgas (1999).

6. In the very early work on impression management, a distinction was not yet made between the objectives of different positive interactions. Only negative impressions in contrast to positive were considered. Typical of these undifferentiated observations was the study by Osgood, Suci, and Tannenbaum (1957), which was based on the assumption that the impression produced by an actor is largely at the level of good versus bad. As the development of impression management progressed over the decades, research found greater differentiation. Various positive and correspondingly different negative interaction targets have now been defined. The researchers, and, in particular, E. E. Jones, devoted themselves to a special (positive) interaction goal with keen interest: the goal of being popular. See E. E. Jones (1990), and also E. E. Jones & Wortman (1973).

7. E. E. Jones (1990), p. 185.

8. Cf., for example, Cialdini & Goldstein (2004); Thacker & Wayne (1995); Eastman (1994). On conversations: Varma, Toh, & Pichler (2006); on salary increases: Tsui & Barry (1986); Appelbaum & Hughes (1998); Orpen (1996); Wayne & Kacmar (1991); Wayne & Ferris (1990); to ingratiate employees: Kipnis, Schmidt, & Wilkinson (1980).

9. E. E. Jones (1964). Tedeschi and Melbug (1984) added favors, which I have included in self-enhancement. According to Drory and Zaidman (1986), the "respect" component should also be added.

10. Girard (1977).

11. Drachman, Carufel, & Inkso (1978).

12. E. E. Jones (1990), p. 183. According to source credibility theory, sources that have a high motivation to influence others are less influential because their motivation is obvious. Cf. Pornpitakpa (2004); Birnbaum & Stegner (1979).

13. E. E. Jones (1990), p. 183.

14. Grant (2014), p. 43.

15. I learned this from Dale Carnegies wonderful classic (Carnegie, 1936/2001, p. 58).

16. See also Nasher (2013), p. 61ff.

17. Ury (2008), p. 82.

18. Grant (2014).

19. Carnegie (1936/2001), p. 89.

20. More on this: Nasher (2013), p. 158ff. On the impact of a favor: Mummendey (1995), p. 157. The principle of reciprocity was probably first examined by Gouldner (1960).

21. Vrij (2008), p. 48; Chartrand & Bargh (1999); Akehurst & Vrij (1999); Baumeister, Hutton, & Tice (1989); DePaulo & Friedman (1998); Dimberg, Thumberg, & Grunedal (2002); Tickle-Degnen (2006).

22. Wheeler & Nelson (2003), p. 14.

23. Tedeschi & Melbug (1984).

24. E. E. Jones (1964).

25. E. E. Jones (1990), p. 183.
26. E. E. Jones (1990), p. 183.
27. Grant (2014), p. 43.
28. See C. R. Berger, Gardner, Parks, Schulman, & Miller (1976), p. 159f.
29. Sokal (1996b).
30. Sokal (1996a); see also Sokal & Bricmont (1998).
31. Tedeschi & Melbug (1984).
32. Godfrey et al. (1986).
33. Shell (2006), p. 142; Cialdini (1993). Also see Newcomb (1961); Byrne (1971); Locke & Horowitz (1990); M. B. Brewer (1979); Ryen & Kahn (1975); Michinov & Monteil (2002); cf. also Lewicki, Barry, & Saunders (2010), p. 237f.
34. Cialdini (1993), p. 173.
35. Oldmeadow et al. (2003).
36. See Gilbert & Horenstein (1975).
37. See S. J. Gilbert (1976).
38. Cf. Cozby (1973); Mummendey (1995), p. 153.
39. See A. Shapiro (1968).
40. See Jourard & Landsman (1960).
41. See also Schulz (2002), p. 221ff.
42. Cf. Fiser & Fiserova (1969), p. 92; H. L. Shapiro (1947), p. 456.
43. Fiske and Cox (1979) even formulated their questions in such a way that attractiveness would actually be completely in the background: they asked the test subjects how they felt in the company of the person described. Still, the first thing described was the appearance.
44. Winston, Strange, O'Doherty, & Dolan (2002); Winkielman, Halberstadt, Fazendeiro, & Catty (2006); Bar, Neta, & Linz (2006); Hassin & Trope (2000); Zebrowitz (1997).
45. Byrne, London, & Reeves (1968); cf. also Coombs & Kenkel (1966); Korabik (1981); Krebs & Adinolfi (1975); Moss (1969); Roff & Brody (1953); Stroebe, Insko, Thompson, & Layton (1971); Patzer (1985), p. 96. On the stronger effect on the other sex: Praxmarer (2011).
46. Adams & Crane (1980).
47. Stephan & Langlois (1984).
48. On school kids: cf. Chaikin, Gillen, Derlega, Heinen, & Wilson (1978); Felton, Koper, Mitchell, & Stinson (2008); Hamermesh & Parker (2005). For comparison of the pupils at different ages: Goebel & Cashen (1979). On college students: cf. Lombardo & Tocci (1979) and current analyses of faculty attractiveness and attractiveness points at ratemyprofessor.com; Riniolo et al. (2006); Liu, Hu, & Furutan (2013).
49. Ritts, Patterson, & Tubb (1992); Adams (1978); M. Ross & Salvia (1975).
50. See Hill & Kahn (1974).
51. Hamermesh & Biddle (1994); Frieze, Olson, & Russell (1991); Hosoda et al. (2003).
52. See Budesheim & DePaola (1994); Sigelman, Thomas, Sigelman, & Ribich (1986); Efran & Patterson (1974); Albright et al. (1997); Todorov, Mandisodza, Goren, & Hall (2005); Lenz & Lawson (2011); Tsfati, Elfassi, & Waismel-Manor (2010); Hoegg & Lewis (2011); Ibrocheva (2009); and also Verhulst, Lodge, & Lavine (2010). It also made no difference whether the

test subjects were aware of other facts about the candidate (Palmer & Peterson, 2012). A study in the United States: Praino, Stockemer, & Ratis (2014). In Australia: King & Leigh (2009), p. 591. In Finland: Berggren, Jordahl, & Poutvaara (2010). And in Germany: Rosar, Klein, & Beckers (2012).

53. When it comes to the world of medicine, physicians give more optimistic diagnoses and prognoses to attractive patients—whether this is beneficial is questionable (see Barocas & Vance, 1974). Less attractive patients are often not even admitted to therapy by therapists—and if they are, they are more likely to be sent to group therapy (see Cavior, 1970). And the list goes on: more attractive people are more likely to be helped by strangers (Benson, Karabenick, & Lerner, 1976). Attractive defendants are less frequently convicted of a crime, and those who are receive a more mild punishment than unattractive ones (see Efran, 1974). For more on the incredible impact of physical attractiveness, see Efran (1974); Hudson & Henze (1969); H. L. Miller & Rivenbark (1970); Perrin (1921); Tesser & Brodie (1971).

54. Chaiken (1979).

55. Cf. Byrne & Clore (1970); Kleck, Richardson, & Ronald (1974); Levinger (1972).

56. Moore, Filippou, & Perrett (2011). Regarding popularity: G. Brewer & Archer (2007); Patzer (1975). The research is based on attribution theory (e.g., Bem, 1972; Heider, 1944, 1946, 1954, 1958; E. E. Jones & Davis, 1965).

57. Cf. Berscheid & Walster (1972) and also Patzer (1985), p. 190. More recent: Lee, Pitesa, Pillutla, & Thau (2015).

58. Cf. A. G. Miller (1970), p. 242.

59. Abramowitz & O'Grady (1991).

60. Cf. Patzer (1985); Bassili (1981); Henss (1989), and also Myers (2005). It is only since Aronson (1969) that social psychology has focused more on attractiveness. The research set in motion by him has defined four principles (cf. Patzer, 1985, p. 42): Attractive people have more social power than unattractive people (Mills & Aronson, 1965; Sigall, Page, & Brown, 1971). If everything else is identical, attractive people are more popular than unattractive people (Byrne, 1971; Byrne et al., 1968; Walster, Aronson, Abrahams, & Rottmann, 1966). More attractive people are attributed with more positive qualities than unattractive people (Dion, Berscheid, & Walster, 1972; A. G. Miller, 1970; Nida & Williams, 1977). More attractive people have a different effect on others and invoke different reactions compared to unattractive people (McGuire, 1969; Sternthal, 1972).

61. Koernig & Page (2002).

62. See Praxmarer (2011).

63. Eagly, Ashmore, Makhijani, & Longo (1991).

64. Todorov et al. (2005).

65. Cf. Cunningham, Barbee, Druen, Roberts, & Wu (1995); Langlois et al. (2000); Perrett, May, & Yoshikawa (1994); Zebrowitz (1997); Baker & Churchill (1977); Murstein (1972); Cross & Cross (1971); Kopera, Maier, & Johnson (1971). In Cross and Cross (1971), there was a great deal of agreement around evaluating the "most attractive" face. However, every face had at least one vote. There is thus great agreement in the evaluation of beauty. At the same time, however, we can still hope that every human being is beautiful to at least one other person, which explains one relationship or the other.

66. See Budge (1981).

67. If you analyze the works of da Vinci, you can see that he actually adhered to this proportion rule with mathematical precision (compare Patzer, 1985, p. 155). Another strictly mathematical approach is applied today by the California beauty surgeon Edward Levin, for whom the proportions are also decisive.

68. Gründl (2013), p. 360.

69. Gründl (2013), p. 354; Perrett et al. (1998). Only the prominent lower jaw is typically male (Alley & Cunningham, 1991; Cunningham, Barbee, & Pike, 1990; Grammer & Thornhill, 1994).

70. Gründl (2013), p. 240; Eibl-Eibesfeldt (1997); Enlow (1989); Lorenz (1943); cf. also Gründl (n.d.c.).

71. Hirschberg (1978). On the eyes: Keating & Doyle (2002).

72. Gründl (2013), p. 305f.; cf. also Berry & Brownlow (1989); Berry & McArthur (1985); Zebrowitz (1997).

73. Gründl (2013), p. 305.

74. Wolf (1991); Gründl (2013), S. 298.

75. Wolf (1991); Gründl (2013), p. 297f.; Alley (1988a); Deutsch, Zalenski, & Clark (1986); England & McClintock (2009); Falser, Bendel, Voller, & Wegner (2008); Giesen (1989); Henss (1992); D. Jones (1995); Teuscher & Teuscher (2007); Wilcox (1997); Deutsch, Clark, & Zalenski (1983); Johnston & Franklin (1993); Braun, Gründl, Marberger, & Scherber (2001).

76. Buss (1989).

77. Gründl (2013), p. 237.

78. Cf. Farkas & Cheung (1981); Peck, Peck, & Kataja (1991); Sackeim (1985); Simmons, Rhodes, Peters, & Koehler (2004).

79. Galton (1878, 1888).

80. Langlois & Roggman (1990); cf. also Grammer (2000), p. 174.

81. Langlois & Roggman (1990); Thornhill & Gangestad (1993).

82. J. Halberstadt & Rhodes (2003). As for the perception of humans: Winkielman et al. (2006); Winkielman, Schwarz, Reber, & Fazendeiro (2003).

83. Grammer & Thornhill (1994); Rhodes, Roberts, & Simmons (1999); Rhodes, Proffitt, Grady, & Sumich (1998); Thornhill & Gangestad (1993).

84. Alley & Cunningham (1991); cf. also Gründl (2013), p. 4ff.

85. Gründl (2013), p. 88f.

86. Gründl (2013), p. 349.

87. Gründl (2013), p. 90.

88. Cf. Nielsen & Kernaleguen (1976).

89. Gründl (2013), p. 93ff. The relevance was ordered after Terry & Brady (1976); Terry & Davis (1976); Terry (1977): first, mouth; second, eyes; third, facial structure; fourth, hair; and fifth, nose. Other factors are skin and teeth.

The full list of factors from Gründl's postdoctoral research project is as follows (Gründl, 2013):

Women

• tanned skin
• darker eyelashes
• darker eyebrows
• lighter sclera (whiteness)
• no dark eye rings
• narrower eyebrows
• eyebrows rising laterally

- eyebrows tapering more laterally
- more lashes
- smaller distance between eyelid and eyelid fold
- more pronounced cheekbones
- more concave cheeks, narrower nasal bridge
- shorter distance between the sides of the nostrils
- shorter philtrum (distance between nose and upper lip)
- fuller lips
- narrower and longer neck
- more pronounced jaw angle
- narrower face (greater ratio of length: width)
- greater ratio of the vertical distance between the vertex and hairline to the forehead height
- shorter middle and lower face in relation to the entire skull
- upper jaw not situated back in relation to the mandible

Men

- tanned skin
- darker eyebrows
- lighter sclera (whiteness)
- denser eyelashes
- longer eyelashes
- more pronounced cheekbones
- more concave cheeks, wider back of the nose
- smaller distance to the outside of the nostrils
- weaker nasolabial folds
- fuller lips
- symmetrical upper lip (even crista philtri)
- narrower neck
- no receding hairline, more acute angle of the jaw
- more prominent chin with greater distance between the mouth and base of the chin
- narrower face (greater ratio of length to width)
- greater ratio of the vertical distance between the vertex and hairline to the forehead height
- longer mandible relative to the upper face
- no receding hairline, less sloping forehead
- less protruding orbital bulge
- less protruding nasal bridge
- concave (instead of convex) curved nasal ridges
- less protruding nasal tip
- contoured (smaller) jaw-neck angle
- longer mandible in the vertical in relation to the upper face

90. Cf. Patzer (1985), p. 149.
91. Cf. Lawson (1971).
92. "Augen und Brauen" (n.d.).
93. Martins, Tiggemann, & Churchett (2008); cf. also Feinman & Gill (1977); Gründl (2013), p. 310; Roll & Verinis (1971).

94. Cf. Hamid (1968); Terry & Kroger (1976); Terry & Zimmermann (1970).
95. Thornton (1943, 1944). Interestingly, Jahoda (1963) found that on average, myopic people are actually more intelligent.
96. Argyle & McHenry (1971); cf. also Argyle (1979). A Japanese study, on the other hand, found that the positive effect of the glasses persists even after three minutes (Saito, 1978).
97. Osborn (1996); Rennenkampff (2004), p. 80.
98. Sobal & Stunkard (1989). Cf. also Gründl (n.d.a.).
99. Andersson (1994); cf. also Gründl (n.d.a.).
100. On the BMI: Fan, Dai, Liu, & Wu (2005); Maisey, Vale, Cornelissen, & Tovee (1999); Swami & Tovee (2006). On the WHR: Furnham, Tan, & McManus (1997); Henss (1995); Singh (1995). On the WCR: Fan et al. (2005); Maisey et al. (1999); Swami & Tovee (2006); Swami et al. (2007); cf. also Tovee, Reinhardt, Emery, & Cornellisen (1998); Tovee, Hancock, Mahmoudi, Singleton, & Cornelissen (2002).
101. Fan et al. (2005); Maisey et al. (1999); Swami & Tovee (2006).
102. Frederick & Haselton (2003); Furnham & Radley (1989); Lavraka (1975); cf. also Swami et al. (2007) and Barber (1995); cf. also W. D. Ross & Ward (1982). Leit, Pope, and Gray (2001) studied Playgirl models from 1973 to 1997.
103. Cf., for example, Maier & Lavrakas (1984); Parsons (1980); Swami, Antonakopoulos, Tovee, & Furnham (2006); Swami, Caprario, Tovee, & Furnham (2006).
104. Yang, Gray, & Pope (2005).
105. Swami et al. (2007); cf. also Maier & Lavrakas (1984); Parsons (1980); Swami, Antonakopoulos, et al. (2006); Swami, Caprario, et al. (2006); Apparala, Reifman, & Munsch (2003).
106. Furnham & Nordling (1998).
107. Swami et al. (2007).
108. Swami & Furnham (2006); Swami & Tovee (2005); Swami, Antonakopoulos, et al. (2006); Swami, Caprario, et al. (2006); J. M. B. Wilson, Tripp, & Boland (2005); Sypeck et al. (2006).
109. Freese and Meland (2002) came to different conclusions regarding the WHRs of the Miss America winners and Playboy models. According to Gründl, "There is a kernel of truth in the theory that the ideal ratio of waist to hip in a woman should be 0.7. But the context is weak. Inflating 0.7 to a 'Magic Number' and making it as an irrefutable fact does not do justice to the truth" ("Taille-Hüfte-Verhältnis," n.d.).
110. Gründl also developed a "beauty formula," a mathematical equation for calculating the attractiveness value of a particular figure. In a multiple regression analysis, the average attractiveness assessment was predicted from the body figure measurements. This regression equation, into which the figure-measured values are applied, is $Y = b0 + b1 * x1 + b2 * x2 + \ldots + bn * xn$. Y is the predicted attractiveness value of the figure under consideration. The x values are values measured from the figure, such as the leg length, and the b values are the constant factors associated with the x values, with which the respective x value is multiplied. Cf. Gründl (n.d.b.).
111. Berscheid & Walster (1972); cf. R. A. Stewart, Powell, & Chetwynd (1979), p. 125.
112. Lee et al. (2015).
113. Feingold (1992); Langlois et al. (2000); Jackson, Hunter, & Hodge (1995); see also Zebrowitz, Hall, Murphy, & Rhodes (2002), p. 239.

114. Zebrowitz et al. (2002), p. 244ff.
115. Zebrowitz et al. (2002), p. 240f.; cf. also Langlois et al. (2000) and Zebrowitz (1997) for an overview of how attractiveness leads to higher intelligence.
116. Mobius & Rosenblat (2006).
117. Kanazawa & Kovar (2004).
118. Others have not found any correlation between attractiveness and intelligence (Feingold, 1992; Langlois et al., 2000; Eagly et al., 1991); a weak one was found by Jackson et al. (1995).
119. Asch (1946); but more accurately: Fiske et al. (2002); Fiske, Xu, Cuddy, & Glick (1999); for the "warmth over competence hypothesis" with the dimensions of warmth (rapport) and efficiency (competence), cf. Abele & Wojciszke (2007); Wojciszke (1994); see also J. Durante & Volpato (2012).
120. Thus, for example, riddled with relativization and thus hardly convincing: Judd, James-Hawkins, Yzerbyt, & Kashima (2005); Kervyn, Yzerbyt & Judd (2010); cf. also F. Durante, Capozza, & Fiske (2010).
121. Richetin, Durante, Mari, Perugini, & Volpato. (2012); cf. also Rosenberg et al. (1968).
122. W.-Y. Lin, Wang, Lin, Lin, & Johnson (2011); cf. also Yzerbyt et al. (2005); Judd et al. (2005).
123. Mills & Aronson (1965); Mills (1966).
124. Reinhard, Messner, & Sporer (2006).
125. Lenz & Lawson (2011).
126. Stockemer & Praino (2015); cf. also Banducci, Karp, Thrasher, & Rallings (2008) and Lenz & Lawson (2011).
127. Chandon & Wansink (2007).

Chapter 8

1. McKenna (2006) gives an exciting insight into the history of business consultants.
2. See Peterson, pp. 1–28, for this entire paragraph, particularly pp. 6–7 and 15–16.
3. Doob & Gross (1968). A very similar experiment was carried out by Joseph Forgas (1976). He compared the different driving methods of Europeans: the most impatient were the Italians (surprise, surprise), who were honking after an average of 5 seconds; the Germans were most patient, with an average of 7.5 seconds.
4. Milgram (1963).
5. Webster & Driskell (1978).
6. Schmid Mast & Hall (2004), p. 146.
7. Bunderson (2003); Oldmeadow et al. (2003), p. 146ff; Fiske et al. (2002). In different cultures: Cuddy et al. (2006); Fiske & Cuddy (2006).
8. Oldmeadow et al. (2003), p. 139; see also Balkwell, Berger, Webster, Nelson-Kilger, & Cashen (1992); Berger, Norman, Balkwell, & Smith (1992).
9. Very convincing: Oldmeadow et al. (2003), p. 138f, referring to the so-called status characteristics theory. It still assumed that there must be a "path of relevance" between the respective status and the perceived competence (see Foddy, 1988; Foddy & Riches, 2000; Norman, Smith, & Berger, 1988). On the individual status characteristics, such as occupation, race, and gender, see Cuddy et al. (2006); Eckes (2002); and Fiske & Cuddy (2006).

10. Mischke (2004); and Michler (2013).
11. Bourdieu (1982).
12. Lefkowitz, Blake, & Mouton (1955).
13. See Mummendey (1995), p. 151.
14. Schmid Mast & Hall (2004); Sybers & Roach (1962); Barnes & Sternberg (1989). Clothing also affects expectations (Rafaeli & Pratt, 1993). With men, a suit and tie influence their perceived—and, indeed, even their actual—status.
15. O'Neal & Lapitsky (1991); Kwon (1994); Kwon & Färber (1992).
16. A study by US authorities came to the conclusion that 75 percent of people assume that being well dressed leads to being perceived as smarter, more diligent, and more popular (Bowman, 1992, p. 39).
17. On formal attire: Rucker, Anderson, & Kangas (1999); on casual wear: Rafaeli, Dutton, Harquail, & Mackie-Lewis (1997). (Peluchette & Karl, 2007).
18. Hoffmann (1981).
19. In men, attractiveness is also a status trait (Schmid Mast & Hall, 2004).
20. Wookey, Graves, & Butler (2009). However, this was not the case for lower positions such as that of secretary. When the secretary was dressed in a "sexy" manner, she was rated as socially more competent, which seemed to be appropriate for the lower position. Similarly: Glick, Larsen, Johnson, & Branstiter (2005).
21. See Nielsen & Kernaleguen (1976); Beckwith (1997), p. 186; Han, Nunes, & Dreze (2010).
22. Booher (2011), p. 20.
23. Kruglanski & Webster (1991); C. E. Miller & Anderson (1979); Schachter (1951). Particularly on status: Cialdini & Goldstein (2004); C. Anderson, Srivastava, Beer, Spataro, & Chatman (2006); J. M. Levine (1989); L. Lin, Dahl, & Argo (2013); Marques, Abrams, & Serôdio (2001); C. P. Wilson (1979).
24. Etzioni (2004); Searcy (2011).
25. Cartwright (1959a); Galinsky, Magee, Gruenfeld, Whitson, & Liljenquist (2008); Haslam (2004); Sherif & Sherif (1964); J. Berger & Ward (2010); Feltovich, Harbaugh, & To (2002); Han et al. (2010).
26. Bellezza, Gino, & Keinan (2014); see D. J. Phillips & Zuckerman (2001); Thompson, Rindfleisch, & Arsel (2006); Van Kleef, Homan, Finkenauer, Gundemir, & Stamkou (2011); Simonson & Nowlis (2000); Arnould & Thompson (2005); Brooks (1981); D. B. Holt (1998); R. A. Peterson & Kern (1996); Solomon (1999). On individualism: Baumeister (1982); Galinsky et al. (2008); Kim & Markus (1999).
27. "Survey finds" (2000). In the study, 44 percent of respondents indicated that a casual dress code led to more delays and absences. At least 30 percent also stated that it led to more flirting behavior. In other words, casual clothing leads to a casual attitude.
28. On piercings and tattoos: Seiter & Hatch (2005). On eyebrow piercings: Acor (2001). See also Karl, McIntyre Hall, & Peluchette (2013); Chen (2007); B. Miller, Niçois, & Eure (2009). A survey ("How companies," 2004) concluded that a total of 72 percent were against body piercings, 69 percent against visible tattoos, 73 percent against unusual hair colors, and 64 percent against unusual hairstyles.
29. See McArthur & Post (1977), p. 531.
30. Kircheisen (1925), p. 272.
31. Aronson & Mills (1959).

32. Gerard & Mathewson (1966).

33. See Young (1965). American fraternities call them "hell weeks." A fraternity at Ohio State University locked two candidates into a storage room for two days. The two were only fed salty food and given two plastic cups to collect their own urine (Cialdini, 1993, p. 87). Germany has a tradition in which applicants to fraternities must complete a certain number of fencing duels, named "academic fencing," in order to become full members. The rather common scar resulting from these dangerous fights is worn with pride.

34. S. Brown (2001).

35. See Schmidt (1971); Schmidt, Schmerl, & Steffens (1971); see also Mummendey (1995), p. 151.

36. According to a study conducted by the online job market Stepstone, senior marketing executives with a postgraduate degree earn an average of 64,862 euros, compared to 48,957 euros without one. There are also differences in industries: for IT executives, the difference is only just under 10 percent; in the financial sector, just under 15 percent (see Naumann, 2015). Another good overview of the differences between industries: Ritter (2013).

37. See Sobelman (1974); Strong, Taylor, Bratton, & Loper (1971).

38. Bryan Huang, former chief of BearingPoint China, says, "How can I face my friends when they are all directors and I'm just a manager?" (Fernández & Underwood, 2006, p. 54).

39. Cialdini (1993), p. 75 ff.

40. See Schwanitz (1999), p. 395ff.

41. See Cialdini & Richardson (1980).

42. See Mummendey (1995), p. 145f.

43. Cialdini et al. (1976).

44. Mummendey (1995), p. 145.

45. Cialdini & de Nicholas (1989).

46. A. A. Harrison, Struthers, & Moore (1988).

47. See Cialdini & Richardson (1980).

48. I thank Dr. Vladimir Donshoi for his inspiring thoughts on this matter.

49. Cialdini et al. (1976).

50. Also found in Spurling (2000).

51. Gladwell (2007), p. 160ff.

52. Fernández & Underwood (2006), p. 84.

53. Fiske & Taylor (1991), pp. 121–22, 144–45.

54. Uzzi, Lancaster, & Dunlap (2007); see also Lancaster & Uzzi (2012).

55. Probably because you can expect valuable rewards from them (see Ridgeway & Johnson, 1990).

56. Bunderson (2003), pp. 563, 578.

57. Pratto, Stallworth, & Sidanius (1997); Nyquist & Spence (1986); Eagly & Blair (1990). On women's modesty: Schmid Mast & Hall (2004), p. 160.

58. Pheterson, Kiesler, & Goldberg (1971).

59. Schmid Mast & Hall (2004), p. 156; and also Amyx & Bristow (2009).

60. McKenna (2006), p. 159.

61. McKenna (2006), p. 8ff. According to recent estimates, there are almost 500,000 consultants worldwide, although it is unclear how narrowly the position is defined (Hari, 2010).

62. McKenna (2006), p. 200.

Conclusion

1. G. Spence (1996).
2. Ridderstråle & Nordström (2000).
3. Knapp (1972).
4. Competence + trustworthiness = credibility (Amyx & Bristow, 2009; see also McGuire, 1969). M. B. Brewer (1997, 1999) considers trustworthiness to be a precondition for successful communication (see also Morgan & Hunt, 1994; Hosmer, 1995; Nooteboom, 1996; Johnson & Lennon, 1999; Das & Teng, 2001; McKnight & Chervany, 2001; Moorman, Zaltman, & Deshpandé, 1992; Gambetta, 1988). Das and Teng (2001) distinguish between *goodwill trust* and *competence trust*. For Todorov, Said, Engell, and Oosterhof (2008), competence is positioned on an axis with confidence and dominance. Finally, trust also has a positive influence on perceived competence (Verhulst et al. 2010).
5. See Poortinga & Pidgeon (2003), p. 962. See also Hosmer (1995).
6. Van Iddekinge, McFarland, & Raymark (2007); A. P. Ellis, West, Ryan, & DeShon (2002).
7. C. K. Stevens & Kristof (1995).
8. Gordon (1996).
9. For this, see Fiske (1998); Diekman & Eagly (2000); Steffens, Schult, & Ebert (2009).
10. Rosen (1981).
11. Simpson (2013). Certainly, due to the fact that buyers did not know the artist really was Banksy, the artworks could have simply looked like Banksy copies.

Epilogue

1. Zaltman (2003), pp. 27, 57.
2. Mead was referring to "symbolic interactionism," a term that probably was first used by Herbert Blumer (cf. Felson, 1981; cf. also Swann, 1987).
3. Goffman (1959).
4. Under the auspices of the Office of Naval Research, a symposium was held at Harvard University in 1957, where, for the first time, questions were discussed under the heading "Person Perception" (Tagiuri & Petrullo, 1958). The list of participants reads like a who's who of the most influential experts in this young field—from Solomon Asch through Fritz Heider to E. E. Jones. See also D. J. Schneider, Hastorf, & Ellsworth (1979); Warr & Knapper (1968).
5. See E. E. Jones (1990); Nisbett & Roll (1980).
6. Rosenfeld et al. (1995). It would seem that the frequently used concept of *self-presentation* is only used here to establish a connection between this research, with strong sociological roots, and the popular self-concept research of modern psychology. See Mummendey (1995), p. 126; D. J. Schneider (1981) is of another opinion; Schlenker (1985); Schlenker & Weigold (1992).
7. See Argyle, Ginsburg, et al. (1981), p. 254; Nemeth & Wachtler (1974), p. 540; Wahrman & Pugh (1972).
8. J. Berger et al. (1977, p. 124), uses a more complex formula: $SSci = [1 - (1 - e(cl)) * (1 - e(c2i)) * (1 - e(c3i))]$. Here, *SSci* stands for "specific status cue

score," the *e* mirrors the different factors, and the *i* stands for the employee in question (cf. also Bunderson, 2003, p. 570).

9. Oldmeadow et al. (2003), p. 141ff.
10. Also known as the *ecological approach* (McArthur & Baron, 1983).
11. D. J. Schneider (1973).
12. Gerard Zaltman of Harvard Business School developed, for this purpose, the so-called *metaphor elicitation technique* (MET) (Zaltman, 2003).
13. Sommer (1988).
14. Quoted in A. Stevens (2018).
15. The description of "stereotypes" concerning human beings goes back to Lippmann (1922). For a good overview: Hilton & von Hippel (1996).
16. Todorov et al. (2005). The following was found to hold true: The higher the perceived competence, the better the candidate's result in the election was. When there was no doubt about the candidate's perceived competence, the candidate won by a landslide.
17. For more detail, see (especially in their literature review) Montaser-Kouhsari, Landy, Heeger, & Larsson (2007).
18. This and other "Gestalt laws" were developed by the Austro-Hungarian psychologist Max Wertheimer to describe our perception under a variety of circumstances (Wertheimer, 1923).

    The Italian psychologist Gaetano Kanizsa (1976), in the context of optical illusions, spoke of "illusory contours." Martin Gründl (personal correspondence), on the other hand, finds that, in this figure, it is more the "good gestalt" that is in play, since, in this case, a white triangle seems to partly conceal the "Line-Triangle" underlying it, and it is easy to see two triangles turned counter to one another here.
19. Based on the model of *cognitive information processing*, impressions are stored in the memory and retrieved again (cf. Wayne & Liden, 1995, p. 235ff.).
20. Thus, for example, Loftus & Palmer (1974); Shaw & Porter (2015).
21. Reynolds & Gifford (2001), p. 198.
22. See Murphy et al. (2003); Ambady, Hallahan, & Rosenthal (1995); Colvin & Bundick (2001); J. A. Hall (1984); J. A. Hall, Carter, & Horgan (2001).
23. Eagly et al. (1991).
24. For a very good overview of their theory, see Kahneman (2011).
25. For detailed argumentation, see D. E. Rosenthal (1976), p. 264ff.
26. O. Peterson, Andrews, & Spain (1956).
27. Murphy (2007) and Reynolds & Gifford (2001).
28. Gifford & Reynolds (2001), p. 197.
29. J. A. Hall (1984); cf. also Murphy et al. (2003), p. 471.
30. Golde (1969), summarized by D. E. Rosenthal (1976, p. 271), who was mainly interested in the competence of lawyers.

BIBLIOGRAPHY

Knowledge can be acquired by a suitable and complete study,
no matter what the starting point is.

—GEORGE GURDJIEFF

Abele, A. E., & Wojciszke, B. (2007). Agency and communion from the perspective of self versus others. *Journal of Personality and Social Psychology, 93,* 751–63.

Abramowitz, I. A., & O'Grady, K. E. (1991). Impact of gender, physical attractiveness, and intelligence on the perception of peer counselors. *Journal of Psychology, 125*(3), 311–26.

Abrams, D. (Ed.). (1993). *Group motivation: Social psychological perspectives.* London: Harvester.

Abrams, D., & Hogg, M. A. (1988). *Social identifications: A social psychology of intergroup relations and group processes.* Florence: Taylor and Francis.

Acor, A. (2001). Employers' perceptions of persons with body art and an experimental test regarding eyebrow piercing. *Dissertation Abstracts International, Section B, 61*(1B), 3885.

Adams, G. R. (1978). Racial membership and physical attractiveness effects on preschool teachers' expectations. *Child Study Journal, 8,* 29–41.

Adams, G. R., & Crane, P. (1980). An assessment of parents' and teachers' expectations of preschool children's social preference for attractive or unattractive children and adults. *Child Development, 5,* 224–31.

Addington, D. (1971). The effect of vocal variations on ratings of source credibility. *Speech Monographs, 38,* 242–47.

Akehurst, L. & Vrij, A. (1999). Creating Suspects in Police Interviews. *Journal of Applied Social Psychology, 29*(1), 190–210.

Albert, H. (1968). *Traktat über kritische Vernunft.* Tübingen, Germany: Mohr Siebeck.

Albert, S., & Dabbs, J. (1970). Physical distance and persuasion. *Journal of Personality and Social Psychology, 15,* 265–70.

Albright, L., Malloy, T. E., Dong, Q., Kenny, D. A., Fang, X., Winquist, L., & Yu, D. (1997). Cross-cultural consensus in personality judgments. *Journal of Personality and Social Psychology, 72*(3), 558–69.

Alley, T. R. (1988a). The effects of growth and aging on facial aesthetics. In T. R. Alley (Ed.), *Social and applied aspects of perceiving faces* (pp. 51–62). Hillsdale, NJ: Lawrence Erlbaum Associates.

Alley, T. R. (Ed.). (1988b). *Social and applied aspects of perceiving faces.* Hillsdale, NJ: Lawrence Erlbaum Associates.

Alley, T. R., & Cunningham, M. R. (1991). Averaged faces are attractive, but very attractive faces are not average. *Psychological Science, 2,* 123–25.

Allport, G. W., & Cantril, H. (1934). Judging personality from voice. *Journal of Social Psychology, 5,* 37–55.

Ambady, N., Bernieri, F. J., & Richeson, J. A. (2000). Toward a histology of social behavior: Judgmental accuracy from thin slices of the behavioral stream. In M. P. Zanna (Ed.), *Advances in experimental social psychology* (Vol. 32, pp. 201–71). San Diego: Academic Press.

Ambady, N., Hallahan, M., & Rosenthal, R. (1995). On judging and being judged accurately in zero-acquaintance situations. *Journal of Personality and Social Psychology, 69,* 538–47.

Ambady, N., & Rosenthal, R. (1992). Thin slices of expressive behavior as predictors of interpersonal consequences: A meta-analysis. *Psychological Bulletin, 111,* 256–74.

Ambady, N., & Rosenthal, R. (1993). Half a minute: Predicting teacher evaluations from thin slices of nonverbal behavior and physical attractiveness. *Journal of Personality and Social Psychology, 64*(3), 431–41.

Amyx, D., Bristow, D., & Robb, J. (2009). Source credibility in attorney advertisements. *Services Marketing Quarterly, 30*(4), 377–96.

Anderson, C., Srivastava, S., Beer, J. S., Spataro, S. E., & Chatman, E. (2006). Knowing your place: Self-perceptions of status in face-to-face groups. *Journal of Personality and Social Psychology, 91*(6), 1094–110.

Anderson, L. D. (1921). Estimating intelligence by means of printed photographs. *Journal of Applied Psychology, 5,* 152–55.

Anderson, N. R. (1991). Decision making in the graduate selection interview: An experimental investigation. *Human Relations, 44,* 403–17.

Anderson, U., Kadous, K., & Koonce, L. (2004). The role of incentives to manage earnings and quantification in auditors' evaluations of management-provided evidence. *Auditing: A Journal of Practice & Theory, 23*(1), 11–27.

Andersson, M. (1994). *Sexual selection.* Princeton, NJ: Princeton University Press.

Ansolabehere, S., Snowberg, E. C., & Snyder, J. M. (2006). Television and the incumbency advantage in U.S. elections. *Legislative Studies Quarterly, 31*(4), 469–90.

Apparala, M. L., Reifman, A., & Munsch, J. (2003). Cross-national comparisons of attitudes towards fathers' and mothers' participants in household tasks and childcare. *Sex Roles, 48,* 189–203.

Appelbaum, S., & Hughes, B. (1998). Ingratiation as a political tactic: Effects within the organization. *Management Decision, 36*(2), 85–95.

Argenti, P.A. & Forman, J. (2002). *The Power of Corporate Communication.* New York: McGraw-Hill.

Argyle, M. (1979). *Körpersprache und Kommunikation.* Paderborn, Germany: Junfermann.

Argyle, M., Alkema, F., & Gilmour, R. (1972). The communication of friendly and hostile attitudes by verbal and non-verbal signals. *European Journal of Social Psychology, 1,* 385–402.

Argyle, M., Furnham, A., & Graham, J. A. (1981). *Social situations.* Cambridge: Cambridge University Press.

Argyle, M., Ginsburg, G. P., Forgas, J. P., & Campbell, A. (1981). Personality constructs in relation to situations. In M. Argyle, A. Furnham, & J. A. Graham, *Social situations* (pp. 252–56). Cambridge: Cambridge University Press.

Argyle, M., & McHenry, R. (1971). Do spectacles really affect judgments of intelligence? *British Journal of Social and Clinical Psychology, 10,* 27–29.

Armstrong, J. S. (1980). Unintelligible management research and academic prestige. *Interfaces, 10*(2), 80–86.

Arnould, E. J., & Thompson, C. J. (2005). Culture consumer theory (CCT): Twenty years of research. *Journal of Consumer Research, 31*(3), 868–81.

Aronson, E. (1969). Some antecedents of interpersonal attraction. In W. J. Arnold & D. Levine (Eds.), *Nebraska symposium on motivation* (Vol. 17, pp. 143–73). Lincoln: University of Nebraska Press.

Aronson, E., & Mills, J. (1959). The effect of severity of initiation on liking for a group. *Journal of Abnormal and Social Psychology, 59,* 177–81.

Asch, S. E. (1946). Forming impressions of personality. *Journal of Abnormal and Social Psychology, 41,* 258–90.

Atkins, C. P. (1993). Do employment recruiters discriminate on the basis of nonstandard dialect? *Journal of Employment Counseling, 30*(3), 108–18.

Atkinson, R. C., & Shiffrin, R. M. (1968). Human memory: A proposed system and its control processes. In K. W. Spence & J. T. Spence (Eds.), *The psychology of learning and motivation* (Vol. 2, pp. 89–195). New York: Academic Press.

Augen und Brauen. (n.d.). *Beautycheck.* Retrieved from http://www.beautycheck.de /cmsms/index.php/augen-und-brauen.

Bacharach, S. B., & Lawler, E. J. (Eds.). (1984). *Research in the sociology of organizations.* Greenwich, CT: JAI Press.

Baker, M. J., & Churchill, G. A., Jr. (1977). The impact of physically attractive models on advertising evaluations. *Journal of Marketing Research, 14,* 538–55.

Balkwell, J. W., Berger, J., Webster, M., Nelson-Kilger, M., & Cashen, J. M. (1992). Processing status information: Some tests of competing theoretical arguments. *Advances in Group Processes, 9,* 1–20.

Banducci, S. A., Karp, J. A., Thrasher, M., & Rallings, C. (2008). Ballot photographs as cues in low-information elections. *Political Psychology, 29*(6), 903–17.

Bar, M., Neta, M., & Linz, H. (2006). Very first impressions. *Emotion, 6*(2), 269–78.

Barber, N. (1995). The evolutionary psychology of physical attractiveness: Sexual selection and human morphology. *Ethology and Sociobiology, 16*(5), 395–424.

Bargh, J. A., Chen, M., & Burrows, L. (1996). Automaticity of social behavior: Direct effects of trait construct and stereotype priming on action. *Journal of Personality and Social Psychology, 71,* 230–44.

Barnes, M. L., & Sternberg, R. J. (1989). Social intelligence and judgment policy of nonverbal cues. *Intelligence, 13,* 263–87.

Barocas, R., & Vance, F. L. (1974). Physical appearance and personal adjustment counseling. *Journal of Counseling Psychology, 21,* 96–100.

Barrett, G. (2005, January 17). Halo cars. Retrieved from http://www.waywordradio .org/halo_car/.

Bassili, J. N. (1981). The attractiveness stereotype: Goodness or glamour? *Basic and Applied Social Psychology, 2,* 235–52.

Bata, T. J., & Sinclair, S. (1990). *Bata: Shoemaker to the world.* Toronto: Stoddart.

Bates, S. (2005). *Speak like a CEO: Secrets for commanding attention and getting results.* New York: McGraw-Hill.

Baumeister, R. F. (1982). A self-presentational view of social phenomena. *Psychological Bulletin, 91*(1), 3–26.

Baumeister, R. F. (1998). The self. In D. T. Gilbert, S. T. Fiske, & G. Lindzey (Eds.), *Handbook of social psychology* (Vol. 1, pp. 680–740). New York: McGraw-Hill.

Baumeister, R. F., Smart, L., & Boden, J. M. (1996). Relation of threatened egotism to violence and aggression: The dark side of high self-esteem. *Psychological Review, 103,* 5–33.

Baumeister, R. F., Tice, D. M., & Hutton, D. G. (1989). Self-Presentational Motivations and Personality Differences in Self-Esteem. *Journal of Personality, 57*(3), 547–79.

Bazil, V. (2005). *Impression management: Sprachliche Strategien für Reden und Vorträge.* Wiesbaden: Gabler.

Beckwith, H. (1997). *Selling the invisible: A field guide to modern marketing.* New York: Warner Books.

Behling, D. U., & Williams, E. A. (1991). Influence of dress on perception of intelligence and expectations of scholastic achievement. *Clothing and Textiles Research Journal, 9,* 1–7.

Bellezza, S., Gino, F., & Keinan, A. (2014). The red sneakers effect: Inferring status and competence from signals of nonconformity. *Journal of Consumer Research, 41*(1), 35–54.

Bem, D. J. (1972). Self-perception theory. In L. Berkowitz (Ed.), *Advances in experimental social psychology* (Vol. 6, pp. 1–62). New York: Academic Press.

Benson, P. L., Karabenick, S. A., & Lerner, R. M. (1976). Pretty pleases: The effects of physical attractiveness, race, and sex on receiving help. *Journal of Experimental Social Psychology, 12,* 409–15.

Berger, C. R., & Bradac, J. (1982). *Language and social knowledge: Uncertainty in interpersonal relations.* London: Arnold.

Berger, C. R., Gardner, R. R., Parks, M. R., Schulman, L., & Miller, G. R. (1976). Interpersonal epistemology and interpersonal communication. In G. R. Miller (Ed.), *Explorations in interpersonal communication* (pp. 149–72). Beverly Hills: Sage.

Berger, J., Fisek, M. H., Norman, R. Z., & Zelditch, M. (1977). *Status characteristics and social interaction: An expectation-states approach.* New York: Elsevier.

Berger, J., Norman, R. Z., Balkwell, J. W., & Smith, R. F. (1992). Status inconsistency in task situations: A test of four status processing principles. *American Sociological Review, 57,* 843–55.

Berger, J., & Ward, M. (2010). Subtle signals of in-conspicuous consumption. *Journal of Consumer Research, 37*(4), 555–69.

Berggren, N., Jordahl, H., & Poutvaara, P. (2010). The looks of a winner: Beauty, gender, and electoral success. *Journal of Public Economics, 94*(1–2), 8–15.

Berkowitz, L. (Ed.). (1965). *Advances in experimental social psychology* (Vol. 2). New York: Academic Press.

Berkowitz, L. (Ed.). (1972). *Advances in experimental social psychology* (Vol. 6). New York: Academic Press.

Berkowitz, L. (Ed.). (1978). *Advances in experimental social psychology* (Vol. 11). New York: Academic Press.

Berkowitz, L. (Ed.). (1980). *Advances in experimental social psychology* (Vol. 13). Orlando: Academic Press.

Berry, D. S., & Brownlow, S. (1989). Were the physiognomists right? Personality correlates of facial babyishness. *Personality and Social Psychology Bulletin, 15,* 266–79.

Berry, D. S., & McArthur, L. Z. (1985). Some components and consequences of a babyface. *Journal of Personality and Social Psychology, 48,* 312–23.

Berscheid, E., & Walster, E. (1972). Beauty and the best. *Psychology Today, 5,* 42–46.

Bierhoff, H.-W. (1989). *Person perception and attribution.* Berlin: Springer.

Birdsell, D. (1998). *Presentation graphics.* New York: McGraw-Hill. Retrieved from http://www.mhhe.com/socscience/comm/luccas/student/birdsetl/birdselll2.html.

Birdwhistell, R. L. (1952). *Introduction to kinesics.* Louisville: University of Kentucky Press.

Birdwhistell, R. L. (1970). *Kinesics and context: Essays on body motion communication.* Philadelphia: University of Pennsylvania Press.

Birnbaum, M. H., & Stegner, S. E. (1979). Source credibility in social judgment: Bias, expertise, and the judge's point of view. *Journal of Personality and Social Psychology, 37*(1), 48–74.

Blaker, N. M., Rompa, I., Dessing, I. H., Vriend, A. F., Herschberg, C., & Van Vugt, M. (2013). The height leadership advantage in men and women: Testing evolutionary psychology predictions about the perceptions of tall leaders. *Group Processes and Intergroup Relations, 16*(1), 17–27.

Bolino, M. C., Varela, J. A., Bande, B., & Turnley, W. H. (2006). The impact of impression-management tactics on supervisor ratings of organizational citizenship behavior. *Journal of Organizational Behavior, 27,* 281–97.

Booher, D. (2011). *Creating personal presence: Look, talk, think, and act like a leader.* San Francisco: Berrett-Koehler.

Borkenau, P., & Liebler, A. (1995). Observable attributes as manifestations and cues of personality and intelligence. *Journal of Personality, 63,* 1–25.

Bottger, P. (1984). Expertise and air time as bases of actual and perceived influence in problem-solving groups. *Journal of Applied Psychology, 69,* 214–21.

Bourdieu, P. (1982). Der Sozialraum und seine Transformationen. In P. Bordieu, *Die feinen Unterschiede: Kritik der gesellschaftlichen Urteilskraft* (pp. 171–210). Frankfurt am Main, Germany: Suhrkamp.

Bowman, J. S. (1992). Dress standards in government: A national survey of state administrators. *Review of Public Personnel Administration, 12,* 35–51.

Bradac, J. J., Hemphill, M. R., & Tardy, C. H. (1981). Language style on trial: Effects of powerful and powerless speech upon judgments of victims and villains. *Western Journal of Speech Communication, 45,* 327–41.

Bradac, J. J., & Mulac, A. (1984). Attributional consequences of powerful and powerless speech styles in a crisis-intervention context. *Journal of Language and Social Psychology, 3,* 1–19.

Braun, C., Gründl, M., Marberger, C., & Scherber, C. (2001). Beautycheck: Ursachen und Folgen von Attraktivität. Projektabschlussbericht. Retrieved from http://www.beautycheck.de/cmsms/index.php/der-ganze-bericht.

Brehm, J. W. (1968). Attitude change from threat to attitudinal freedom. In A. G. Greenwald, T. C. Brock, & J. M. Ostrom (Eds.), *Psychological foundations of attitudes* (pp. 277–96). New York: Academic Press.

Brehm, J. W. (1978). *A theory of psychological reactance.* New York: Academic Press.

Brescoll, V., & Uhlmann, E. (2008). Can an angry woman get ahead? Status conferral, gender, and expression of emotion in the workplace. *Psychological Science, 19,* 268–75.

Brewer, G., & Archer, J. (2007). What do people infer from facial attractiveness? *Journal of Evolutionary Psychology, 5*(1–4), 39–49.

Brewer, M. B. (1979). In-group bias in the minimal group situation: A cognitive-motivational analysis. *Psychological Bulletin, 86*, 307–24.

Brewer, M. B. (1997). On the social origins of human nature. In C. McGarty & S. A. Haslam (Eds.), *The message of social psychology: Perspectives on mind in society* (pp. 54–62). Cambridge, MA: Blackwell.

Brewer, M. B. (1999). The psychology of prejudice: Ingroup love or outgroup hate? *Journal of Social Issues, 55*, 429–44.

Bromley, D. B. (1993). *Reputation, image and impression management.* Chichester, UK: John Wiley & Sons.

Brooks, J. (1981). *Showing off in America: From conspicuous consumption to parody display.* Boston: Little, Brown.

Brown, B. (1969). The social psychology of variations in French Canadian speech. *Dissertation Abstracts International: Section B. Sciences and Engineering, 30*, 3093B.

Brown, B. L., Strong, W. J., & Rencher, A. C. (1975). Accoustic determinants of perceptions of personality from speech. *International Journal of Sociology of Language, 6*, 11–32.

Brown, S. (2001). Torment your customers (they'll love it). *Harvard Business Review, 79*(9). Retrieved from https://hbr.org/2001/10/torment-your-customers-theyll-love-it.

Buckalew, L. W., & Ross, S. (1981). Relationship of perceptual characteristics to efficacy of placebos. *Psychological Reports, 49*(3), 955–61.

Budesheim, T. L., & DePaola, S. J. (1994). Beauty or the beast? The effects of appearance, personality, and issue information on evaluations of political candidates. *Personality and Social Psychology Bulletin, 20*, 339–48.

Budge, H. S. (1981). *Dimensions of physical attractiveness: How others see us* (Unpublished doctoral dissertation). University of Utah, Salt Lake City.

Bugental, D. E., Kaswan, J. W., & Love, L. R. (1970). Perception of contradictory meanings conveyed by verbal and nonverbal channels. *Journal of Personality and Social Psychology, 16*, 647–55.

Bunderson, J. S. (2003). Recognizing and utilizing expertise in work groups: A status characteristics perspective. *Administrative Science Quarterly, 48*, 557–91.

Buss, D. M. (1989). Sex differences in human mate preferences: Evolutionary hypotheses tested in 37 cultures. *Behavioural and Brain Sciences, 12*, 1–49.

Buss, D. M. (2000). The evolution of happiness. *American Psychologist, 55*, 15–23.

Byrne, D. (1971). *The attraction paradigm.* New York: Academic Press.

Byrne, D., & Clore, G. L. (1970). A reinforcement model of evaluative responses. *Personality: An International Journal, 1*, 103–28.

Byrne, D., London, C., & Reeves, K. (1968). The effects of physical attractiveness, sex, and attitude similarity on interpersonal attraction. *Journal of Personality, 36*, 259–71.

Campbell, Joseph (1949). *The Hero with a Thousand Faces.* Princeton, NJ: Princeton University Press.

Cargile, A. C. (2000). Evaluations of employment suitability: Does accent always matter? *Journal of Employment Counseling, 37*(3), 165–77.

Carnegie, D. (1936/2001). *How to win friends and influence people.* New York: Simon & Schuster.

Carney, D. R., Cuddy, A. J. C., & Yap, A. J. (2010). Power Posing: Brief Nonverbal Displays Affect Neuroendocrine Levels and Risk Tolerance. *Psychological Science, 21*, 1363–68.

Cartwright, D. (1959a). A field theoretical conception of power. In D. Cartwright (Ed.), *Studies in social power* (pp. 86–103). Ann Arbor: University of Michigan Press.

Cartwright, D. (Ed.). (1959b). *Studies in social power.* Ann Arbor: University of Michigan Press.

Carver, C. S., Lawrence, J. W., & Scheier, M. F. (1999). Self-discrepancies and affect: Incorporating the role of feared selves. *Personality and Social Psychological Bulletin, 25,* 783–92.

Castiglione, B. (1999). *Der Hofmann: Lebensart in der Renaissance.* Berlin: Wagenbach.

Cavior, N. (1970). *Physical attractiveness, perceived attitude similarity, and interpersonal attraction among fifth and eleventh grade boys and girls* (Unpublished doctoral dissertation). University of Houston.

Chabris, C., & Simons, D. (2009). *The invisible gorilla and other ways our intuitions deceive us.* New York: Crown.

Chaikin, A. L., Gillen, B., Derlega, V. J., Heinen, J. R. K., & Wilson, M. (1978). Students' reactions to teachers' physical attractiveness and nonverbal behavior: Two exploratory studies. *Psychology in Schools, 15,* 588–95.

Chaiken, S. (1979). Communicator physical attractiveness and persuasion. *Journal of Personality and Social Psychology, 37,* 1387–97.

Chandon, P., & Wansink, B. (2007). The biasing health halos of fast-food restaurant health claims: Lower calorie estimate and higher side-dish consumption intentions. *Journal of Consumer Research, 34*(3), 301–14.

Chartrand, T. L. & Bargh, J. A. (1999). The chameleon effect: The perception-behavior link and social interaction. *Journal of Personality and Social Psychology, 76*(6), 893–910.

Cheetham, G., & Chivers, G. (1996). Towards a holistic model of professional competence. *Journal of European Industrial Training, 20,* 20–30.

Chen, H. H. (2007). Tattoo survey results: Vault explains it all for you. Retrieved from http://www.vault.com/nr/main_article_detail.jsp?article_id=5319842&ht_type=5.

Cialdini, R. B. (1993). *Influence: The psychology of persuasion.* New York: William Morrow.

Cialdini, R. B., Borden, R. J., Thorne, A., Walker, M. R., Freeman, S., & Sloan, L. R. (1976). Basking in reflected glory: Three (football) field studies. *Journal of Personality and Social Psychology, 34,* 366–74.

Cialdini, R. B., Cacioppo, J. T., Bassett, R., & Miller, J. A. (1978). Low-ball procedure for producing compliance: Commitment then cost. *Journal of Personality and Social Psychology 36*(5), 463–76.

Cialdini, R. B., & de Nicholas, M. E. (1989). Self-presentation by association. *Journal of Personality and Social Psychology, 57,* 626–31.

Cialdini, R. B., & Goldstein, N. J. (2004). Social influence: Compliance and conformity. *Annual Review of Psychology, 55*(1974), 591–621.

Cialdini, R. B., & Richardson, K. D. (1980). Two indirect tactics of image management: Basking and blasting. *Journal of Personality and Social Psychology, 39,* 406–15.

Clance, P. R., & Imes, S. A. (1978). The imposter phenomenon in high achieving women: Dynamics and therapeutic intervention. *Psychotherapy: Theory, Research and Practice, 15*(3), 241–47.

Clark, M. S., Pataki, S. P., & Carver, V. H. (1996). Some thoughts and findings on self-presentation of emotions in relationships. In G. J. O. Fletcher & J. Fitness (Eds.),

Knowledge structures in close relationships: A social psychological approach (pp. 247–74). Mahwah, NJ: Lawrence Erlbaum Associates.

Clark, T., & Salaman, G. (1998). Telling tales: Management gurus' narratives and the construction of managerial identity. *Journal of Management Studies, 35*(2), 85–107.

Coates, J. (Ed.). (1998). *Language and gender: A reader.* Oxford: Blackwell.

Collins, J. (2001). *Good to great: Why some companies make the leap . . . and others don't.* New York: HarperCollins.

Colvin, C. R., & Bundick, M. S. (2001). In search of the good judge of personality: Some methodological and theoretical concerns. In J. A. Hall & F. J. Bernieri (Eds.), *Interpersonal sensitivity: Theory and measurement* (pp. 47–65). Mahwah, NJ: Lawrence Erlbaum Associates.

Condon, J. C., Jr. (1977). *Interpersonal communication.* New York: Macmillan.

Connolly-Ahern, C., & Broadway, S. C. (2007). The importance of appearing competent: An analysis of corporate impression management strategies on the World Wide Web. *Public Relations Review, 33*(3), 343–45.

Cook, W. C. (1939). The judgment of intelligence from photographs. *Journal of Abnormal and Social Psychology, 34,* 384–89.

Coombs, R. H., & Kenkel, W. F. (1966). Sex differences in dating aspirations and satisfaction with computer-selected partners. *Journal of Marriage and the Family, 28,* 62–66.

Cornelissen, J. (2014). *Corporate Communicaton. A Guide to Theory & Practice.* London: Sage.

Cozby, P. C. (1973). Self-disclosure: A literature review. *Psychological Bulletin, 79,* 73–91.

Cravens, K., Oliver, E. G., & Ramamoorti, S. (2003). The reputation index: Measuring and managing corporate reputation. *European Management Journal, 21,* 201–12.

Cross, J. F., & Cross, J. (1971). Age, sex, race, and the perception of facial beauty. *Developmental Psychology, 5,* 433–39.

Crusco, A. H. & Wetzel, C. G. (1984). The Midas Touch. *Personality and Social Psychology Bulletin, 10*(4), 512–17.

Cuddy, A. J. C, Fiske, S. T., Glick, P (2007). The BIAS Map: Behaviors from Intergroup Affect and Stereotypes. *Journal of Personality and Social Psychology, 92,* 527–41.

Culbert, S. A. (1968). Trainer self-disclosure and member growth in T-groups. *Journal of Applied Behavioral Science, 4,* 47–73.

Cunningham, M. R., Barbee, A. P., Druen, P. B., Roberts, A. R., & Wu, C.-H. (1995). Their ideas of beauty are, on the whole, the same as ours: Consistency and variability in the cross-cultural perception of female physical attractiveness. *Journal of Personality and Social Psychology, 68,* 261–79.

Cunningham, M. R., Barbee, A. P., & Pike, C. L. (1990). What do women want? Facialmetric assessment of multiple motives in the perception of male facial physical attractiveness. *Journal of Personality and Social Psychology, 59,* 61–72.

Cutler, B. L., Dexter, H. R., Penrod, S. D. (1990). Nonadversarial methods for sensitizing jurors to eyewitness evidence. *Journal of Applied Social Psychology, 20*(13–14), 1197.

Cutler, B. L., Penrod, S. D., Stuve, T. E., Roesch, R. (1988). Juror Decision Making in Eyewitness Identification Cases. *Law and Human Behavior, 12*(1), 41–55.

Darby, B. W., & Schlenker, B. R. (1982). Children's reaction to apologies. *Journal of Personality and Social Psychology, 8,* 377–83.

Darley, J. M., & Goethals, J. R. (1980). People's analysis of the causes of ability-linked performances. In L. Berkowitz (Ed.), *Advances in experimental social psychology* (Vol. 13, pp. 2–37). Orlando: Academic Press.

Das, T. K., & Teng, B.-S. (2001). Trust, control and risk in strategic alliances: An integrated framework. *Organization Studies, 22*(2), 251–83.

Davis, F. (1971). *Inside intuition.* New York: Signet Books.

Davis Polk & Wardwell. (2004). Report of Davis Polk & Wardwell to the Shell Group Audit Committee. Retrieved from: http://www.shellnews.net/classactiondocs/Binder1_405-6_OCR.PDF.

Deck, L. P. (1968). Buying brains by the inch. *Journal of the College and University Personnel Association, 19,* 33–37.

De Craen, A. J. M., Roos, P. J., de Vries, A. L., & Kleijnen, J. (1996). Effect of colour of drugs: Systematic review of perceived effect of drugs and of their effectiveness. *British Medical Journal, 313*(7072), 1624–26.

Delamater, R. J., & McNamara, J. R. (1987). Expression of anger: Its relationship to assertion and social desirability among college women. *Psychological Reports, 61*(1), 131–34.

DePaolo, B. M., & Friedman, H. S. (1998). *Nonverbal Communication.* New York: McGraw-Hill.

De Rivera, J. (1977). *A structural theory of the emotions.* New York: International Universities Press.

Deussen, P. (Ed.). (1913). *Arthur Schopenhauers sämtliche Werke* (Vol. 4). Munich: Piper.

Deutsch, F. M., Clark, M. E., & Zalenski, C. M. (1983). Is there a double standard of aging? In T. R. Alley (Ed.), *Social and applied aspects of perceiving faces* (pp. 36–89). Hillsdale, NJ: Lawrence Erlbaum Associates.

Deutsch, F. M., Zalenski, C. M., & Clark, M. E. (1986). Is there a double standard of aging? *Journal of Applied Social Psychology, 16,* 771–85.

Diekman, A. B., & Eagly, A. H. (2000). Stereotypes as dynamic constructs: Women and men of the past, present, and future. *Personality and Social Psychology Bulletin, 26,* 1171–88.

Dijksterhuis, A., & van Knippenberg, A. (1998). The relation between perception and behavior, or how to win a game of Trivial Pursuit. *Journal of Personality and Social Psychology, 74*(4), 865–77.

Dimberg, U., Thunberg, M., & Grunedal, S. (2002). Facial reactions to emotional stimuli: Automatically controlled emotional responses. *Cognition and Emotion, 16*(4), 449–71.

Dion, K., Berscheid, E., & Walster, E. (1972). What is beautiful is good. *Journal of Personality and Social Psychology, 24*(3), 285–90.

Dipboye, R. L. (1989). Threats to the incremental validity of interviewer judgments. In R. W. Eder & G. R. Ferris (Eds.), *The employment interview: Theory, research, and practice* (pp. 45–60). Newbury Park, CA: Sage.

Dixon, J. A., & Mahoney, B. (2004). The effect of accent evaluation and evidence on a suspect's perceived guilt and criminality. *Journal of Social Psychology, 144*(1), 63–73.

Dobelli, R. (2011). *Die Kunst des klaren Denkens*. Freiburg, Germany: Herder.

Doob, A. N., & Gross, A. E. (1968). Status of frustrator as an inhibitor of horn-honking responses. *Journal of Social Psychology, 76*, 213–18.

Dovidio, J. F., & Ellyson, S. L. (1982). Decoding visual dominance: Attributions of power based on relative percentages of looking while speaking and looking while listening. *Social Psychology Quarterly, 45*, 106–13.

Drachman, D., Carufel, A. de, & Inkso, C. A. (1978). The extra credit effect in interpersonal attraction. *Journal of Experimental Social Psychology, 14*, 458–67.

Drory, A., & Zaidman, N. (1986). Impression management behavior: Effects of the organizational system. *Journal of Managerial Psychology, 22*(3), 290–308.

Durante, F., Capozza, D., & Fiske, S. T. (2010). The stereotype content model: The role played by competence in inferring group status. *Testing, Psychometrics, Methodology in Applied Psychology, 17*, 1–13.

Durante, J., & Volpato, S. (2012). Primacy of warmth versus competence: A motivated bias? *Journal of Social Psychology, 152*(4), 417–35.

Dutton, D. G., & Aron, A. P. (1974). Some evidence for heightened sexual attraction under conditions of high anxiety. *Journal of Personality and Social Psychology, 30*, 510–17.

Eagly, A. H., & Acksen, B. A. (1971). The effect of expecting to be evaluated on change toward favorable and unfavorable information about oneself. *Sociometry, 34*, 411–22.

Eagly, A. H., Ashmore, R. D., Makhijani, M. G., & Longo, L. C. (1991). What is beautiful is good, but . . . : A meta-analytic review of research on the physical attractiveness stereotype. *Psychological Bulletin, 110*(1), 109–28.

Eagly, A. H., & Blair, T. J. (1990). Gender and leadership style: A meta-analysis. *Psychological Bulletin, 108*, 233–56.

Eastman, K. (1994). In the eyes of the beholder: An attributional approach to ingratiation and organizational behavior. *Academy of Management Journal, 37*(5), 1379–91.

Eckes, T. (2002). Paternalistic and envious gender stereotypes: testing predictions from the stereotype content model. *A Journal of Research, 99*(16).

Eder, R. W., & Ferris, G. R. (Eds.). (1989). *The employment interview: Theory, research, and practice*. Newbury Park, CA: Sage.

Efran, M. G. (1974). The effect of physical appearance on the judgment of guilt, interpersonal attraction, and severity of recommended punishment in a simulated jury task. *Journal of Research in Personality, 8*, 45–54.

Efran, M. G., & Patterson, E. W. J. (1974). Voters vote beautiful: The effect of physical appearance on a national election. *Canadian Journal of Behavioural Science/Revue Canadienne des Sciences du Comportement 6*(4), 352–56.

Efron, D. (1941). *Gesture and environment*. New York: King's Crown.

Eibl-Eibesfeldt, I. (1997). *Die Biologie des menschlichen Verhaltens: Grundriß der Humanethologie*. Weyarn, Germany: Seehamer.

Ekman, P. (2001). *Telling lies: Clues to deceit in the marketplace, politics, and marriage*. New York: W. W. Norton.

Ekman, P., & Friesen, W. V. (1969). The repertoire of nonverbal behavior: Categories, origins, usage, and coding. *Semiotica, 1*, 49–98.

Ekman, P., Levenson, R. W., & Friesen, W. (1983). Autonomic nervous system activity distinguishes among emotions. *Science, 221*(4616), 1208–10.

Ellis, A. P., West, B. J., Ryan, A. M., & DeShon, R. P. (2002). The use of impression management tactics in structured interviews: A function of question type. *Journal of Applied Psychology, 87*, 1200–1208.

Ellis, D. S. (1967). Speech and social status in America. *Social Forces, 45*(3), 431–37.

Ellis, J. B., & Wittenbaum, G. M. (2000). Relationships between self-construal and verbal promotion. *Communication Research, 27*, 704–22.

Empson, L. (Ed.). (2007). *Managing the modern law firm.* Oxford: Oxford University Press.

England, P., & McClintock, E. A. (2009). The gendered double standard of aging in U.S. marriage markets. *Population and Development Review, 35*, 797–816.

Enlow, D. H. (1989). *Handbuch des Gesichtswachstums.* Berlin: Quintessenz.

Ericsson, A. K., Prietula, M. J., & Cokely, E. T. (2007). The making of an expert. *Harvard Business Review, 7.* Retrieved from https://hbr.org/2007/07/the-making-of-an-expert.

Etzioni, A. (2004). The post affluent society. *Review of Social Economy, 62*(3), 407–20.

Evans, H. (2004). *They made America: Two centuries of innovators from the steam engine to the search engine.* New York: Little, Brown.

Evans, R. (1971). *Richard Evans' quote book.* Salt Lake City: Publisher's Press.

Exline, R. V. (1963). Explorations in the process of person perception: Visual interaction in relation to competition, sex, and the need for affiliation. *Journal of Personality and Social Psychology, 31*, 1–20.

Exline, R. V., Gray, D., & Schuette, D. (1965). Visual behavior in a dyad as affected by interview content and sex of respondent. *Journal of Personality and Social Psychology, 1*, 201–09.

Exline, R. V., & Winters, L. C. (1965). Affective relations and mutual glances in dyads. In S. Tomkins & C. Izard (Eds.), *Affect cognition and personality* (pp. 319–30). New York: Springer.

Eysenck, H. J., & Nias, D. K. B. (1988). *Astrology: Science or superstition?* London: Pelican.

Falser, G., Bendel, M., Voller, D., & Wegner, A. (2008). Women's attractiveness depends more on their age than men's: New evidence for a double standard of aging. *International Journal of Psychology, 43*(3–4), 76.

Fan, J. T., Dai, W., Liu, F., & Wu, J. (2005). Visual perception of male body attractiveness. *Proceedings of the Royal Society B, 272*, 219–26.

Fanelli, A., & Misangyi, V. F. (2006). Bringing out charisma: CEO charisma and external stakeholders. *Academy of Management Review, 31*, 1049–61.

Farkas, L. G., & Cheung, G. (1981). Facial asymmetry in healthy North American Caucasians: An anthropometrical study. *Angle Orthodontist, 51*, 70–77.

Fast, N., & Chen, S. (2009). When the boss feels inadequate: Power, incompetence, and aggression. *Psychological Science, 20*(11), 1406–13.

Feingold, A. (1992). Good looking people are not what we think. *Psychological Bulletin, 111*, 304–41.

Feinman, S., & Gill, G. W. (1977). Females' response to males' beardedness. *Perceptual and Motor Skills, 44*, 533–34.

Feldman, S. D. (1971). *The presentation of shortness in everyday life: Height and heightism in American society: Toward a sociology of stature.* Paper presented at the meeting of the American Sociological Association, Denver.

Felson, R. B. (1981). An interactionist approach to aggression. In J. T. Tedeschi (Ed.), *Impression management theory and social psychological research* (pp. 181–99). New York: Academic Press.

Felton, J., Koper, P. T., Mitchell, J., & Stinson, M. (2008). Attractiveness, easiness and other issues: Student evaluations of professors on Ratemyprofessors.com. *Assessment & Evaluation in Higher Education, 33,* 45–61.

Feltovich, N., Harbaugh, R., & To, T. (2002). Too cool for school? Signaling and countersignaling. *RAND Journal of Economics, 4*(33), 630–49.

Fernández, J. A., & Underwood, L. (2006). *China CEO: voices of experience from 20 international business leaders.* Singapore: Wiley & Sons.

Ferris, G. R., & Judge, T. A. (1991). Personnel/human resources management: A political influence perspective. *Journal of Management, 17,* 447–88.

Ferris, G. R., Judge, T. A., Rowland, K. M., & Fitzgibbons, D. E. (1994). Subordinate influence and the performance evaluation process: Test of a model. *Organizational Behavior and Human Decision Processes, 58,* 101–35.

Fischer, A. H. (Ed.). (2001). *Gender and emotion: Social psychological perspectives.* New York: Cambridge University Press.

Fiser, I., & Fiserova, O. (1969). Beauty and cosmetics in ancient India. *New Orient, 5,* 92–94.

Fiske, S. T. (1998). Stereotyping, prejudice, and discrimination. In D. T. Gilbert & G. Lindzey (Eds.), *The handbook of social psychology* (4th ed., Vols. 1 and 2, pp. 357–411). New York: McGraw-Hill.

Fiske, S. T., & Cox, M. G. (1979). Person concepts: The effect of target familiarity and descriptive purpose on the process of describing others. *Journal of Personality, 47,* 136–61.

Fiske, S. T., Cuddy, A. J. C., & Glick, P. (2007). Universal dimensions of social perception: Warmth and competence. *Trends in Cognitive Sciences, 11,* 77–83.

Fiske, S. T., Cuddy, A. J. C., Glick, P., & Xu, J. (2002). A model of (often mixed) stereotype content: Competence and warmth respectively follow from perceived status and competition. *Journal of Personality and Social Psychology, 82*(6), 878–902.

Fiske, S. T., & Taylor, S. E. (1991). *Social cognition.* New York: McGraw-Hill.

Fiske, S. T., Xu, J., Cuddy, A. J. C., & Glick, P. (1999). (Dis)respecting versus (dis)liking: Status and interdependence predict ambivalent stereotypes of competence and warmth. *Journal of Social Issues, 55,* 473–89.

Fletcher, G. J. O., & Fitness, J. (Eds.). (1996). *Knowledge structures in close relationships: A social psychological approach.* Mahwah, NJ: Lawrence Erlbaum Associates.

Foddy, M. (1988). Paths of relevance and evaluative competence. In M. Foschi (Ed.), *Status generalization: New theory and research* (pp. 232–47). Stanford, CA: Stanford University Press.

Foddy, M., & Riches, P. (2000). The impact of task and categorical cues on social influence: Fluency and ethnic accent as cues to competence in task groups. *Advances in Group Processes, 17,* 103–30.

Forgas, J. P. (1976). An unobtrusive study of reactions to national stereotypes in four European countries. *Journal of Social Psychology, 99,* 37–42.

Forgas, J. P. (1999). *Soziale Interaktion und Kommunikation: Eine Einführung in die Sozialpsychologie.* Weinheim, Germany: Beltz.

Foschi, M. (Ed.). (1988). *Status generalization: New theory and research.* Stanford, CA: Stanford University Press.

Foster, J. (2013, February 12). Why narcissism leads to success. Retrieved from http://wallstreetinsanity.com/why-narcissism-leads-to-success/.

Frank, J. D. (1961). *Persuasion and healing*. Baltimore: Johns Hopkins University Press.

Freese, J. & Meland, S. (2002). Seven tenths incorrect: Heterogeneity and change in the waist-to-hip ratios of Playboy centerfold models and Miss America Pageant winners. *Journal of Sex Research, 39*(2), 133–38.

Frieze, I. H., Olson, J. E., & Russell, J. (1991). Attractiveness and income for men and women in management. *Journal of Applied Social Psychology, 21,* 1039–57.

Fuertes, J. N., Potere, J. C., & Ramirez, K. Y. (2002). Effects of speech accents on interpersonal evaluations: Implications for counseling practice and research. *Cultural Diversity and Ethnic Minority Psychology, 8*(4), 346–56.

Furnham, A., & Nordling, R. (1998). Cross-cultural differences in preferences for specific male and female body shapes. *Personality and Individual Differences, 25,* 635–48.

Furnham, A., & Radley, S. (1989). Sex differences in the perception of male and female body shapes. *Personality and Individual Differences, 10*(6), 653–62.

Furnham, A., Tan, T., & McManus, C. (1997). Waist-to-hip ratio and preferences for body shape: A replication and extension. *Personality and Individual Differences, 22,* 539–49.

Gaines-Ross, L. (2000). CEO reputation: A key factor in shareholder value. *Corporate Reputation Review, 3,* 366–70.

Galinsky, A. D., Magee, J. C., Gruenfeld, D. H., Whitson, J., & Liljenquist, K. (2008). Power reduces the press of the situation: Implications for creativity, conformity, and dissonance. *Journal of Personality and Social Psychology, 95*(6), 1450–66.

Galton, F. (1878). Composite portraits. *Journal of the Anthropological Institute of Great Britain & Ireland, 8,* 132–44.

Galton, F. (1888). Personal identification and description. *Proceedings of the Royal Institution of Great Britain, 12,* 346–60.

Gambetta, D. (Ed.). (1988). *Trust: Making and breaking organizations*. New York: Basil Blackwell.

Gaskill, P. C., Fenton, N., & Porter, J. P. (1927). Judging the intelligence of boys from their photographs. *Journal of Applied Psychology, 11,* 394–403.

Gerard, H. B., & Mathewson, G. C. (1966). The effects of severity of initiation on liking for a group: A replication. *Journal of Experimental Social Psychology, 2*(3), 278–87.

Giesen, C. B. (1989). Aging and attractiveness: Marriage makes a difference. *International Journal of Aging & Human Development, 29,* 83–94.

Gilbert, D. T., & Lindzey, G. (Eds.). (1998). *The handbook of social psychology* (4th ed.). New York: McGraw-Hill.

Gilbert, S., & Horenstein, D. (1975). The Communication of Self-Disclosure: Level versus Valence. *Human Communication Research, 1*(4), 316.

Gilbert, S. J. (1976). Empirical and theoretical extensions of self-disclosure. In G. R. Miller (Ed.), *Explorations in interpersonal communication* (pp. 197–216). Beverly Hills: Sage.

Giles, H. (1970). Evaluative reactions to accents. *Educational Review, 22,* 211–27.

Giles, H. (1971). Patterns of evaluation to RP: South Welsh and Somerset accented speech. *British Journal of Social and Clinical Psychology, 10*(3), 280–81.

Giles, H. (1973). Communicative effectiveness as a function of accented speech. *Speech Monographs, 40,* 330–31.

Giles, H., & Coupland, N. (1991). *Language: Contexts and consequences.* Milton Keynes, UK: Open University Press.

Giles, H., & Johnson, P. (1981). The role of language in ethnic group relations. In J. C. Turner & H. Giles (Eds.), *Intergroup behavior* (pp. 199–243). Oxford: Blackwell.

Giles, H., & Johnson, P. (1987). Ethnolinguistic identity theory: A social psychological approach to language maintenance. *International Journal of the Sociology of Language, 68,* 69–99.

Giles, H., & Powesland, P. F. (1975). *Speech style and social evaluation.* London: Academic Press.

Giles, H., & St. Clair, R. (Eds.). (1979). *Language and social psychology.* Vol. 1 in P. von Trudgill (Series Ed.), *Language in Society.* Baltimore: University Park Press.

Girard, J. (1977). *How to sell anything to anybody.* New York: Simon & Schuster.

Gladwell, M. (2007). *Blink: The power of thinking without thinking.* New York: Back Bay Books.

Glanzer, M., & Cunitz, A. R. (1966). Two storage mechanisms in free recall. *Journal of Verbal Learning and Verbal Behaviour, 5,* 351–60.

Glick, P., Larsen, S., Johnson, C., & Branstiter, H. (2005). Evaluations of sexy women in low- and high-status jobs. *Psychology of Women Quarterly, 29,* 389–95.

Gluszek, A., & Dovidio, J. F. (2010). The way they speak: A social psychological perspective on the stigma of nonnative accents in communication. *Personality and Social Psychology Review, 14*(2), 214–37.

Godfrey, D. K., Jones, E. E., & Lord, C. G. (1986). Self-promotion is not ingratiating. *Journal of Personality and Social Psychology, 50,* 106–15.

Goebel, B. L., & Cashen, V. M. (1979). Age, sex, and attractiveness as factors in student ratings of teachers: A developmental study. *Journal of Educational Psychology, 71,* 646–53.

Goeudevert, D. (1996). *Wie ein Vogel im Aquarium.* Berlin: Rowohlt.

Goffman, E. (1959). *The presentation of self in everyday life.* Garden City, NY: Doubleday.

Golde, R. (1969). *Can you be sure of your experts? A complete manual on how to choose and use doctors, lawyers, brokers, and all the other experts in your life.* New York: Macmillan.

Gordon, R. A. (1996). Impact of ingratiation on judgments and evaluations: A meta-analytic investigation. *Journal of Personality and Social Psychology, 71,* 54–70.

Gottschalk, L. A., & Auerbach, A. H. (Eds.). (1966). *Methods of research in psychotherapy.* New York: Appleton-Century-Crofts.

Gouldner, A. W. (1960). The norm of reciprocity: A preliminary statement. *American Sociological Review, 25,* 1976–77.

Grammer, K. (2000). *Signale der Liebe: Die biologischen Gesetze der Partnerschaft.* Munich: dtv.

Grammer, K., & Thornhill, R. (1994). Human (homo sapiens) facial attractiveness and sexual selection: The role of symmetry and averageness. *Journal of Comparative Psychology, 108,* 233–42.

Grant, A. (2014). Seven sneaky tactics that sway: Beware of flattery and ingratiation in disguise. *Psychology Today, 47*(2), 43–44.

Greenwald, A. G., Brock. T. C., & Ostrom, J. M. (Eds.). (1968). *Psychological foundations of attitudes.* New York: Academic Press.

Gross, D. (1996). *Forbes greatest business stories of all time.* New York: John Wiley & Sons.

Grout, J., & Perrin, S. (2006). *Mind games: Inspirational lessons from the world's finest sports stars.* London: Capstone.

Gründl, M. (n.d.a.). Ergebnisse zur Schönheit der Figur. *Beautycheck.* Retrieved from http://www.beautycheck.de/cmsms/index.php/ergebnisse-zur-figur.

Gründl, M. (n.d.b.). Formel für die Figur—Hintergrund, *Beautycheck.* Retrieved from http://www.beautycheck.de/cmsms/index.php/formel-fuer-die-figur—hintergrund.

Gründl, M. (n.d.c.). Kindchenschema, *Beautycheck.* Retrieved from http://www.beautycheck.de/cmsms/index.php/kindchenschema.

Gründl, M. (2013). *Determinanten physischer Attraktivität: Der Einfluss von Durchschnittlichkeit, Symmetrie und sexuellem Dimorphismus auf die Attraktivität von Gesichtern* (Unpublished dissertation). University of Regensburg, Germany.

Gründl, M., Braun, C., & Marberger, C. (2003). Das Geheimnis der Schönheit. Retrieved from http://www.stmwfk.bayern.de/downloads/aviso/2003_1aviso08–19.pdf.

Gueguen, N., Coyle, T., Craig, C., Bootsma, R., Mouchnino, L. (2004). Is perception of upper body orientation based on the inertia tensor? *Experimental Brain Research, 156*(4), 471–77.

Gurnee, H. (1934). An analysis of the perception of intelligence in the face. *Journal of Social Psychology, 5,* 82–89.

Halberstadt, A. G., & Saitta, M. B. (1987). Gender, nonverbal behavior, and perceived dominance: A test of the theory. *Journal of Personality and Social Psychology, 53,* 257–72.

Halberstadt, J., & Rhodes, G. (2003). It's not just average faces that are attractive: Computer-manipulated averageness makes birds, fish, and automobiles attractive. *Psychonomic Bulletin and Review, 10,* 149–56.

Hall, E. T. (1959). *The silent language.* Garden City, NY: Doubleday.

Hall, E. T. (1963). A system for the notation of proxemic behavior. *American Anthropologist, 65,* 1003–26.

Hall, E. T. (1966). *The hidden dimension.* Garden City, NY: Doubleday.

Hall, J. A. (1984). *Nonverbal sex differences: Communication accuracy and expressive style.* Baltimore: Johns Hopkins University Press.

Hall, J. A., & Bernieri, F. J. (Eds.). (2001). *Interpersonal sensitivity: Theory and measurement.* Mahwah, NJ: Lawrence Erlbaum Associates.

Hall, J. A., Carter, J. D., & Horgan, T. G. (2001). Gender differences in nonverbal communication of emotion. In A. H. Fischer (Ed.), *Gender and emotion: Social psychological perspectives* (pp. 97–117). New York: Cambridge University Press.

Hamermesh, D. S., & Biddle, J. E. (1994). Beauty and the labor-market. *American Economic Review, 84*(5), 1174–94.

Hamermesh, D. S., & Parker, A. M. (2005). Beauty in the classroom: Instructors' pulchritude and putative pedagogical productivity. *Economics of Education Review, 24,* 369–76.

Hamid, P. (1968). Style of dress as a perceptual cue in impression formation. *Perceptual and Motor Skills, 26,* 904–6.

Hamm, S., & Greene, J. (2004, October 24). The man who could have been Bill Gates. *Bloomberg News.* Retrieved from http://www.bloomberg.com/news/articles/2004-10-24/the-man-who-could-have-been-bill-gates.

Han, Y. J., Nunes, J. C., & Dreze, X. (2010). Signaling status with luxury goods: The role of brand prominence. *Journal of Marketing, 74*(7), 15–30.

Hare, A. & Bales, R. (1963). Seating position and small group interaction. *Sociometry, 26*(4), 480–86.

Hareli, S., Berkovitch, N., Livnat, L., & David, S. (2013). Anger and shame as determinants of perceived competence. *International Journal of Psychology, 48*(6), 1080–89.

Hari, J. (2010, August 19). The management consultancy scam. *Independent.* Retrieved from http://www.independent.co.uk/voices/commentators/johann-hari/johann-hari -the-management-consultancy-scam-2057127.html.

Harrison, A. A., Struthers, N. J., & Moore, M. (1988). On the conjunction of national holidays and reported birthdates: One more path to reflected glory? *Social Psychology Quarterly, 51*(4), 365–70.

Harrison, R. P. (1979). The face in face to face interaction. In G. R. Miller (Ed.), *Explorations in interpersonal communication* (pp. 217–36). Beverly Hills: Sage.

Haselton, M. G. (2003). The sexual overperception bias: Evidence of a systematic bias in men from a survey of naturally occurring events. *Journal of Research in Personality, 37*(1), 34–47.

Hash, R. B., Munna, R. K., Vogel, R. L., & Bason, J. J. (2003). Does Physician Weight Affect Perception of Health Advice. *Preventive Medicine, 36*(1), 41–44.

Haslam, A. S. (2004). *Psychology in organizations: The social identity approach.* London: Sage.

Hasoda, M., Stone-Romero, E. F., & Coats, G. (2003). The effects of physical attractiveness on job-related outcomes: A meta-analysis of experimental studies. *Personnel Psychology, 56*(2), 431–62.

Hassin, R., & Trope, Y. (2000). Facing faces: Studies on the cognitive aspects of physiognomy. *Journal of Personality and Social Psychology, 78*(5), 837–52.

Heider, F. (1944). Social perception and phenomenal causality. *Psychological Review, 51*, 358–74.

Heider, F. (1946). Attitudes and cognitive organization. *Journal of Psychology, 21*, 107–12.

Heider, F. (1954). Perceiving the other person. Paper presented at the American Psychological Association Symposium on Theory and Research in Interpersonal Perception, 1954. In R. Tagiuri & L. Petrullo (Eds.), *Person perception and interpersonal behavior* (pp. 22–26). Stanford, CA: Stanford University Press.

Heider, F. (1958). *The psychology of interpersonal relations.* New York: Wiley.

Hellweg, S. A., Pfau, M., & Brydon, S. B. (1992). *Televised presidential debates: Advocacy in contemporary America.* New York: Praeger.

Henley, M. (1973). Status and sex: Some touching observations. *Bulletin of the Psychonomic Society, 2*(2), 91–93.

Henss, R. (1989). *Attraktivität und Körpergröße: Eine Pilot-Studie.* Saarbrücken, Germany: Universität des Saarlandes.

Henss, R. (1992). *Spieglein, Spieglein an der Wand . . .* Weinheim, Germany: Psychologie Verlags Union.

Henss, R. (1995). Waist-to-hip ratio and attractiveness: Replication and extension. *Personality and Individual Differences, 19*, 479–88.

Higgins, E. T. (1987). Self-discrepancy: A theory relating self and affect. *Psychological Review, 94*, 319–40.

Hill, M. K., & Kahn, A. (1974). *Physical attractiveness and proximity in the attribution of success.* Paper presented at the meeting of the Midwestern Psychological Association, Chicago.

Hilton, J. L., & von Hippel, W. (1996). Stereotypes. *Annual Review of Psychology, 47*(1), 237–71.

Hirschberg, N., Jones, L. E., & Haggerty, M. (1978). What's in a face: Individual differences in face perception. *Journal of Research in Personality, 12*(4), 488–99.

Hirschi, A., & Jaensch, V. (2015). Narcissism and career success: Occupational self-efficacy and career engagement as mediators. *Personality and Individual Differences, 77*, 205–8.

Hoegg, J., & Lewis, M. (2011). The impact of candidate appearance and advertising strategies on election results. *Journal of Marketing Research, 48*(5), 895–905.

Hoffmann, H.-J. (1981). Kommunikation mit Kleidung. *Communications, 7*(2–3), 269–90.

Hofstede, G. (2001). *Culture's consequences: Comparing values, behaviors, institutions, and organizations across nations* (2nd ed.). Thousand Oaks, CA: Sage.

Hogg, M. A., & Abrams, D. (1993). Towards a single-process uncertainty-reduction model of social motivation in groups. In D. Abrams (Ed.), *Group motivation: Social psychological perspectives* (pp. 173–90). London: Harvester.

Holbrook, M. B. (Ed.). (1999). *Consumer value: A framework for analysis and research.* London: Routledge.

Holt, D. B. (1998). Does cultural capital structure American consumption? *Journal of Consumer Research, 25*(1), 1–25.

Holt, J. (2005). Time bandits: What were Einstein and Gödel talking about? *New Yorker, 28*, 80–85.

Hornik, J. (1992). Tactile Stimulation and Consumer Response. *Journal of Consumer Research, 19*(3), 449–58.

Hosman, L. A., & Siltanen, S. A. (1991). *The attributional and evaluative consequences of powerful and powerless speech styles. An examination of the "control of others" and "control of self" explanations.* Paper presented at the meeting of the Speech Communication Association, Atlanta.

Hosman, L. A., & Wright, J. W., II. (1987). The effects of hedges and hesitations on impression formation in a simulated courtroom context. *Western Journal of Speech Communication, 51*, 173–88.

Hosmer, L. T. (1995). Trust: The connecting link between organizational theory and philosophical ethics. *Academy of Management Review, 20*(2), 379–403.

Hossain, T. M. (2010). Hot or not: An analysis of online professor-shopping behavior of business students. *Journal of Education for Business, 85*, 165–67.

How companies are dealing with workplace body art issues. (2004). *HR Focus 81, 9.*

Hubbard, B. M. (2003). Conscious evolution: the next stage of human development. *Systems Research and Behavioral Science, 20*(4), 359.

Hubbertz, H. (2006). Corporate Citizenship und die Absorption von Unsicherheit. *Sozialwissenschaften und Berufspraxis, 29*(2), 298–314.

Hudson, J. W., & Henze, L. S. (1969). Campus values in male selection: A replication. *Journal of Marriage and the Family, 31*, 772–75.

Hume, D. (1779, 1993). *Dialoge über natürliche Religion.* Hamburg, Germany: Meiner.

Hutton, A., Miller, G., & Skinner, D. (2003). The role of supplementary statements with management earnings forecasts. *Journal of Accounting Research, 41*(5), 867–90.

Ibrocheva, E. (2009). Of beauty and politics: Women, politics and the media in post communist Bulgaria. *Controversia: An International Journal of Debate and Democratic Renewal, 6*(1), 85–96.

Iconic Albuquerque photo re-created. (2008, June 25). *Microsoft News*. Retrieved from https://news.microsoft.com/2008/06/25/iconic-albuquerque-photo-re-created/#sm .000dmub02uk3fhp116k1n1lka253i.

Jackson, L. A., Hunter, J. E., & Hodge, C. N. (1995). Physical attractiveness and intellectual competence: A meta-analytic review. *Social Psychology Quarterly, 58*, 108–22.

Jahoda, G. (1963). Refractive errors, intelligence and social mobility. *British Journal of Social and Clinical Psychology, 1*, 96–106.

Jamieson, D. W., Lydon, J. E., Stewart, G., & Zanna, M. P. (1987). Pygmalion revisited: New evidence for student expectancy effects in the classroom. *Journal of Educational Psychology, 79*, 461–66.

Jobs, S. (2005, June 14). "You've got to find what you love," Jobs says. Retrieved from https://news.stanford.edu/2005/06/14/jobs-061505/.

Johnson, K., & Lennon, S. (Eds.). (1999). *Appearance and power: Dress, body, culture*. New York: Berg.

Johnston, M. R., & Franklin, M. (1993). Is beauty in the eye of the beholder? *Ethology and Sociobiology, 14*, 183–99.

Jones, D. (1995). Sexual selection, physical attractiveness, and facial neoteny: Cross-cultural evidence and implications. *Current Anthropology, 36*, 723–48.

Jones, E. E. (1964). Karl E. Zener 1903–1964. *Journal of Personality, 32*(4), 511–13.

Jones, E. E. (1989). The framing of competence. *Personality and Social Psychology Bulletin, 15*, 477–92.

Jones, E. E. (1990). *Interpersonal perception*. New York: Freeman.

Jones, E. E., & Davis, K. E. (1965). From acts to dispositions: The attribution process in person perception. In L. Berkowitz (Ed.), *Advances in experimental social psychology* (pp. 219–66). New York: Academic Press.

Jones, E. E., & Pittman, T. S. (1982). Toward a general theory of strategic self presentation. In J. Suls (Ed.), *Psychological perspectives on the self* (Vol. 1, pp. 231–62). Hillsdale, NJ: Lawrence Erlbaum Associates.

Jones, E. E., & Wortman, C. (1973). *Ingratiation: An attributional approach*. Morristown, NJ: General Learning.

Jones, R. R. (1973). Linguistic standardisation and national development. *International Journal of Psychology, 8*, 51–54.

Joule, R. V., & Beauvois, J. L. (1998). *Kurzer Leitfaden der Manipulation zum Gebrauch für ehrbare Leute*. Berlin: Aufbau.

Jourard, S., & Landsman, M. (1960). Cognition, cathexes and the "dyadic effect" in men's self-disclosing behavior. *Merrill-Palmer Quarterly, 6*, 178–86.

Judd, C. M., James-Hawkins, L. J., Yzerbyt, V. Y., & Kashima, Y. (2005). Fundamental dimensions of social judgment: Understanding the relations between judgments of competence and warmth. *Journal of Personality and Social Psychology, 89*, 899–913.

Judge, T. A., & Cable, D. M. (2004). Effect of physical height on workplace success and income: Preliminary test of a theoretical model. *Journal of Applied Psychology, 89*(3), 428–41.

Judge, T. A., & Ferris, G. R. (1993). Social context of performance evaluation decisions. *Academy of Management Journal, 36*, 80–105.

Jungbauer-Gans, M., Berger, R., & Kriwy, P. (2005). Machen Kleider Leute? Ergebnisse eines Feldexperiments zum Verkäuferverhalten / Does Clothing Make the Man? Conclusions from a Field Experiement on the Behavior of Sales Assistants. *Zeitschrift für Soziologie, 34*(4), 311–22.

Kadous, K., Koonce, L., & Towry, K. (2005). Quantification and persuasion in managerial judgement. *Contemporary Accounting Research, 22*(3), 643–86.

Kahneman, D. (2011). *Thinking, fast and slow.* New York: Farrar, Straus & Giroux.

Kahneman, D., & Tversky, A. (1979). Prospect theory: An analysis of decision under risk. *Econometrica, 47*, 263–92.

Kanazawa, S., & Kovar, J. L. (2004). Why beautiful people are more intelligent. *Intelligence, 32*(3), 227–43.

Kanizsa, G. (1976). Subjective contours. *Scientific American, 234*(4), 48–52.

Karl, K. A., McIntyre Hall, L., & Peluchette, J. V. (2013). City employee perceptions of the impact of dress and appearance: You are what you wear. *Public Personnel Management, 42*(3), 452–70.

Karrass, C. L. (1996). *In business as in life: You don't get what you deserve, you get what you negotiate.* Beverly Hills: Stanford St. Press.

Keating, C. F., & Doyle, J. (2002). The faces of desirable mates and dates contain mixed social status cues. *Journal of Experimental Social Psychology, 38*, 414–24.

Keating, C. F., Mazur, A., Segall, M. H., Cysneiros, P. G., Kilbride, J. E., Leahy, P., . . . Wirsing, R. (1981). Culture and the perception of social dominance from facial expression. *Journal of Personality and Social Psychology, 40*, 615–26.

Kendon, A. (1967). Some functions of gaze-direction in social interaction. *Acta Psychologica, 15*, 192–238.

Kenrick, D. T., & Cialdini, R. B. (1977). Romantic attraction: Misattribution versus reinforcement explanations. *Journal of Personality and Social Psychology, 35*(6), 381–91.

Kernis, M. H., & Grannemann, B. D. (1990). Excuses in the making: A test and extension of Darley and Goethals' attributional model. *Journal of Experimental Social Psychology, 26*(4), 337–49.

Kernis, M. H., Grannemann, B. D., & Barclay, L. C. (1989). Stability and level of self-esteem as predictors of anger arousal and hostility. *Journal of Personality and Social Psychology, 56*, 1013–22.

Kervyn, N., Yzerbyt, V., & Judd, C. M. (2010). Compensation between warmth and competence: Antecedents and consequences of a negative relation between the two fundamental dimensions of social perception. *European Review of Social Psychology, 21*, 155–87.

Kim, H., & Markus, H. R. (1999). Deviance or uniqueness, harmony or conformity? A cultural analysis. *Journal of Personality and Social Psychology, 77*(4), 785–800.

King, A., & Leigh, A. (2009). Beautiful politicians. *Kyklos, 62*(4), 579–93.

Kipnis, D., Schmidt, S., & Wilkinson, I. (1980). Intraorganizational influence tactics: Explorations in getting one's way. *Journal of Applied Psychology, 65*(4), 440–52.

Kircheisen, F. M. (1925). *Napoleon I: Sein Leben und seine Zeit* (Vol. 5). Munich: Georg Müller.

Kleck, R. E., Richardson, S. A., & Ronald, L. (1974). Physical appearance cues and interpersonal attraction in children. *Child Development, 43*, 305–10.

Kleinfield, N. R. (1993, January 17). Buttonholes to go. *New York Times*. Retrieved from http://www.nytimes.com/1993/01/17/style/buttonholes-to-go.html?page wanted=all.

Kleinke, C. L., Berger, D. E., & Staneski, R. A. (1975). Evaluation of an interviewer as a function of interviewer gaze, reinforcement of subject gaze, and interviewer attractiveness. *Journal of Personality and Social Psychology, 31,* 115–22.

Klofstad, C. A., Anderson, R. C., & Peters, S. (2012). Sounds like a winner: Voice pitch influences perception of leadership capacity in both men and women. *Proceedings of the Royal Society B: Biological Sciences* 297:2698–704.

Klofstad, C. A., Anderson, R. C., & Nowicki, S. (2015). Perceptions of competence, strength, and age influence voters to select leaders with lower-pitched voices. *PLoS ONE* 10:e0133779.

Knapp, M. L. (1972). *Nonverbal communication in human interaction.* New York: Holt, Rinehart & Winston.

Knouse, S. B. (1994). Impressions of the resume: The effects of applicant education, experience, and impression management. *Journal of Business & Psychology, 9*(1), 33–45.

Koernig, S. K., & Page, A. L. (2002). What if your dentist looked like Tom Cruise? Applying the match-up hypothesis to a service encounter. *Psychology & Marketing,* • *19*(1), 91–110.

Kopera, A. A., Maier, R. A., & Johnson, J. E. (1971). Perception of physical attractiveness: The influence of group interaction and group coaction on ratings of the attractiveness of photographs of women. *Proceedings of the 79th Annual Convention of the American Psychological Association, 6,* 317–18.

Korabik, K. (1981). Changes in physical attractiveness and interpersonal attraction. *Basic and Applied Social Psychology, 2,* 59–65.

Krebs, D., & Adinolfi, A. A. (1975). Physical attractiveness, social relations, and personality style. *Journal of Personality and Social Psychology, 31,* 245–53.

Kruglanski, A. W., & Webster, D. M. (1991). Group members' reactions to opinion deviates and conformists at varying degrees of proximity to decision deadline and of environmental noise. *Journal of Personality and Social Psychology, 61*(2), 212–25.

Kwon, Y. H. (1994). The influence of appropriateness of dress and gender on the self-perception of occupational attributes. *Clothing and Textiles Research Journal, 12,* 33–37.

Kwon, Y. H., & Färber, A. (1992). Attitudes toward appropriate clothing in perception of occupational attributes. *Perceptual and Motor Skills, 74,* 163–69.

Laird, D. A., & Remmers, H. (1924). A study of estimates of intelligence from photographs. *Journal of Experimental Psychology, 7,* 429–46.

Laird, J. D. (1974). Self-attribution of emotion: The effect of expressive behavior on the quality of emotional experience. *Journal of Personality and Social Psychology, 29,* 475–86.

Lakoff, R. (1973). Language and woman's place. *Language and Society, 2,* 45–79.

Lancaster, R., & Uzzi, B. (2012). Legally charged: Embeddedness and profits in large law firms. *Sociological Focus, 45*(1), 1–22.

Langlois, J. H., Kalakanis, L., Rubenstein, A. J., Larson, A., Hallam, M., & Smoot, M. (2000). Maxims or myths of beauty? A meta-analytic and theoretical review. *Psychological Bulletin, 126,* 390–423.

Langlois, J. H., & Roggman, L. A. (1990). Attractive faces are only average. *Psychological Science, 1,* 115–21.

Lanzetta, J. T., Cartwright-Smith, J., & Kleck, R. E. (1976). Effects of nonverbal dissimulation on emotional experience and autonomic arousal. *Journal of Personality and Social Psychology, 33,* 354–70.

Latham, G. P., & Wexley, K. N. (1981). *Increasing productivity through performance appraisal.* Reading, MA: Addison-Wesley.

Lavrakas, P. J. (1975). Female preferences for male physiques. *Journal of Research in Personality, 9*(4), 324–34.

Lawson, E. (1971). Haircolor, personality and the observer. *Psychological Reports, 28,* 311–22.

Leary, M. R., & Tangney, J. P. (Eds.). *Handbook of self and identity.* New York: Guilford Press.

Le Deist, F. D., & Winterton, J. (2005). What is competence? *Human Resource Development International, 8,* 27–46.

Lee, S., Pitesa, M., Pillutla, M., & Thau, S. (2015). When beauty helps and when it hurts: An organizational context model of attractiveness discrimination in selection decisions. *Organizational Behavior and Human Decision Processes, 128,* 15–28.

Lefkowitz, M., Blake, R. R., & Mouton, J. S. (1955). Status factors in pedestrian violation of traffic signals. *Journal of Abnormal and Social Psychology, 51,* 704–6.

Leit, R. A., Pope, H. G., & Gray, J. J. (2001). Cultural expectations of muscularity in men: The evolution of playgirl centerfolds. *International Journal of Eating Disorders, 29,* 90–93.

Lenz, G. S., & Lawson, C. (2011). Looking the part: Television leads less informed citizens to vote based on candidate's appearance. *American Journal of Political Science, 55*(3), 574–89.

Lerner, M. J. (1980). *The belief in a just world: A fundamental delusion.* New York: Plenum.

Lev-Ari, S., & Keysar, B. (2010). Why don't we believe non-native speakers? The influence of accent on credibility. *Journal of Experimental Social Psychology, 46*(6), 1093–96.

Levine, J. M. (1989). Reaction to opinion deviance in small groups. In P. B. Paulus (Ed.), *Psychology of group influence* (pp. 187–231). Hillsdale, NJ: Lawrence Erlbaum Associates.

Levine, S. P., & Feldman, R. S. (1997). Self-presentational goals, self-monitoring, and nonverbal behavior. *Basic and Applied Social Psychology, 19,* 505–18.

Levinger, G. (1972). Little sand box and big quarry: Comment on Byrne's paradigmatic spade for research on interpersonal attraction. *Representative Research in Social Psychology, 3,* 3–19.

Lewicki, R. J., Barry, B., & Saunders, D. M. (2010). *Negotiation* (international, 6th ed.). New York: McGraw Hill.

Liepman, H. (1957). *Rasputin: Heiliger oder Teufel.* Gütersloh, Germany: Bertelsmann.

Lin, L., Dahl, D. W., & Argo, J. J. (2013). Do the crime, always do the time? Insights into consumer-to-consumer punishment decisions. *Journal of Consumer Research, 40*(1), 64–77.

Lin, W.-Y., Wang, J.-W., Lin, H.-Y., Lin, H.-T., & Johnson, B. T. (2011). When low-warmth targets are liked: The roles of competence, gender, and relative status. *Journal of Psychology, 145*(3), 247–65.

Lindsay, R., Martin, R., Webber, L. (1994). Default values in eyewitness descriptions. *Law and Human Behavior, 18*(5), 527–41.

Lindzey, G., & Aronson, E. (Ed.). (1969). *Handbook of social psychology* (2nd ed., Vol. 3). Reading, MA: Addison-Wesley.

Lippmann, W. (1922). *Public opinion*. New York: Harcourt, Brace.

Littlepage, G., Robison, W., & Reddington, K. (1997). Effects of task experience and group experience on group performance, member ability, and recognition of expertise. *Organizational Behavior and Human Decision Processes, 69,* 133–47.

Litzmann, B. (1927). *Clara Schumann, Johannes Brahms: Briefe aus den Jahren 1853–1896* (Vol. 2). Leipzig: Breitkopf & Härtel.

Liu, J., Hu, J., & Furutan, O. (2013). The influence of student perceived professors' "hotness" on expertise, motivation, learning outcomes, and course satisfaction. *Journal of Education for Business, 88,* 94–100.

Locke, K. D., & Horowitz, L. M. (1990). Satisfaction in interpersonal interactions as a foundation of similarity in level of dysphoria. *Journal of Personality and Social Psychology, 58*(5), 823–31.

Loftus, E. F., & Palmer, J. C. (1974). Reconstruction of auto-mobile destruction: An example of the interaction between language and memory. *Journal of Verbal Learning and Verbal Behavior, 13,* 585–89.

Lombardo, J. P., & Tocci, M. E. (1979). Attribution of positive and negative characteristics of instructors as a function of attractiveness and sex of instructor and sex of subject. *Perceptual and Motor Skills, 48,* 491–94.

Lorenz, K. (1943). Die angeborenen Formen möglichen Verhaltens. *Zeitschrift für Tierpsychologie, 5,* 235–409.

Lubker, J. R., Watson II, J. C., Visek, A. J., & Geer, J. R. (2005). Physical appearance and the perceived effectiveness of performance enhancement consultants. *The Sport Psychologist, 19*(4), 448–58.

Luhmann, N. (1984). *Soziale Systeme: Grundriß einer allgemeinen Theorie.* Frankfurt am Main, Germany: Suhrkamp.

Lütge, C. (2002). *Popper: Ein moralisierender Individualethiker?* Talk at the Karl Popper Centenary Congress, Vienna.

Mahoney, E. R., & Finch, M. D. (1976). Body cathexis and self-esteem: A reanalysis of the differential contribution of specific body aspects. *Journal of Social Psychology, 99,* 251–58.

Maier, R., & Lavrakas, P. J. (1984). Attitudes toward women, personality rigidity, and idealized physique preferences in males. *Sex Roles, 2,* 425–33.

Maisey, D. M., Vale, E. L. E., Cornelissen, P. L., & Tovee, M. J. (1999). Characteristics of male attractiveness for women. *Lancet, 353,* 1500.

Maner, J. K., Kenrick, D. T., Becker, D. V., Robertson, T. E., Hofer, B., Neuberg, S. L., . . . Schaller, M. (2005). Functional projection: How fundamental social motives can bias interpersonal perception. *Journal of Personality and Social Psychology, 88,* 63–78.

Mannix, E., Neale, M., & Anderson, C. (Eds.). (2007). *Research on managing groups and teams: Affect and groups.* London: Elsevier.

Marques, J., Abrams, D., & Serôdio, R. G. (2001). Being better by being right: Subjective group dynamics and derogation of in-group deviants when generic norms are undermined. *Journal of Personality and Social Psychology, 81*(3), 436–47.

Martins, Y., Tiggemann, M., & Churchett, L. (2008). Hair today, gone tomorrow: A comparison of body hair removal practices in gay and heterosexual men. *Body Image, 5,* 312–16.

Mayo, J., White, O., & Eysenck, H. J. (1978). An empirical study of the relation between astrological factors and personality. *Journal of Social Psychology, 105,* 229–36.

McArthur, L. Z., & Baron, R. M. (1983). Toward an ecological theory of social perception. *Psychological Review, 90,* 215–38.

McArthur, L. Z., & Post, D. L. (1977). Figural emphasis and person perception. *Journal of Experimental Social Psychology, 13,* 520–35.

McCornack, S. A., & Levine, T. R. (1990). When lovers become leary: The relationship between suspicion and accuracy in detecting deception. *Communication Monographs, 57,* 219–30.

McCornack, S. A., & Parks, M. R. (1986). Deception detection and relational development: The other side of trust. In M. McLaughlin (Ed.), *Communication yearbook 9* (pp. 377–89). Beverly Hills: Sage.

McGarty, C., & Haslam, S. A. (Eds.) (1997). *The message of social psychology: Perspectives on mind in society.* Cambridge, MA: Blackwell.

McGarty, C., Turner, J. C., Oakes, P. J., & Haslam, S. A. (1993). The creation of uncertainty in the influence process: The roles of stimulus information and disagreement with similar others. *European Journal of Social Psychology, 23,* 17–38.

McGuire, W. J. (1969). The nature of attitudes and attitude change. In G. Lindzey & E. Aronson (Eds.), *Handbook of social psychology* (2nd ed., Vol. 3, pp. 136–314). Reading, MA: Addison-Wesley.

McKenna, C. D. (2006). *The world's newest profession: Management consulting in the twentieth century.* New York: Cambridge University Press.

McKnight, D. H., & Chervany, N. L. (2001). What trust means in e-commerce customer relationships: An interdisciplinary conceptual typology. *International Journal of Electronic Commerce, 6*(2), 35–59.

McLaughlin, M. (Ed.). (1986). *Communication yearbook 9.* Beverly Hills: Sage.

Mead, G. H. (1934). *Mind, self, and society.* Chicago: University of Chicago Press.

Mehrabian, A. (1968). Inference of attitudes from the posture, orientation, and distance of a communicator. *Journal of Consulting and Clinical Psychology, 32,* 296–308.

Mehrabian, A. (1970). A semantic space for nonverbal behavior. *Journal of Consulting and Clinical Psychology, 35,* 248–57.

Mehrabian, A. (1971). *Silent messages.* Belmont, CA: Wadsworth.

Mehrabian, A. (1972). *Nonverbal communication.* Chicago: Aldine-Atherton.

Mehrabian, A. (2009). Silent messages: A wealth of information about nonverbal communication (body language). Retrieved from http://kaaj.com/psych/smorder.html.

Mehrabian, A., & Ferris, S. R. (1967). Inference of attitudes from nonverbal communication in two channels. *Journal of Consulting Psychology, 31*(3), 248–52.

Mellers, B. A., Stone, E., Murray, T., Minster, A., Rohrbaugh, N., Bishop, M., . . . Tetlock, P. E. (2015). Identifying and cultivating "superforecasters" as a method of improving probabilistic predictions. *Perspectives in Psychological Science, 10,* 267–81.

Merton, R. K. (1968). *Social theory and social structure.* New York: Free Press.

Metcalfe, A. W. (1992). The curriculum vitae: Confessions of a wage-labourer. *Work, Employment & Society, 6,* 619–41.

Michinov, E. & Monteil, J. M. (2002). The similarity-attraction relationship revisited: divergence between the affective and behavioral facets of attraction. *European Journal of Social Psychology, 32*(4), 485–500.

Michler, I. (2013, August 3). Die Statussymbole der Deutschen sind unbezahlbar. *Welt am Sonntag*. Retrieved from https://www.welt.de/wirtschaft/article118660732/Die -Statussymbole-der-Deutschen-sind-unbezahlbar.html.

Mikulincer, M. (1998). Adult attachment style and individual differences in functional versus dysfunctional experiences of anger. *Journal of Personality and Social Psychology, 74*(2), 513–24.

Milgram, S. (1963). Behavioral study of obedience. *Journal of Abnormal and Social Psychology, 67*, 371–78.

Miller, A. G. (1970). Role of physical attractiveness in impression formation. *Psychonomic Science, 19*, 241–43.

Miller, B., Niçois, K. M., & Eure, J. (2009). Body art in the workplace: Piercing employment possibilities? *Personnel Review, 38*, 621–64.

Miller, C. E., & Anderson, P. D. (1979). Group decision rules and the rejection of deviates. *Social Psychology Quarterly, 42*(4), 354–63.

Miller, G. F., & Todd, P. M. (1998). Mate choice turns cognitive. *Cognitive Sciences, 2*, 190–98.

Miller, G. R., & Hewgill, M. A. (1964). The effect of variations in nonfluency on audience ratings of source credibility. *Quarterly Journal of Speech, 50*, 36–44.

Miller, G. R., & Stiff, J. B. (1993). *Deceptive communication*. Thousand Oaks, CA: Sage.

Miller, H. L., & Rivenbark, W. (1970). Sexual differences in physical attractiveness as a determinant of heterosexual likings. *Psychological Reports, 27*, 701–2.

Miller, N., Maruyama, B., Beaber, R. J., & Valone, K. (1975). *Between people: A new analysis of interpersonal communication*. Chicago: Science Research Associate.

Mills, J. (1966). Opinion change as a function of the communicator's desire to influence and liking for the audience. *Journal of Experimental Social Psychology, 2*, 152–59.

Mills, J., & Aronson, E. (1965). Opinion change as a function of the communicator's attractiveness and desire to influence. *Journal of Personality and Social Psychology, 1*, 173–77.

Mischke, R. (2004, July 10). Ich fahre—also bin ich. *Die Welt*. Retrieved from https://www.welt.de/print-welt/article326407/Ich-fahre-also-bin-ich.html.

Mobius, M. M., & Rosenblat, T. S. (2006). Why beauty matters. *American Economic Review, 96*(1), 222–35.

Montaser-Kouhsari, L., Landy, M. S., Heeger, D. J., & Larsson, J. (2007). Orientation-selective adaptation to illusory contours in human visual cortex. *Journal of Neuroscience, 27*, 2186–95.

Moore, F. R., Filippou, D., Perrett, D. I. (2011). Intelligence and attractiveness in the face: Beyond the attractiveness halo effect. *Journal of Evolutionary Psychology, 9*(3), 205–17.

Moorman, C., Zaltman, G., & Deshpandé, R. (1992). Relationships between providers and users of market research: The dynamics of trust within and between organizations. *Journal of Marketing Research, 29*(3), 314–28.

Morgan, R. M., & Hunt, S. (1994). The commitment-trust theory of relationship marketing. *Journal of Marketing, 58*(3), 20–38.

Morris, L. (1999). *The knowledge channel: Corporate strategies for the Internet*. San Jose, CA: toExcel.

Moss, M. K. (1969). *Social desirability, physical attractiveness, and social choice* (Unpublished doctoral dissertation). Kansas State University.

Mott, P. (1972). *The characteristics of effective organizations*. New York: Harper & Row.

Mulac, A. (1975). Evaluation of the speech dialect attitudinal scale. *Speech Monographs, 42*, 184–89.

Mulac, A. (1976). Assessment and application of the revised speech dialect attitudinal scale. *Communication Monographs, 43*, 238–45.

Mulac, A., & Rudd, M. J. (1977). Effects of selected American regional dialects upon regional audience members. *Communication Monographs, 44*(3), 185–95.

Mummendey, H.-D. (1995). *Psychologie der Selbstdarstellung*. Göttingen, Germany: Hogrefe.

Murdock, B. B. (1962). The serial position effect of free recall. *Journal of Experimental Psychology, 64*, 482–88.

Murphy, N. (2007). Appearing smart: The impression management of intelligence, person perception accuracy, and behavior in social interaction. *Personality and Social Psychology Bulletin, 33*, 325–39.

Murphy, N., Hall, J., & Colvin, R. (2003). Accurate intelligence assessments in social interactions: Mediators and gender effects. *Journal of Personality, 71*(3), 465–93.

Murstein, B. I. (1972). Physical attractiveness and marital choice. *Journal of Personality and Social Psychology, 22*, 8–12.

Myers, D. G. (2005). *Social psychology* (8th ed.). New York: McGraw-Hill.

Naftulin, D. H., Ware, J. E., Jr., & Donnelly, F. A. (1973). The Doctor Fox lecture: A paradigm of educational seduction. *Journal of Medical Education, 48*, 630–35.

Nasher, J. (2010). *Durchschaut: Das Geheimnis, kleine und große Lügen zu entlarven*. Munich: Heyne.

Nasher, J. (2013). *Deal! Du gibst mir, was ich will*. Frankfurt: Campus.

Nasher, J. (2015). *Entlarvt! Wie Sie in jedem Gespräch die ganze Wahrheit sehen*. Frankfurt: Campus.

Naumann, A. (2015, January 17). In diesen Branchen zahlt sich ein Doktortitel aus. *Welt*. Retrieved from https://www.welt.de/wirtschaft/karriere/bildung/article136475552/In -diesen-Branchen-zahlt-sich-ein-Doktortitel-aus.html.

Nemeth, C., & Wachtler, J. (1974). Creating the perceptions of consistency and confidence: A necessary condition for minority influence. *Sociometry, 37*, 529–40.

Newcomb, T. M. (1961). *The acquaintance process*. New York: Holt, Rinehart and Winston.

Ng, S. H., & Bradac, J. J. (1993). *Power in language: Verbal communication and social influence*. Thousand Oaks, CA: Sage.

Nida, S. A., & Williams, J. E. (1977). Sex-stereotyped traits, physical attractiveness, and interpersonal attraction. *Psychological Reports, 41*, 1311–22.

Nielsen, J. P. & Kernaleguen, A. (1976). Influence of Clothing and Physical Attractiveness in Person Perception. *Perceptual and Motor Skills, 42*, 775–80.

Nisbett, R. E., & Roll, L. (1980). *Human inference strategies and shortcomings of social judgment*. Englewood Cliffs, NJ: Prentice-Hall.

Nöllke, M. (2002). *Anekdoten, Geschichten, Metaphern für Führungskräfte*. Freiburg, Germany: Haufe-Mediengruppe.

Nooteboom, B. (1996). Trust, opportunism and governance: A process and control model. *Organization Studies, 17*(6), 985–1010.

Norman, R. Z., Smith, R., & Berger, J. (1988). The processing of inconsistent status information. In M. Foschi (Ed.), *Status generalization: New theory and research* (pp. 169–87). Stanford, CA: Stanford University Press.

Nyquist, L. V., & Spence, J. T. (1986). Effects of dispositional dominance and sex role expectations on leadership behaviors. *Journal of Personality and Social Psychology, 50,* 87–93.

O'Barr, W., & Atkins, B. (1998). "Women's language" or "powerless language"? In J. Coates (Ed.), *Language and gender: A reader.* Oxford: Blackwell.

O'Driscoll, M. P., Humphries, M., & Larsen, H. H. (1991). Managerial activities, competence and effectiveness: Manager and subordinate perceptions. *International Journal of Human Resource Management, 2*(3), 313–26.

Oldmeadow, J., Platow, M. J., Foddy, M., & Anderson, D. (2003). Self-categorization, status and social influence. *Social Psychology Quarterly, 66*(2), 138–52.

O'Neal, G. S., & Lapitsky, M. (1991). Effects of clothing as nonverbal communication on credibility of the message source. *Clothing and Textiles Research Journal, 9,* 28–34.

Orpen, C. (1996). The effects of ingratiation and self-promotion tactics on employee career success. *Social Behavior and Personality, 24*(3), 213–14.

Osborn, D. R. (1996). Beauty is as beauty does? Makeup and posture effects on physical attractiveness judgments. *Journal of Applied Social Psychology, 26*(1), 31–51.

Osgood, C. E., Suci, G. J., & Tannenbaum, P. H. (1957). *The measurement of meaning.* Urbana: University of Illinois Press.

Pancer, S. M., & Meindl, J. R. (1978). Length of hair and beardedness as determinants of personality impressions. *Perceptual and Motor Skills, 46,* 1328–30.

Parsons, J. H. (Ed.). (1980). *The psychobiology of sex differences and sex roles.* Washington, DC: Hemisphere.

Patzer, G. L. (1975). *Determinants of judgments of physical attractiveness and the attribution of sexual attitudes to strangers* (Unpublished master's thesis). Pittsburg State University.

Patzer, G. L. (1985). *The physical attractiveness phenomena.* New York: Plenum Press.

Paulus, P. B. (Ed.). (1989). *Psychology of group influence.* Hillsdale, NJ: Lawrence Erlbaum Associates.

Pease, A., & Pease, B. (2004). *The definitive book of body language: The hidden meaning behind people's gestures and expressions.* New York: Random House/Bantam Dell.

Peck, S., Peck, L., & Kataja, M. (1991). Skeletal asymmetry in esthetically pleasing faces. *Angle Orthodontist, 61,* 43–48.

Peluchette, J., & Karl, K. (2007). The impact of workplace attire on employee self-perceptions. *Human Resource Development Quarterly, 18,* 345–58.

Perrett, D. I., Lee, K. J., Penton-Voak, I., Rowland, D., Yoshikawa, S., Burt, D. M., . . . Akamatsu, S. (1998). Effects of sexual dimorphism on facial attractiveness. *Nature, 394,* 884–87.

Perrett, D. I., May, K. A., & Yoshikawa, S. (1994). Facial shape and judgments of female attractiveness. *Nature, 368,* 239–42.

Perrin, F. A. C. (1921). Physical attractiveness and repulsiveness. *Journal of Experimental Psychology, 4,* 203–17.

Peter, L. J., & Hull, R. (1969). *The Peter Principle: Why things always go wrong.* New York: William Morrow.

Peters, T. (2006, May 1). The work matters: On self-reliance, becoming a "change insurgent," and the power of peculiarities [PowerPoint presentation]. Retrieved from http://tompeters.com/slides/topic-presentations/.

Peterson, J. B. (2018). *12 Rules for Life—An Antidote to Chaos.* Toronto: Random House Canada.

Peterson, O., Andrews, L., & Spain, R. (1956). An analytical study of North Carolina general practice, 1953–1954. *Journal of Medical Education, 31*(2), 1–165.

Peterson, R. A., & Kern, R. M. (1996). Changing high-brow taste: From snob to omnivore. *American Sociological Review, 61*(5), 900–907.

Peterson, R. D., & Palmer, C. L. (2012). Beauty and the Pollster: The Impact of Halo Effects on Perceptions of Political Knowledge and Sophistication. *Midwest Political Science Association*, Retrieved from: https://web.archive.org/web/20140309 023825/http://cas.illinoisstate.edu/clpalme/research/documents/Beauty_and_the _Pollster_revision.pdf.

Pheterson, G. I., Kiesler, S. B., & Goldberg, P. A. (1971). Evaluation of the performance of women as a function of their sex, achievement, and personal history. *Journal of Personality and Social Psychology, 19*, 114–18.

Phillips, A. P., & Dipboye, R. L. (1989). Correlational tests of predictions from a process model of the interview. *Journal of Applied Psychology, 74*, 41–52.

Phillips, D. J., & Zuckerman, E. W. (2001). Middle-status conformity: Theoretical restatement and empirical demonstration in two markets. *American Journal of Sociology, 107*(2), 379–429.

Pintner, R. (1918). Intelligence as estimated from photographs. *Psychological Review, 25*, 286–96.

Plassmann, H., O'Doherty, J., Shiv, B., & Rangel, A. (2008). Marketing actions can modulate neural representations of experienced pleasantness. *Proceedings of the National Academy of Sciences, 105*(3), 1050–54.

Pollach, I., & Kerbler, E. (2011). Appearing competent: A study of impression management in U.S. and European CEO profiles. *Journal of Business Communication, 48*(4), 355–72.

Poortinga, W., & Pidgeon, N. F. (2003). Exploring the Dimensionality of Trust in Risk Regulation. *Risk Analysis, 23*(5), 961–72.

Popper, K. R. (1969). *Conjectures and refutations.* London: Routledge & Kegan Paul.

Popper, K. R. (1987). *Das Elend des Historizismus* (6th ed.). Tübingen, Germany: Mohr Siebeck.

Pornpitakpan, C. (2004). The persuasiveness of source credibility: A critical review of five decades' evidence. *Journal of Applied Social Psychology, 34*(2), 243–81.

Porter, T. (1995). *Trust in numbers.* Princeton, NJ: Princeton University Press.

Potter, S. (1962). *Threeupmanship.* New York: Holt, Rinehart & Winston.

Powelz, M. (2011, May 15). Der beliebteste Nachrichten-Star. *TV Digital.* Retrieved from http://www.tvdigital.de/magazin/specials/aktionen/der-beliebteste-nachrichten-star.

Power, T. G., Hildebrandt, K. A., & Fitzgerald, H. E. (1982). Adults' responses to infants varying in facial expression and perceived attractiveness. *Infant Behavior and Development, 5*, 33–44.

Pozo-Muñoz, C., Rebolloso-Pacheco, E., & Fernández-Ramírez, B. (2000). The "ideal teacher": Implications for student evaluation of teacher effectiveness. *Assessment & Evaluation in Higher Education, 25*(3), 253–63.

Praino, R., Stockemer, D., & Ratis, J. (2014). Looking good or looking competent? Physical appearance and electoral success in the 2008 congressional elections. *American Politics Research, 42*(6), 1096–117.

Pratto, F., Stallworth, L. M., & Sidanius, J. (1997). The gender gap: Differences in political attitudes and social dominance orientation. *British Journal of Social Psychology, 36,* 49–68.

Praxmarer, S. (2011). How a presenter's perceived attractiveness affects persuasion for attractiveness-unrelated products. *International Journal of Advertising, 30*(5), 839–65.

Pyszczynski, T., Greenberg, J., & Goldenberg, J. L. (2003). Freedom versus fear: On the defense, growth, and expansion of the self. In M. R. Leary & J. P. Tangney (Eds.), *Handbook of self and identity* (pp. 314–43). New York: Guilford Press.

Radmacher, S. A., & Martin, D. J. (2001). Identifying significant predictors of student evaluations of faculty through hierarchical regression analysis. *Journal of Psychology, 135,* 259–68.

Rafaeli, A., Dutton, J., Harquail, C., & Mackie-Lewis, S. (1997). Navigating by attire: The use of dress by administrative employees. *Academy of Management Journal, 40,* 19–45.

Rafaeli, A., & Pratt, M. (1993). Tailored meanings: On the meaning and impact of organizational dress. *Academy of Management Review, 18,* 32–55.

Rajagopalan, N., & Datta, D. K. (1996). CEO characteristics: Does industry matter? *Academy of Management Journal, 39,* 197–215.

Rakic, T., Steffens, M. C., & Mummendey, A. (2011a). Blinded by the accent! The minor role of looks in ethnic categorization. *Journal of Personality and Social Psychology, 100*(1), 16–29.

Rakic, T., Steffens, M. C., & Mummendey, A. (2011b). When it matters how you pronounce it: The influence of regional accents on job interview outcome. *British Journal of Psychology, 102,* 868–83.

Ralston, S. M., & Kirkwood, W. G. (1999). The trouble with applicant impression management. *Journal of Business and Technical Communication, 13,* 190–207.

Raymond, E. S. (Ed.). (2003). FUD. In *The jargon file* (Version 4.4.7). Retrieved from http://www.catb.org/jargon/oldversions/jarg447.txt.

Reelection rates over the years. (n.d.). Retrieved from http://www.opensecrets.org /bigpicture/reelect.php.

Reinhard, M. A., Messner, M., & Sporer, S. L. (2006). Explicit persuasive intent and its impact on success at persuasion: The determining roles of attractiveness and likeableness. *Journal of Consumer Psychology, 16*(3), 249–59.

Rennenkampff, A. von. (2004). *Aktivierung und Auswirkungen geschlechtsstereotyper Wahrnehmung von Führungskompetenz im Bewerbungskontext* (Unpublished doctoral dissertation). University of Mannheim, Germany.

Reynolds, D. J., & Gifford, R. (2001). The sounds and sights of intelligence: A lens model channel analysis. *Personality and Social Psychology Bulletin, 27,* 187–200.

Rhodes, G., Proffitt, F., Grady, J. M., & Sumich, A. (1998). Facial symmetry and the perception of beauty. *Psychonomic Bulletin & Review, 5*(4), 659–69.

Rhodes, G., Roberts, J., & Simmons, L. W. (1999). Reflections on symmetry and attractiveness. *Psychology, Evolution, & Gender, 1,* 279–95.

Richardson, K. D., & Cialdini, R. B. (1981). Basking and blasting: Tactics of indirect self-presentation. In J. T. Tedeschi (Ed.), *Impression management theory and social psychological research* (pp. 41–53). New York: Academic Press.

Riches, P., & Foddy, M. (1989). Ethnic accent as a status cue. *Social Psychology Quarterly, 52,* 197–206.

Richetin, J., Durante, F., Mari, S., Perugini, M., & Volpato, C. (2012). Primacy of Warmth Versus Competence: A Motivated Bias. *The Journal of Social Psychology, 152*(4), 417–35.

Ridderstråle, J., & Nordström, K. (2000). *Funky business: Talent makes capital dance.* Edinburgh: Pearson Education.

Ridgeway, C., & Johnson, C. (1990). What is the relationship between socioemotional behavior and status in task groups? *American Journal of Sociology, 95,* 1189–212.

Riniolo, T. C., Johnson, K. C., Sherman, T. R., & Misso, J. A. (2006). Hot or not: Do professors perceived as physically attractive receive higher student evaluations? *Journal of General Psychology, 133,* 19–34.

Ritter, J. (2013, October 15). Wem bringt der Doktortitel was? *ZEIT Online.* Retrieved from http://www.zeit.de/campus/2013/06/service-promotion-faecher/komplettansicht.

Ritts, V., Patterson, M. L., & Tubbs, M. E. (1992). Expectations, impressions, and judgments of physically attractive students: A review. *Review of Educational Research, 62,* 413–26.

Roberts, J. V., & Herman, C. P. (1986). The psychology of height: An empirical review. In C. O. Herman, M. P. Zanna, & E. T. Higgnis (Eds.), *The Ontario Symposium: Vol. 3. Physical appearance, stigma and social behavior* (pp. 113–40). Hillsdale, NJ: Lawrence Erlbaum Associates.

Robinson, W. P., & Giles, H. (Ed.) (2001). *The new handbook of language and social psychology.* New York: John Wiley.

Rodriguez Mosquera, P. M. R., Fischer, A. H., Manstead, A. S. R., & Zaalberg, R. (2008). Attack, disapproval, or withdrawal? The role of honour in anger and shame responses to being insulted. *Cognition and Emotion, 22*(8), 1471–98.

Rodriguez Mosquera, P. M. R., Manstead, A. S. R., & Fischer, A. H. (2002). The role of honour concerns in emotional reactions to offences. *Cognition and Emotion, 16,* 143–63.

Roff, M., & Brody, D. S. (1953). Appearance and choice status during adolescence. *Journal of Psychology, 36,* 347–56.

Roll, S., & Verinis, J. S. (1971). Stereotypes of scalp and facial hair as measured by the semantic differential. *Psychological Reports, 28,* 975–80.

Rosar, U., Klein, M., & Beckers, T. (2008). The frog pond beauty contest: Physical attractiveness and electoral success of the constituency candidates at the North Rhine-Westphalia state election 2005. *European Journal of Political Research, 47*(1), 64–79.

Rosar, U., Klein, M., & Beckers, T. (2012). Magic Mayors: Predicting Electoral Success from Candidates' Physical Attractiveness under the Conditions of a Presidential Electoral System. *German Politics, 21*(4), 372–91.

Rosen, S. (1981). The economics of superstars. *American Economic Review, 71*(5), 845–58.

Rosenberg, S., Nelson, C., & Vivekananthan, P. (1968). A multidimensional approach to the structure of personality impressions. *Journal of Personality and Social Psychology, 9,* 283–94.

Rosenfeld, P., Giacalone, R. A., & Riordan, C. A. (1995). *Impression management in organizations: Theory, measurement, and practice.* London: Routledge.

Rosenthal, D. E. (1976). Evaluating the competence of lawyers. *Law & Society Review, 11*(2), 257–85.

Rosenthal, R. (1973). The Pygmalion Effect lives. *Psychology Today, 7,* 56–63.

Rosenzweig, P. (2007). *The Halo Effect . . . and the eight other business delusions that deceive managers.* New York: Free Press.

Ross, L. (1977). The intuitive psychologist and his shortcomings: Distortions in the attribution process. In L. Berkowitz (Ed.), *Advances in experimental social psychology* (pp. 173–220). New York: Academic Press.

Ross, M., & Salvia, J. (1975). Attractiveness as a biasing factor in teacher judgments. *American Journal of Mental Deficiency, 80,* 96–98.

Ross, W. D., & Ward, R. (1982). Human proportionality and sexual dimorphism. In R. L. Hall (Ed.), *Sexual dimorphism in Homo sapiens: A question of size* (pp. 317–61). New York: Praeger.

Rothman, N. B., & Wiesenfeld, B. M. (2007). The social consequences of expressing emotional ambivalence in groups and teams. In E. Mannix, M. Neale, & C. Anderson (Eds.), *Research on managing groups and teams: Affect and groups* (pp. 205–308). London: Elsevier.

Rowe, P. M. (1989). Unfavorable information and interview decisions. In R. W. Eder & G. R. Ferris (Eds.), *The employment interview: Theory, research, and practice* (pp. 77–89). Newbury Park, CA: Sage.

Rucker, M., Anderson, E., & Kangas, A. (1999). Clothing, power and the workplace. In K. Johnson & S. Lennon (Eds.), *Appearance and power: Dress, body, culture* (pp. 59–77). New York: Berg.

Rushkoff, D. (2000). *Der Anschlag auf die Psyche.* Stuttgart, Germany: Deutsche Verlags–Anstalt.

Ryan, E. B. (1979). Why do low-prestige language varieties persist? In P. von Trudgill (Series Ed.), H. Giles & R. St. Clair (Vol. Eds.), *Language in Society: Vol. 1. Language and social psychology* (pp. 145–47). Baltimore: University Park Press.

Ryan, E. B., & Carranza, M. A. (1975). Evaluative reactions of adolescents toward speakers of standard English and Mexican American accented English. *Journal of Personality and Social Psychology, 31*(5), 855–63.

Ryan, E. B., & Giles, H. (Eds.). (1982). *Attitudes toward language variation.* London: Edward Arnold.

Ryan, E. B., Giles, H., & Sebastian, R. J. (1982). An integrative perspective for the study of attitudes toward language variation. In E. B. Ryan & H. Giles (Eds.), *Attitudes toward language variation* (pp. 1–19). London: Edward Arnold.

Ryan, E. B., & Sebastian, R. J. (1976). Social class effects on evaluation reactions towards accented speakers. Unpublished manuscript, University of Notre Dame, Indiana.

Ryen, A. H., & Kahn, A. (1975). Effects of intergroup orientation on group attitudes and proximic behavior. *Journal of Personality and Social Psychology, 31,* 302–10.

Sackeim, H. A. (1985). Morphologic asymmetries of the face: A review. *Brain and Cognition, 4,* 296–312.

Saito, K. (1978). An experimental study of personality judgments: Effect of wearing glasses. *Japanese Journal of Experimental Social Psychology, 17,* 121–27.

Salter, C. (2007). Lessons from the tarmac. *Fast Company, 2,* 31–32.

Sandberg, J., & Pinnington, A. H. (2009). Professional competence as ways of being: An existential ontological perspective. *Journal of Management Studies, 46,* 1138–70.

Segal, R., Raglan, F. R. S., & Rank, O. (1990). *Quest of the Hero*. Princeton, NJ: Princeton University Press.

Schachter, S. (1951). Deviation, rejection, and communication. *Journal of Abnormal and Social Psychology, 46*(2), 190–208.

Scheflen, A. E. (1964). The significance of posture in communication systems. *Psychiatry, 27*, 316–31.

Scheflen, A. E. (1965). *Behavioral Studies Monograph: Vol. 1. Stream and structure of communicational behavior: Context analysis of a psychotherapy session*. Philadelphia: Eastern Pennsylvania Psychiatric Institute.

Scheflen, A. E. (1966). Natural history method in psychotherapy: Communicational research. In L. A. Gottschalk & A. H. Auerbach (Eds.), *Methods of research in psychotherapy* (pp. 263–89). New York: Appleton-Century-Crofts.

Scherer, K. (1979). Voice and speech correlates of perceived social influence in simulated juries. In P. von Trudgill (Series Ed.), H. Giles & R. St. Clair (Vol. Eds.), *Language in Society: Vol. 1. Language and social psychology* (pp. 88–120). Baltimore: University Park Press.

Scherer, K. R. (1979). *Nonverbale Kommunikation: Forschungsberichte zum Interaktionsverhalten*. Weinheim: Beltz.

Schlenker, B. R. (1985). *The self and social life*. New York: McGraw-Hill.

Schlenker, B. R., & Darby, B. W. (1981). The use of apologies in social predicaments. *Social Psychology Quarterly, 44*, 271–78.

Schlenker, B. R., & Leary, M. (1982). Audiences' reactions to self-enhancing, self-denigrating, and accurate self-presentations. *Journal of Experimental Social Psychology, 18*, 89–104.

Schlenker, B. R., & Weigold, M. F. (1992). Interpersonal processes involving impression regulation and management. *Annual Review of Psychology, 43, 133*(36).

Schmid Mast, M., & Hall, J. A. (2004). Who is the boss and who is not? Accuracy of judging status. *Journal of Nonverbal Behavior, 28*(3), 145–65.

Schmidt, H. D. (1971). Experimente zur Prestige-Beeinflußbarkeit: I. Co-Judge-Suggestibilität und Persönlichkeit. *Archiv für Psychologie, 123*, 49–64.

Schmidt, H. D., Schmerl, C., & Steffens, K. H. (1971). Experimente zur Prestige-Beeinflußbarkeit: II. Dimensionen der Prestige-Beeinflußbarkeit. *Archiv für Psychologie, 123*, 97–119.

Schneider, D. J. (1973). Implicit personality theory: A review. *Psychological Bulletin, 79*, 294–309.

Schneider, D. J. (1981). Tactical self-presentations: Toward a broader conception. In J. T. Tedeschi (Ed.), *Impression management theory and social psychological research* (pp. 23–53). New York: Academic Press.

Schneider, D. J., Hastorf, A. H., & Ellsworth, P. C. (1979). *Person perception*. Reading, MA: Addison-Wesley.

Schneider, F. W., Gruman, J. A., & Coutts, L. M. (2012). *Applied social psychology: Understanding and addressing social and practical problems* (2nd ed.). Thousand Oaks, CA: Sage.

Schopenhauer, A. (1913a). *Parerga und Paralipomena: Kleine philosophische Schriften* (Vol. 1). In P. Deussen (Ed.), *Arthur Schopenhauers sämtliche Werke* (Vol. 4, pp. 159–221). Munich: Piper. (Original work published 1851).

Schopenhauer, A. (1913b). Über die Universitätsphilosophie. In A. Schopenhauer, *Parerga und Paralipomena: Kleine philosophische Schriften* (Vol. 1), in P. Deussen (Ed.), *Arthur Schopenhauers sämtliche Werke* (Vol. 4, pp. 182–83). Munich: Piper. (Original work published 1851).

Schulz, M. (2002). Venus unterm Faltenhobel. *Der Spiegel, 41,* 212–28.

Schuman, M. A. (2008). *Bill Gates: Computer mogul and philanthropist.* Berkeley Heights, NJ: Enslow.

Schwanitz, D. (1999). *Bildung: Alles, was man wissen muss.* Frankfurt: Eichborn.

Scott, L. M., & Batra, R. (Eds.). (2003). *Persuasive imagery: A consumer response perspective.* Mahwah, NJ: Lawrence Erlbaum Associates.

Searcy, T. (2011, November 8). The new rules on dressing for success. *CBS Moneywatch.* Retrieved from http://www.cbsnews.com/news/the-new-rules-on-dressing-for -success/.

Seiter, J. S., & Hatch, S. (2005). Effect of tattoos on perceptions of credibility and attractiveness. *Psychological Reports, 96*(3), 1113–20.

Sereno, K. K., & Hawkins, G. J. (1967). The effects of variations in speaker's nonfluency upon audience ratings of attitude toward the speech topic and speaker's credibility. *Speech Monographs, 34,* 58–64.

Shapiro, A. (1968). The relationship between self concept and self disclosure. *Dissertation Abstracts International, 39*(3B), 1180–81.

Shapiro, H. L. (1947). From the neck up. *Natural History, 56,* 456–65.

Shaw, J., & Porter, S. (2015). Constructing rich false memories of committing crime. *Psychological Science, 26*(3), 291–301.

Shell, G. R. (2006). *Bargaining for advantage: Negotiation strategies for reasonable people* (2nd ed.). New York: Penguin Books.

Shell, G. R., & Moussa, M. (2007). *The art of woo: Using strategic persuasion to sell your ideas.* New York: Portfolio.

Shelly, R. K. (2001). How performance expectations arise from sentiments. *Social Psychology Quarterly, 64*(1), 72–87.

Sherif, M. (1935). A study of some social factors in perception. *Archives of Psychology, 27*(187), 17–22.

Sherif, M., & Sherif, C. W. (1964). *Reference groups.* New York: Harper & Row.

Siegfried, J. J. (1970). A First Lessen in Econometrics. *Journal of Political Economy, 78,* 1378–79.

Sigall, H., Page, R., & Brown, A. (1971). The effects of physical attraction and evaluation on effort expenditure and work output. *Representative Research in Social Psychology, 2,* 19–25.

Sigelman, C. K., Thomas, D. B., Sigelman, L., & Ribich, F. D. (1986). Gender, physical attractiveness, and electability: An experimental investigation of voter biases. *Journal of Applied Social Psychology, 16,* 229–48.

Simmons, L. W., Rhodes, G., Peters, M., & Koehler, N. (2004). Are human preferences for facial symmetry focused on signals of developmental instability? *Behavioral Ecology, 15,* 864–71.

Simonson, I., & Nowlis, S. M. (2000). The role of explanations and need for uniqueness in consumer decision making: Unconventional choices based on reasons. *Journal of Consumer Research, 27*(1), 49–68.

Simpson, D. (2013, October 15). Big-ticket graffiti artist Banksy says he offered paintings for $60 in Central Park. *CNN.com*. Retrieved from http://edition.cnn.com/2013/10/14/living/banksy-street-art-sale/.

Sinaceur, M., & Tiedens, L. Z. (2006). Get mad and get more than even: When and why anger expression is effective in negotiations. *Journal of Experimental Social Psychology, 42,* 314–22.

Singh, D. (1995). Female judgment of male attractiveness and desirability for relationships: Role of waist-to-hip ratio and financial status. *Journal of Personality and Social Psychology, 69,* 1089–101.

Snyder, M., & Cantor, N. (1979). Testing hypotheses about other people: The use of historical knowledge. *Journal of Experimental Social Psychology, 15,* 330–42.

Sobal, J., & Stunkard, A. J. (1989). Socioeconomic status and obesity: A review of the literature. *Psychological Bulletin, 105,* 260–75.

Sobelman, S. A. (1974). The effects of verbal and nonverbal components on the judge level of counselor warmth. *Dissertation abstracts International, 35,* 273A.

Sokal, A. D. (1996a). A physicist experiments with cultural studies. *Lingua Franca, 6,* 62–64.

Sokal, A. D. (1996b). Transgressing the boundaries: Towards a transformative hermeneutics of quantum gravity. *Social Text, 46/47,* 217–52.

Sokal, A. D., & Bricmont, J. (1998). *Fashionable nonsense: Postmodern intellectuals' abuse of science.* New York: Picador.

Solomon, M. R. (1999). The value of status and the status of value. In M. B. Holbrook (Ed.), *Consumer value: A framework for analysis and research* (p. 224). Abingdon, UK: Routledge.

Sommer, R. (1969). *Personal space: The behavioral basis of design.* Englewood Cliffs, NJ: Prentice Hall.

Sommer, R. (1988). The personality of vegetables: Botanical metaphors for human characteristics. *Journal of Personality, 56*(4), 665–83.

Spence, G. (1996). *How to argue and win every time.* New York: St. Martin Griffin.

Spence, G. (2006). *Win your case: How to present, persuade, and prevail.* New York: St. Martin Griffin.

Spence, K. W., & Spence, J. T. (Eds.). (1968). *The psychology of learning and motivation* (Vol. 2). New York: Academic Press.

Spinath, F. M., & Angleitner, A. (2004). Thin slices of behavior as cues of personality and intelligence. *Journal of Personality and Social Psychology, 86,* 599–614.

Spurling, H. (2000, December 24). The wickedest man in Oxford. *New York Times*. Retrieved from http://www.nytimes.com/books/00/12/24/reviews/001224.24spurlit.html.

Steffens, M. C., Schult, J. C., & Ebert, I. D. (2009). Feminization of management leads to backlash against agentic applicants: Lack of social skills, not gender, determines low hirability judgments in student samples. *Psychology Science Quarterly, 51,* 16–46.

Stephan, C. W., & Langlois, J. H. (1984). Baby beautiful: Adult attributions of infant competence as a function of infant attractiveness. *Child Development, 55,* 576–85.

Sternthal, B. (1972). *Persuasion and the mass communications process* (Unpublished doctoral dissertation). Ohio State University, Columbus.

Stevens, A. (2018, January 8). Are gummy bear flavors just fooling our brains? *NPR*. Retrieved from https://www.npr.org/sections/thesalt/2018/01/08/575406711/are -gummy-bear-flavors-just-fooling-our-brains.

Stevens, C. K., & Kristof, A. L. (1995). Making the right impression: A field study of applicant impression management during job interviews. *Journal of Applied Psychology, 80,* 587–606.

Steward, A. L. & Lupfer, M. (1987). Touching as Teaching: The Effect of Touch in Student's Perceptions and Performance. *Journal of Applied Social Psychology, 17*(9), 800–9.

Stewart, M. A., Ryan, E. B., & Giles, H. (1985). Accent and social class effects on status and solidarity evaluations. *Personality and Social Psychology Bulletin, 11*(1), 98–105.

Stewart, R. A., Powell, G. E., & Chetwynd, S. J. (1979). *Person perception and stereotyping.* Westmead, UK: Saxon House.

Stiff, J. B., Kim H. J., & Ramesh, C. (1992). Truth biases and aroused suspicion in relational deception. *Communication Research, 19,* 326–45.

Stockemer, D., & Praino, R. (2015). Blinded by beauty? Physical attractiveness and candidate selection in the U.S. House of Representatives. *Social Science Quarterly, 96,* 430–43.

Stone, J., & Cooper, J. (2001). A self-standards model of cognitive dissonance. *Journal of Experimental Social Psychology, 37,* 228–43.

Strack, F., Stepper, L. L., & Martin, S. (1988). Inhibiting and facilitating conditions of the human smile: A non-obtrusive test of the facial-feedback hypothesis. *Journal of Personality and Social Psychology, 54,* 768–77.

Strodtbeck, F. & Hook, L. (1961). The social dimension of a twelve-man jury table. *Sociometry, 24*(4), 397–415.

Stroebe, W., Hewstone, M., & Stephenson, G. M. (Eds.). (1996). *Sozialpsychologie: Eine Einführung.* Berlin: Springer.

Stroebe, W., Insko, C. A., Thompson, V. D., & Layton, B. D. (1971). Effects of physical attractiveness, attitude similarity, and sex on various aspects of interpersonal attraction. *Journal of Personality and Social Psychology, 18,* 79–91.

Strong, S. R., Taylor, R. G., Bratton, J. C., & Loper, R. G. (1971). Nonverbal behavior and perceived counselor characteristics. *Journal of Counseling Psychology, 18*(6), 554–61.

Stulp, G., Buunk, A. P., Verhulst, S., & Pollet, T. V. (2012). Tall claims? Sense and nonsense about the importance of height of US presidents. *Leadership Quarterly, 24,* 159–71.

Sugrue, T. (1999). Remarks of Thomas Sugrue: 11th Annual FT World Mobile Communications Conference, November 10–11, 1999. Retrieved from http://wireless.fcc .gov/statements/11-10-99.html.

Survey finds tardiness and absenteeism up at workplaces that dress down. (2000, June 15). Retrieved from http://www.jacksonlewis.com/news/survey-finds-tardiness -and-absenteeism-workplaces-dress-down.

Swami, V., Antonakopoulos, N., Tovee, M. J., & Furnham, A. (2006). A critical test of the waist-to-hip ratio hypothesis of female physical attractiveness in Britain and Greece. *Sex Roles, 54,* 201–11.

Swami, V., Caprario, C., Tovee, M. J., & Furnham, A. (2006). Female physical attractiveness in Britain and Japan: A cross-cultural study. *European Journal of Personality, 20,* 69–81.

Swami, V., Furnham, A., Shah, K. (2006). Body weight, waist-to-hip ratio and breast size correlates of ratings of attractiveness and health. *Personality and Individual Differences, 41*(3), 443–54.

Swami, V., Smith, J., Tsiokris, A., Georgiades, C., Sangareau, Y., Tovée, M. J., & Furnham, A. (2007). Male physical attractiveness in Britain and Greece: A cross-cultural study. *Journal of Social Psychology, 147*(1), 15–26.

Swami, V., & Tovee, M. J. (2006). Does hunger influence judgements of female physical attractiveness? *British Journal of Psychology, 97,* 353–63.

Swann, W. B. (1987). Identity negotiation: Where two roads meet. *Journal of Personality and Social Psychology, 53,* 1038–51.

Swann, W. B., & Ely, R. J. (1984). A battle of wills: Self-verification versus behavioral confirmation. *Journal of Personality and Social Psychology, 91,* 457–77.

Sybers, R., & Roach, M. E. (1962). Sociological research: Clothing and human behavior. *Journal of Home Economics, 54,* 184–87.

Sypeck, M. F., Gray, J. J., Etu, S. F., Ahrens, A. H., Mosimann, J. E., & Wiseman, C. V. (2006). Cultural representations of thinness in women, redux: Playboy magazine's depiction of beauty from 1979 to 1999. *Body Image, 3,* 229–35.

Tagiuri, R., & Petrullo, L. (Eds.). (1958). *Person perception and interpersonal behavior.* Stanford, CA: Stanford University Press.

Taille-Hüfte-Verhältnis. (n.d.). *Beautycheck.* Retrieved from http://www.beautycheck.de /cmsms/index.php/taille-huefte-verhaeltnis.

Tangney, J. P. (1996). Conceptual and methodological issues in the assessment of shame and guilt. *Behaviour Research and Therapy, 34,* 741–54.

Tanner, B., & Chartrand, T. (2006). The convincing chameleon: The impact of mimicry on persuasion. *NA—Advances in Consumer Research, 33,* 409–12.

Taylor, D. M., Bassili, J. N., & Aboud, F. E. (1973). Dimensions of ethnic identity: An example from Quebec. *Journal of Social Psychology, 89*(2), 185–92.

Taylor, D. M., & Gardner, R. C. (1970). Bicultural communication: A study of communicational efficiency and person perception. *Canadian Journal of Behavioural Science, 2,* 67–81.

Tecce, J. J. (2004). *Body language in presidential debates as a predictor of election results, 1960–2004.* Unpublished manuscript, Boston College.

Tedeschi, J. T. (Ed.). (1981). *Impression management theory and social psychological research.* New York: Academic Press.

Tedeschi, J. T., & Melbug, V. (1984). Impression management and influence in the organization. In S. B. Bacharach & E. G. Lawler (Eds.), *Research in the sociology of organizations* (pp. 293–322). Greenwich, CT: JAI Press.

Tedeschi, J. T., & Riess, M. (1981). Identities, the phenomenal self, and laboratory research. In J. T. Tedeschi (Ed.), *Impression management theory and social psychological research* (pp. 3–22). New York: Academic Press.

Tedeschi, J. T., Schlenker, B. R., & Bonoma, T. V. (1971). Cognitive dissonance: Private ratiocination or public spectacle? *American Psychologist, 26,* 685–95.

Terry, R. L. (1977). Further evidence on components of facial attractiveness. *Perceptual and Motor Skills, 45,* 130.

Terry, R. L., & Brady, C. S. (1976). Effects of framed spectacles and contact lenses on self-ratings of facial attractiveness. *Perceptual and Motor Skills, 42,* 789–90.

Terry, R. L., & Davis, J. S. (1976). Components of facial attractiveness. *Perceptual and Motor Skills, 42,* 918.

Terry, R. L., & Kroger, D. L. (1976). Effects of eye correctives on ratings of attractiveness. *Perceptual and Motor Skills, 42,* 562.

Terry, R. L., & Zimmermann, D. J. (1970). Anxiety induced by contact lenses and framed spectacles. *Journal of American Optometric Association, 41,* 257–59.

Tesser, A., & Brodie, M. (1971). A note on the evaluation of a computer date. *Psychonomic Science, 23,* 300.

Tetlock, P. E. (2005). *Expert political judgment: How good is it? How can we know?* Princeton, NJ: Princeton University Press.

Tetlock, P. E., Mellers, B., Rohrbaugh, N., & Chen, E. (2014). Forecasting tournaments: Tools for increasing transparency and the quality of debate. *Current Directions in Psychological Science, 23*(4), 290–95.

Teuscher, U., & Teuscher, C. (2007). Reconsidering the double standard of aging: Effects of gender and sexual orientation on facial attractiveness ratings. *Personality and Individual Differences, 42,* 631–39.

Thacker, R., & Wayne, S. (1995). An examination of the relationship between upward influence tactics and assessments of promotability. *Journal of Management, 21*(4), 739–56.

"The Triumph of the Nerds"; program transcripts, Part II (1996). Retrieved from http://www.pbs.org/nerds/part2.html.

Thompson, C. J., Rindfleisch, A., & Arsel, Z. (2006). Emotional branding and the strategic value of the doppelgänger brand image. *Journal of Marketing, 70*(1), 50–64.

Thorndike, E. L. (1920). A constant error in psychological ratings. *Journal of Applied Psychology, 4,* 25–29.

Thornhill, R., & Gangestad, S. W. (1993). Human facial beauty: Averageness, symmetry, and parasite resistance. *Human Nature, 4*(3), 237–69.

Thornton, G. R. (1943). The effect upon judgments of personality traits of varying a single factor in a photograph. *Journal of Social Psychology, 18,* 127–48.

Thornton, G. R. (1944). The effect of wearing glasses on judgements of personality traits of persons seen briefly. *Journal of Applied Psychology, 28,* 203–07.

Tickle-Degnen, L., Puccinelli, N. M., Rosenthal, R. (2006). Effect of Target Position and Target Task on Judge Sensitivity to Felt Rapport. *Journal of Nonverbal Behavior, 30*(2), 95–95.

Tiedens, L. Z. (2001). Anger and advancement versus sadness and subjugation: The effect of negative emotion expressions on social status conferral. *Journal of Personality and Social Psychology, 80,* 86–94.

Tiedens, L. Z., Ellsworth, P. C., & Mesquita, B. (2000). Stereotypes about sentiments and status: Emotional expectations for high- and low-status group members. *Personality and Social Psychology Bulletin, 26,* 500–74.

Tigue, C. C., Borak, D. J., O'Connor, J. J. M., Schandl, C., & Feinberg, D. R. (2012). Voice pitch influences voting behavior. *Evolution and Human Behavior* 33:210–16.

Todorov, A., Mandisodza, A. N., Goren, A., & Hall, C. C. (2005). Inferences of competence from faces predict election outcomes. *Science, 308,* 1623–26.

Todorov, A., Said, C. P., Engell, A. D., & Oosterhof, N. N. (2008). Understanding evaluation of faces on social dimensions. *Trends in Cognitive Sciences, 12*(12), 455–60.

Tomikins, S., & Izard, C. (Eds.). (1965). *Affect cognition and personality.* New York: Springer.

Tovee, M. J., Hancock, P., Mahmoudi, S., Singleton, B. R. R., & Cornelissen, P. L. (2002). Human female attractiveness: Waveform analysis of body shape. *Proceedings of the Royal Society B, 269,* 2205–13.

Tovee, M. J., Reinhardt, S., Emery, J., Cornelissen, P. (1998). Optimum body-mass index and maximum sexual attractiveness. *Lancet, 352,* 548.

Tsfati, Y., Elfassi, D. M., & Waismel-Manor, I. (2010). Exploring the association between Israeli legislators' physical attractiveness and their television news coverage. *International Journal of Press/Politics, 15*(2), 175–92.

Tsui, A. S., & Barry, B. (1986). Interpersonal affect and rating errors. *Academy of Management Journal, 29,* 586–99.

Turner, J. C. (1991). *Social influence.* Pacific Grove, CA: Brooks/Cole.

Turner, J. C., & Oakes, P. J. (1989). Self-categorization theory and social influence. In P. B. Paulus (Ed.), *Psychology of group influence* (pp. 233–75). Hillsdale, NJ: Erlbaum.

Tversky, A., & Kahneman, D. (1991). Loss aversion in riskless choice: A reference dependent model. *Quarterly Journal of Economics, 106,* 1039–61.

Ulmer, R. R., Sellnow, T. L., & Seeger, M. W. (2007). *Effective Crisis Communication: Moving From Crisis to Opportunity.* Thousand Oaks, CA: Sage.

Ury, W. (2008). *The power of a positive no: Save the deal, save the relationship—and still say no.* New York: Random House.

Uzzi, B., Lancaster, R., & Dunlap, S. (2007). Your client relationships and reputation: Weighing the worth of social ties: Embeddedness and the price of legal services in the large law firm market. In L. Empson (Ed.), *Managing the modern law firm* (pp. 91–116). Oxford: Oxford University Press.

Van Iddekinge, C. H., McFarland, L. A., & Raymark, P. H. (2007). Antecedents of impression management use and effectiveness in a structured interview. *Journal of Management, 33,* 752–73.

Van Kleef, G. A., Homan, A. C., Finkenauer, C., Gundemir, S., & Stamkou, E. (2011). Breaking the rules to rise to power: How norm violators gain power in the eyes of others. *Social Psychological and Personality Science, 2*(5), 500–507.

Van Vugt, M., Hogan, R., & Kaiser, R. B. (2008). Leadership, followership, and evolution: Some lessons from the past. *American Psychologist, 63*(3), 182–96.

Varma, A., Toh, S., & Pichler, S. (2006). Ingratiation in job applications: Impact on selection decisions. *Journal of Managerial Psychology, 21*(3), 200–210.

Verhulst, B., Lodge, M., & Lavine, H. (2010). The attractiveness halo: Why some candidates are perceived more favorably than others. *Journal of Nonverbal Behavior, 34*(2), 111–17.

Vogler, C. (1998). *The Writer's Journey: Mythic Structure For Writers.* Studio City, CA: Michael Wiese Productions.

Vonk, R. (1999). Impression formation and impression management: Motives, traits and likeability inferred from self-promoting and self-deprecating behavior. *Social Cognition, 17,* 390–412.

Vrij, A. (2008). *Detecting lies and deceit: Pitfalls and opportunities.* Chichester, UK: John C. Wiley.

Waber, R. L., Shiv, B., Carmon, Z., & Ariely, D. (2008). Commercial features of placebo and therapeutic efficacy. *JAMA: Journal of the American Medical Association, 299,* 1016–17.

Wahrman, R., & Pugh, M. D. (1972). Competence and conformity: Another look at Hollander's study. *Sociometry, 35,* 376–86.

Waldmann, D. A., Ramirez, G. G., House, R. J., & Puranam, P. (2001). Does leadership matter? CEO leadership attributes and profitability under conditions of perceived environmental uncertainty. *Academy of Management Journal, 44,* 134–43.

Waller, D., & Younger, R. (2017). *The reputation game: The art of changing how people see you.* London: One World.

Walster, E., Aronson, V., Abrahams, D., & Rottmann, L. (1966). Importance of physical attractiveness in dating behavior. *Journal of Personality and Social Psychology, 4,* 508–16.

Walther, G. (1996). *Sag, was du meinst, und du bekommst, was du willst.* Düsseldorf, Germany: Econ.

Warr, P. B., & Knapper, C. (1968). *The perception of people and events.* New York: Wiley.

Watson, O. (1972). *Proxemic behaviours: Cross-cultural study.* The Hague: Mouton.

Watson, O., & Graves, T. (1966). Quantitative research in proxemic behavior. *American Anthropologist, 68,* 971–85.

Wayne, S. J., & Ferris, G. R. (1990). Influence tactics, affect, and exchange quality in supervisor-subordinate interactions: A laboratory experiment and field study. *Journal of Applied Psychology, 75,* 487–99.

Wayne, S. J., & Kacmar, K. (1991). The effects of impression management on the performance appraisal process. *Organizational Behavior and Human Decision Processes, 48*(1), 70–88.

Wayne, S. J., & Liden, R. (1995). Effects of impression management on performance ratings: A longitudinal study. *Academy of Management Journal, 38*(1), 232–60.

Webster, M., & Driskell, J. E. (1978). Status generalizations: A review and some new data. *American Sociological Review, 43,* 220–36.

Weibel, D., Wissmath, B., & Groner, R. (2008). How gender and age affect newscasters' credibility: An investigation in Switzerland. *Journal of Broadcasting & Electronic Media, 52*(3), 466–484.

Weiner, B. (1986). *An attributional theory of motivation and emotion.* New York: Springer.

Weingarten, G. (2007, April 8). Pearls before breakfast: Can one of the nation's great musicians cut through the fog of a D.C. rush hour? *Washington Post.* Retrieved from https://www.washingtonpost.com/lifestyle/magazine/pearls-before-breakfast-can -one-of-the-nations-great-musicians-cut-through-the-fog-of-a-dc-rush-hour-lets -find-out/2014/09/23/8a6d46da-4331-11e4-b47c-f5889e061e5f_story.html.

Weinraub, B. (2000). The George Clooney Interview. *Playboy* (US edition), *47* (7), 67–74.

Wertheimer, M. (1923). Untersuchungen zur Lehre von der Gestalt II, in Psychologische Forschung, Vol. 4, 301–350.

Wheeler, M. A., & Nelson, D. (2003, February). Nonverbal communication in negotiation. Harvard Business School Background Note 903-081. (Revised September 2009).

White, G., Fishbein, S., & Rutstein, J. (1981). Passionate love and the misattribution of arousal. *Journal of Personality and Social Psychology, 41*(1), 56–62.

Wilcox, S. (1997). Age and gender in relation to body attitudes: Is there a double standard of aging? *Psychology of Women Quarterly, 21,* 549–65.

Wilkinson, A. (1965). Spoken English. *Educational Review, Supplement, 17*(2), 2.

Williams, R. G., & Ware, J. E. (1976). Validity of student ratings of instruction under different incentive conditions: A further study of the Dr. Fox Effect. *Journal of Educational Psychology, 68,* 48–56.

Williams, W. M., & Ceci, S. J. (1997). How'm I doing? *Change, 29,* 13–24.

Willis, F. & Hamm, H. (1980). The use of interpersonal touch in securing compliance. *Journal of Nonverbal Behavior, 5*(1), 49–55.

Wilson, C. P. (1979). *Jokes: Form, content, use, and function.* London: Academic Press.

Wilson, J. M. B., Tripp, D. A., & Boland, F. J. (2005). The relative contributions of waist-to-hip ratio and body mass index to judgements of attractiveness. *Sexualities, Evolution and Gender, 7,* 245–67.

Wilson, P. R. (1968). Perceptual distortion of height as a function of ascribed academic status. *Journal of Social Psychology, 74,* 97–102.

Winkielman, P., Halberstadt, J., Fazendeiro, T., & Catty, S. (2006). Prototypes are attractive because they are easy on the mind. *Psychological Science, 17*(9), 799–806.

Winkielman, P., Schwarz, N., Reber, R., & Fazendeiro, T. A. (2003). Cognitive and affective consequences of visual fluency: When seeing is easy on the mind. In L. M. Scott & R. Batra (Eds.), *Persuasive imagery: A consumer response perspective* (pp. 75–89). Mahwah, NJ: Lawrence Erlbaum Associates.

Winston, J. S., Strange, B. A., O'Doherty, J., & Dolan, R. J. (2002). Automatic and intentional brain responses during evaluation of trustworthiness of faces. *Nature Neuroscience, 5*(3), 277–83.

Wojciszke, B. (1994). Multiple meanings of behavior: Construing actions in terms of competence and morality. *Journal of Personality and Social Psychology, 67,* 222–32.

Wojciszke, B. (2005). Affective concomitants of information on morality and competence. *European Psychologist, 10,* 60–70.

Wojciszke, B., Bazinska, R., & Jaworski, M. (1998). On the dominance of moral categories in impression formation. *Personality and Social Psychology Bulletin, 24,* 1245–57.

Wolf, N. (1991). *The beauty myth: How images of beauty are used against women.* New York: W. Morrow.

Wookey, M. L., Graves, N. A., & Butler, J. C. (2009). Effects of a sexy appearance on perceived competence of women. *Journal of Social Psychology, 149,* 116–18.

Yang, C.-F. J., Gray, P., & Pope, H. G. (2005). Male body image in Taiwan versus the West: Yanggang Zhiqi meets the Adonis complex. *American Journal of Psychiatry, 162,* 263–69.

Young, F. W. (1965). *Initiation ceremonies.* New York: Bobbs-Merrill.

Yzerbyt, V., Provost, V., & Corneille, O. (2005). Not competent but warm . . . Really? Compensatory stereotypes in the French-speaking world. *Group Processes & Intergroup Relations, 8*(3), 291–308.

Zaidel, S. F., & Mehrabian, A. (1969). The ability to communicate and infer positive and negative attitudes facially and vocally. *Journal of Experimental Research in Personality, 3,* 233–41.

Zaltman, G. (2003). *How customers think: Essential insights into the mind of the markets.* Boston: Harvard Business School Press.

Zanna, M. P. (Ed.). (2000). *Advances in experimental social psychology* (Vol. 32). San Diego: Academic Press.

Zebrowitz, L. A. (1997). *Reading faces: Window to the soul?* Boulder, CO: Westview Press.

Zebrowitz, L. A., Hall, J. A., Murphy, N. A., & Rhodes, G. (2002). Looking smart and looking good: Facial cues to intelligence and their origins. *Personality and Social Psychology Bulletin, 28,* 238–49.

Zuckerman, M., & Driver, R. E. (1989). What sounds beautiful is good: The vocal attractiveness stereotype. *Journal of Nonverbal Behavior, 13*(2), 67–82.

INDEX

ABOUT THE AUTHOR

Jack Nasher-Awakemian is an international authority on reading and influencing people.

He is a negotiation adviser and founder of the NASHER Negotiation Institute, a management professor, and an internationally best-selling author. Nasher has helped car manufacturers, pharmaceutical companies, and start-ups all over the world improve their negotiation processes.

Educated at Oxford University and trained at Wall Street's leading law firm, Skadden, and Germany's Mission to the UN in New York City, Nasher was the youngest appointee to full professorship at the esteemed Munich Business School in 2011 at the age of 31. He is currently a visiting faculty member of Stanford University.

His books are best sellers and have appeared in Germany, Russia, China, and many other countries. Articles from and about him have appeared in leading publications, such as the *Harvard Business Manager* and the *Huffington Post*.

He is an avid mentalist and regularly demonstrates his mind mysteries at the world-renowned Magic Castle in Hollywood.

Nasher is an award-winning researcher and a principle practitioner of the Association of Business Psychology.

Download a free one-page overview of the book here:
www.JackNasher.com/convinced.
On the website, you may also request a talk or negotiation
seminar.

When I buy a new book, I always read the last page first, that way in case I die before I finish, I know how it ends.

—NORA EPHRON

Berrett–Koehler
Publishers

Berrett-Koehler is an independent publisher dedicated to an ambitious mission: *Connecting people and ideas to create a world that works for all.*

We believe that the solutions to the world's problems will come from all of us, working at all levels: in our organizations, in our society, and in our own lives. Our BK Business books help people make their organizations more humane, democratic, diverse, and effective (we don't think there's any contradiction there). Our BK Currents books offer pathways to creating a more just, equitable, and sustainable society. Our BK Life books help people create positive change in their lives and align their personal practices with their aspirations for a better world.

All of our books are designed to bring people seeking positive change together around the ideas that empower them to see and shape the world in a new way.

And we strive to practice what we preach. At the core of our approach is Stewardship, a deep sense of responsibility to administer the company for the benefit of all of our stakeholder groups including authors, customers, employees, investors, service providers, and the communities and environment around us. Everything we do is built around this and our other key values of quality, partnership, inclusion, and sustainability.

This is why we are both a B-Corporation and a California Benefit Corporation—a certification and a for-profit legal status that require us to adhere to the highest standards for corporate, social, and environmental performance.

We are grateful to our readers, authors, and other friends of the company who consider themselves to be part of the BK Community. We hope that you, too, will join us in our mission.

A BK Business Book

We hope you enjoy this BK Business book. BK Business books pioneer new leadership and management practices and socially responsible approaches to business. They are designed to provide you with groundbreaking and practical tools to transform your work and organizations while upholding the triple bottom line of people, planet, and profits. High-five!

To find out more, visit **www.bkconnection.com.**

Berrett–Koehler
Publishers

Connecting people and ideas
to create a world that works for all

Dear Reader,

Thank you for picking up this book and joining our worldwide community of Berrett-Koehler readers. We share ideas that bring positive change into people's lives, organizations, and society.

To welcome you, we'd like to offer you a free e-book. You can pick from among twelve of our bestselling books by entering the promotional code **BKP92E** here: http://www.bkconnection.com/welcome.

When you claim your free e-book, we'll also send you a copy of our e-newsletter, the *BK Communiqué*. Although you're free to unsubscribe, there are many benefits to sticking around. In every issue of our newsletter you'll find

- A free e-book
- Tips from famous authors
- Discounts on spotlight titles
- Hilarious insider publishing news
- A chance to win a prize for answering a riddle

Best of all, our readers tell us, "Your newsletter is the only one I actually read." So claim your gift today, and please stay in touch!

Sincerely,

Charlotte Ashlock
Steward of the BK Website

Questions? Comments? Contact me at bkcommunity@bkpub.com.